D0353240

THE GAA IMMORTALS

The GAA Immortals

100 Gaelic Games Legends

John Scally

BLACK & WHITE PUBLISHING

First published 2017
by Black & White Publishing Ltd
Nautical House, 104 Commercial Street
Edinburgh EH6 6NF

1 3 5 7 9 10 8 6 4 2   17 18 19 20

ISBN: 978 1 78530 133 9

Copyright © John Scally 2017

The right of John Scally to be identified as the author of
this work has been asserted by him in accordance with the
Copyright, Designs and Patents Act 1988.

All rights reserved.
No part of this publication may be reproduced,
stored in a retrieval system, or transmitted in any form,
or by any means, electronic, mechanical, photocopying,
recording or otherwise, without permission
in writing from the publisher.

The publisher has made every reasonable effort
to contact copyright holders of images in this book.
Any errors are inadvertent and anyone who for any reason
has not been contacted is invited to write to the publisher
so that a full acknowledgment can be made
in subsequent editions of this work.

A CIP catalogue record for this book is available from the British Library.

Typeset by Iolaire, Newtonmore
Printed and bound by CPI Group (UK) Ltd. Croydon, CR0 4YY

To Amelia Naughton
May your days be merry and bright

ACKNOWLEDGEMENTS

This book has been more than twenty years in the making. I have had the great good fortune to meet many of the greats of both football and hurling, including some who have passed on to their eternal reward such as Tony Keady, Dermot Earley, Jack Lynch, Seán Purcell, Enda Colleran, John Wilson and Eddie Boyle, and this books draws heavily on interviews with them. There are too many to name individually, but I am grateful for all their insights. I am also very honoured that the legendary Seán Boylan agreed to write the foreword for this book.

I'd like to say thanks to the wonderfully hospitable Kathryn Brennan of Castle Bookshop in Castlebar for her ongoing love affair with books. And thanks to Simon Hess, Campbell Brown and all at Black & White Publishing for their help.

As a small boy, the first name I ever associated with St Brigid's club was Pat Dennehy who sadly died this summer. He devoted his life to the club he loved so well. May he rest in peace. While this book was being written, we lost a great Roscommon woman, Annie Loftus-Conroy, after a rich life, well lived. She will be much missed.

CONTENTS

FOREWORD

Many people can remember where they were when hearing of famous events in world history, like the assassination of John F. Kennedy or Nelson Mandela being released from prison. Similarly, GAA fans will in years to come recall their whereabouts when watching great victories in Croke Park.

Meath's 1987 All-Ireland triumph is a favourite memory from the twenty-three years I managed the team. That was an amazing day because it had been twenty years since the previous All-Ireland triumph and some of the greatest footballers to put on a Meath jersey had achieved what they'd always wanted – for a long time, it looked as if it might never happen for them. The biggest disappointments included losing the 1991 final to Down. We couldn't take from Down's performance but it would have been the icing on the cake if the lads had got the All-Ireland after playing ten games. But they got a lot of credit for the way they conducted themselves in defeat. The All-Ireland final defeat against Galway in 2001 was another big disappointment; we just didn't perform on the day.

Nothing adorns the rich history of the GAA like a great player. Like me, they all had good days and bad days.

This book is a celebration of the greats of the GAA. I hope you enjoy it.

Seán Boylan, September 2017

Introduction

If talent were water, I would have enough to fill a thimble. Hence my failure to make it as a footballer or hurler. When I was in my early twenties, I got involved in writing about sport and one of the first people I spoke with was the late Raymond Smith – who at the time was to the print media what Micheál O'Muircheartaigh is to broadcasting. He told me the story of how Hill 16 got its name – how it was built with the rubble from the 1916 Rising – and he told me about the time he had a drink with a man who got five shillings for wheeling the rubble into Croke Park. I immediately accepted his version as the Gospel truth — the only problem was I discovered the hill was actually built in 1915. I would have bet my house that the story was true, so it was such a shock when I found out it was not! I almost had to go into therapy.

Stories like these, though, add to the mythology of the GAA. However, nothing adds more to the lore and legend of Gaelic games than great players. Since Adam was a boy, great players have had the power to make the heart skip a beat. Joe Brolly tells a story of the admiration GAA stars attract. When he was playing for Celtic, Neil Lennon invited Anthony Tohill over for a visit. Lennon brought him to meet Martin O'Neill, who was managing the club at the time. O'Neill was having a glass of wine with the Rangers manager Alex McLeish. The future Irish manager leapt off his chair and ran over and kissed Tohill's shoes, saying to Alex: 'On your knees, boy, and pay homage to a real star.'

Of course they have also added to the gaiety of the nation for those of us barely fit enough to move when going down an escalator. Witness Pat Spillane's dismissal of the Tommy Murphy Cup as the 'Tommy Cooper Cup' and to a younger audience 'the Tommy Tiernan Cup'.

John B. Keane, one of the greatest Irish writers, was once asked how he wished to be remembered. Rather than pointing to his many great plays and his impact on the literary landscape, his response looked to a specific split-second in his life when he was twenty-three years old. He answered he only wanted to be remembered 'as the player who scored the winning point in the North Kerry intermediate football final against Duagh in 1951'.

This book is a celebration of such men and women. The problem, though, is twofold. Who do you put in? Who do you leave out? The difficulties of attempting the task of selecting 100 GAA Immortals are greatly magnified when one attempts the hazardous task of selecting the greatest players over different eras. It was much harder to decide who to exclude than to include. I could have easily filled this book with just Kerry footballers and Kilkenny hurlers. However, as the GAA is a national movement I wanted all the thirty-two counties to be included.

Historically the high-profile players of past and present get acres of space in the national media while often remarkable players lose out because they have never won an All-Ireland medal. The tragedy is that their stories are often forgotten. So many heroic players' stories are woven almost anonymously in the tapestry of GAA history even though they deserve individual recognition. This book makes some attempt to redress that balance.

I knew that I would upset many people not for those I chose to include but for the many greats of the GAA who I reluctantly had to exclude. I did not wish to compound the problem by arranging the book in terms of the greatness of the players. That is why I deliberately chose to have a random structure so as not to take on the additional burden of designing the list in terms of greatness or by seeming to imply that one code is superior to the other. I make no apologies for trying to get the greatest possible diversity of profiles and if I have strained the definition of 'GAA Immortal' in certain instances then so be it.

Nothing passes a winter's evening more pleasantly for GAA fans than picking their dream teams. I invited all of my interviewees to pick their dream teams. Many kindly agreed to do so. Some were understandably wary of losing too many old friends and declined.

The book is weighted to include people who in their different ways were innovators like Jim McGuinness and Pat Gilroy who changed the face of football management; Stephen Cluxton who transformed the face of goalkeeping, Angela Downey who redefined the game of camogie and of course Davy Fitzgerald who redefined . . . everything!

A number of options presented themselves in the writing of the book, but I opted for a personal style of portrait, showing their characters, the controversies they faced and sometimes created, and their triumphs and setbacks through their own eyes or those who played against them. I am grateful to the many players who shared their stories with me. However, I think it would not be in his interest to name the prominent player, with a tongue as sharp as a blade, who asked me: 'What do you call a beautiful woman on the arm of an Armagh footballer?'

———

'A tattoo.'

Neither can I name the multi-All-Ireland-winning Kerry footballer who when asked why he did not go to the funeral of a former player of some repute answered: 'Sure he only had two All-Ireland medals. If I was going to funerals for lads with only two All-Ireland medals, I would be going to funerals every day.'

Another player I cannot name is the All-Ireland medal winner who became an undertaker. His first client was a woman who had lost her husband at a young age and was very distressed that the new undertaker had laid him out in grey, as she hated the colour on him. The second client was a woman who had lost her 30-year-old son. She was similarly very distressed that the All-Ireland winner had laid him out in brown, as she hated the colour on him.

The great hurler appeased both of them and said he would just do a swap. A few weeks later he met up with Christy Ring and was explaining the adjustment to his new life. He told the story of his first two clients. Christy nodded his head solemnly: 'Ah, I see. You swapped the suits. That was very resourceful of you.'

'Not at all,' replied the hurler. 'It was much easier to swap their heads.'

I hope these portraits will in some way capture the unique magic and humour of the GAA.

John Scally, September 2017

1

THE MASTER OF THE SWERVE

Dick Fitzgerald: 1903–1923

While many Irish sportsmen fought and died on the Western Front and at Gallipoli, some chose the path of radical nationalism. Seán Etchingham of the Wexford GAA was such a man. He proposed in November 1914 that the GAA establish rifle clubs so that members could defend Ireland. A speaker at the meeting expressed concern that the weather might not be suitable for rifle training. Etchingham was infuriated and responded: 'Do you want special weather for war? This opportunity – the like of which you have not had for a century – may pass; an opportunity that may not occur again.'

In the wake of the 1916 Easter Rising, more than 1,800 Irishmen were rounded up and detained without trial at a prisoner-of-war camp near the Welsh village of Frongoch, which had previously been used to detain Germans. Over the next six months, the internees of what was known as the 'University of Revolution', which included a who's who in the struggle for independence, including Michael Collins, Richard Mulcahy, Terence MacSwiney and Sam Maguire, formed deep chains of friendship while sharing their skills and knowledge of football and revolution.

The lessons of the Rising had been learnt and Republican networks were strengthened within Frongoch's North and South camps. Michael Collins was one of the prime movers in the establishment of a league competition between four teams called after the leaders of the Rising. Eventually these games morphed into inter-county contests. Since so many players from Kerry and Louth were in the camp, it was decided to contest an unofficial Wolfe Tone (at the time a major competition in the GAA) final between the two sides.

An unusual marketing strategy was pursued for the game. Posters were put up around the camp saying: 'Wives and sweethearts should be left at home.'

The Kerry team in Frongoch was captained by Dick Fitzgerald. He famously wrote *How to Play Gaelic Football*, the first handbook of its kind in the GAA. Fitzgerald won five All-Ireland championships and became the first man to captain a county to consecutive All-Irelands in 1913 and 1914.

Although Limerick won the first All-Ireland in 1887, Gaelic football really came of age in 1903, when Kerry won their first All-Ireland. They beat Kildare in a three-game saga which grabbed the public imagination. Kerry won the first game, but the match was replayed because they had been awarded a controversial goal. So intense was the second game, which finished in a draw, that the referee collapsed at the end. On the third occasion Kerry were comprehensive winners by 0–8 to 0–2.

The following year saw the first taster of what would become one of the great rivalries in the GAA when Kerry beat Dublin to claim their second All-Ireland. By now Fitzgerald had emerged as the first true star of Gaelic football, notably when he appeared to defy the laws of physics in one of the Kildare games when he pointed a late free only yards from the touchline.

Fitzgerald saw football in very spiritual terms, creating a sense of the immutable bond that victory brings, a feeling of kinship that goes beyond professional loyalty, a camaraderie that overcomes differences of age, sex, even previous fallings out. This was particularly important in Kerry in the 1920s and 1930s, when memories of the civil war lingered very powerfully. Neighbours who had shot at one another displayed a greater desire to forgive and forget when gathered around the goalposts than when gathered around the altar. Fitzgerald's philosophy was that love of country draws its strength and vitality from love of neighbours, fellow parishioners and fellow countrymen and women; from love of the traditions, culture and way of life associated with one's home and place of origin: that a club or county provides a sense of importance, belonging and identity, shared goals, a pride and a purpose. His code was not to talk the talk but walk the walk.

Fitzgerald's influence came not just from his achievements on the playing field. He was pivotal to the decision that Kerry should wear the green and gold, organised street leagues, trained Clare to an All-Ireland in 1917, refereed two All-Irelands and acted as a delegate to Congress.

Success in Gaelic football is about history and geography – about being in the right place at the right time. Fitzgerald was the right man for his time and was destined to remain one of the chosen few whose name would live on when his stay in this valley of tears had ended.

Tragedy darkened his door in 1929 when his beloved wife

Kitty died, and Fitzgerald himself would pass away prematurely the following year, two days before the All-Ireland final, at the age of forty-six, when he fell from the roof of the Killarney courthouse, a short distance from where he was born. On the Sunday thousands kneeled outside the church of his commemorative mass. Fitzgerald was a selector with the Kerry team that year and after the Artane Boys' Band had played the national anthem before the All-Ireland final between Kerry and Monaghan, they played Chopin's 'Funeral March'. Kerry did what the occasion demanded and routed Monaghan by eighteen points.

The most obvious reason for Kerry's success has been a phenomenal array of fantastic footballers, from Dick Fitzgerald to Paddy Kennedy to Seamus Moynihan. Dick's name lives on in Fitzgerald Stadium in Killarney, opened in 1936. His legacy is to make the green and gold synonymous with Gaelic football.

2

THE RING MASTER

Christy Ring: 1939–1964

It was a funeral like no other.

Raymond Smith wrote: 'Christy Ring, the undisputed genius of three decades of competitive hurling, yesterday drew the crowds for the last time. But never did they turn out in such spontaneous tribute as they did for the final, sad procession, as the nation's superb hurler went back to the soil of his native Cloyne.'

He had lived a public life, but his death, at the age of fifty-eight, was nearly a private affair. He fell down in a quiet street in Cork and a passing teacher, Patricia Horgan, softly whispered an act of contrition into his ear as he took his last breath and prepared to meet his God.

His former teammate and the then Taoiseach Jack Lynch delivered a heartfelt eulogy: 'As a hurler he had no peer. As long as young men will match their hurling skills against each other on Ireland's green fields, as long as young boys bring their camáns for the sheer thrill of the tingle on their fingers of the impact of ash with leather, as long as hurling is played, the story of Christy Ring will be told. And that will be forever.'

He was carried to his last resting place on the shoulders of his teammates, one of whom, Paddy Barry, was heard to remark: 'We carried him at last.' One observer said that the crowd was the biggest in Cork since the funeral for 'the martyr Lord Mayor Tomás Mac Curtain'.

Ring has a special place in the annals of the GAA. He first sprang to prominence in 1935 when at the age of sixteen he played for Cork Minors. In his twenty-four years playing for the Cork seniors he would amass eight All-Ireland winners' medals, nine Munster championships, three league medals and a staggering eighteen Railway Cups – when it was a premier competition. He retired in 1964 when the Cork selectors dropped him, aged forty-three. His best guess was that he had played more than 1,200 games. He left behind a treasure trove of memories but a small archive of interviews because, as he famously said, 'All my talking was done on the field with a hurley.'

His special status with hurling fans was most tellingly revealed on the day of a Munster final when a Cork fan met him and two of his teammates. She sprinkled holy water on his colleagues but assured the wizard of Cloyne, 'Ringy, you don't need any of this!'

One of the many stories told about Ring is when once, as he was leading his team out of the tunnel, he turned them back to the dressing room even though they were halfway out. Then he took off his Cork jersey, held it up and asked his players to look at the colour and what it meant to them. After that the team went out with fire in their bellies and played out of their skins.

He was not a man to call a spade an argicultural implement. In Ring's days as a selector Cork's ace forward Seánie O'Leary got a belt of a hurley across the nose and was withdrawing from the field when Ring shouted at him, 'Get back out there. You don't play hurling with your nose.'

Few hurlers are better equipped to evaluate Ring's career than Tipperary's greatest hurling legend, John Doyle. 'Christy Ring was by far the best hurler I ever saw. He had unbelievable skill and could do anything with a ball. He only thought or dreamed about hurling. Once, after we beat Cork in a Munster final in Thurles, I saw him in Hayes Hotel telling another Cork player what they needed to do to beat us the following year. How could you keep a man like that down?

'He was also a very tough hurler. I think back to a great tussle between Christy and another Tipperary player in a game in Cork. Though I was not involved in the scuffle, I happened to be lying on the ground close to it and I got a fierce belt of a hurl as they both drew on the ball together. As a result I needed four stiches on my chin and ended up with a scar for life.

'He was a true perfectionist. He was always trying to perfect and practise his skills. The interesting thing was that unlike most players, the older he got the better he performed.

'I saw a side to Christy that few hurling fans got to see. He was a very kind, helpful person. Back in the 1960s I ran for the Senate and I went down to Cork to do some canvassing. I went into Johnny Quirke's pub and there, sitting in the corner, drinking a mineral, was Christy. When I explained what I was doing, he immediately volunteered to go canvassing with me and we went around all his friends, who not only promised to vote for me but actually did. It was a mark of the man that he was so generous with his time.'

3

EVERYONE SAY JAYO

Jason Sherlock: 1995–2010

In 1995 Jason Sherlock became the GAA's first pin-up boy when at just nineteen years of age he helped Dublin to win their first All-Ireland footall final in twelve years. His was fame of pop-star proportions after his bootless goal against Laois, his decisive goal against Cork in the All-Ireland semi-final and his pass to Charlie Redmond for the winning goal against Tyrone in the All-Ireland final. Nobody had ever seen any thing like it. Hence Marty Morrissey's unique question in the post-match interview: 'Is there a lady in your life?'

To his credit Jason turned defence into attack: 'I know you with the girls, Marty.'

One of the big hits of the time was the Outhere Brothers' 'Boom, Boom, Boom'. On Hill 16 this was adapted to 'Boom, boom, boom, everybody say Jayo'. This was a long way from the GAA of Christy Ring and Mick O'Connell.

Jayo's high profile over his fifteen years playing for the Dubs, though, came with a price, particularly when Dublin's form began to dip. 'I came from Finglas. I had a mother and

I had no father in the household. My father was from Hong Kong, so I looked different and Dublin or Ireland were in a place where we didn't understand other cultures in our society,' he says. 'Growing up had its challenges. I would have felt sport was a great outlet because I was invisible. If you were good at sport, people didn't really care what size or shape you were.

'I grew up wanting to be accepted, and winning an All-Ireland at that stage probably was the start of being accepted, and when that happened my focus in what I wanted to achieve probably wavered. But as things changed in the Dublin context and we started to lose games, I was singled out and things went back to the old days.'

By his own admission it took Jason a couple of years to come to terms with the situation he was in at the time: 'Looking back now, I was never the biggest, I was never the strongest, but I like to think I had an aptitude and I wanted to commit. After two years I did commit everything I had to play for fifteen years. I probably didn't get the trophies I wanted, but, in saying that, I gave everything to be the best footballer I could be and also to try and encourage and bring my teammates on as well.'

Since his retirement Jason has taken on the role of mental health campaigner. A case in point was his role in Cycle Against Suicide, a charity event where people cycled around the country stopping at schools to talk to transition years.

'I stood up with a microphone in front of 400 transition-year girls out in Bray who wouldn't have a clue who I am and I just talked about growing up and how hard it was to feel accepted and how it made me feel. I talked about how I dealt with it or didn't deal with it because it is important to share and ask for help,' he says.

'I wasn't sure how it would be received, but afterwards a 14-year-old girl came up to me in tears and said, "I know exactly what you mean, and you have really made me feel better," and she gave me a hug. That was very powerful for me because I'm sure for any sportsperson at the end of their career it is hard to comprehend what value you have outside the sport – that was something I had to come to terms with. To get a message like that was a very powerful thing and I was delighted. From there I moved into talking about racism and what I have encountered.'

When Jason first began speaking about racism, he talked to his family about what it was like for them when he was growing up.

'My uncle said we didn't see you as different, we saw you as a Dub. That's the way we treated you and that's the way we wanted you to see yourself,' he says. 'Now, that was noble and what they thought was right, but what it did was force me into a situation where I couldn't understand why people saw me as different because I just saw myself as a Dub. If I had it around again, I would have liked my family to say, "Yeah, you are different, and it's OK to be different, and we celebrate that." Then I might have been able to rationalise the negativity and abuse that I got a bit better.'

Over the years Jason experienced racism on a verbal and physical level and did not know how to deal with it. He believes this affected his self-esteem and made him paranoid. In 2013 he was the victim of racial abuse online after his appearance on RTÉ's *Up for the Match* programme on the eve of the All-Ireland final between Dublin and Mayo. A message posted by another player on Twitter said: 'Sherlock you na Fianna reject … Back to Asia with you, you don't belong here.'

'There was a time when I would have been a victim of that, but I retweeted it because I don't want to be a victim any more,' Jason says. Then some positives emerged out of a horrible situation. 'It was great to get the support that I got. The club he played for contacted me and he was suspended. Him and his parents wanted to apologise, which was noble of him. So I met him. One thing I asked him was, when he saw the abuse he was getting, how did he feel? He said he felt pretty bad. I told him he'd done something to warrant that. But imagine if you didn't do anything and people abused you anyway and you woke up to that abuse every day, can you imagine what effect that has on you as a person?'

Jason believes the answer is to be found in education.

'I think the GAA should take a more active leadership role on this. We all know how big and important a part of Irish society it is and they could take the bull by the horns and stamp this out.

'I know racism is part of a bigger issue in the GAA, sport and society, and I think education is the crucial thing. Someone like me is not going to get any satisfaction if someone racially abuses me and the referee hears it and suspends him because the damage is already done. It's not the punishment and the procedures but education which is more important. We need to seriously up our game in this respect. I think the GAA is a powerful tool and they have the opportunity to grasp the nettle. Irish society will be much the better if they do.'

4

JEEPERS KEEPERS

Davy Fitzgerald: 1990–2008

Davy Fitzgerald holds a unique place in the annals of Clare hurling. He won two All-Irelands as a player and another as manager.

Davy was central to the drama of Clare's All-Ireland win in 1995, as Anthony Daly recalled for me: 'There was a bit of magic in the air in Croke Park that day. It just seemed the way things fell into place. When the All-Ireland started, everything was going grand. Seánie McMahon scored two great points to set us off. We were doing everything we planned. It was a war of attrition. We were blocking them and hooking them.

'Then just before half-time disaster struck. Michael Duignan came along under the Cusack Stand and he seemed to try and lob the ball over the bar, but it fell short. Fitzie tried to control the ball with his hurley, which was unusual for him, but the sliotar skidded off and into the net. It looked like the classic sucker punch that could destroy us, if there was any fragile area in our make-up that would undo us. But we never dropped our heads.

'We came out and hurled away and got the break with the goal two minutes from the end. Offaly got the goal just before half-time – everyone says that's a great time to get a goal but it is probably a better time to get one with two minutes to go.'

Once at the summit in 1995 the Clare team was unlikely to be a wilting flower. It had been getting them there that had been the problem.

Fitzgerald was the one player who provided a litmus test for Ger Loughnane as to his team's psychological state. 'I always judged things by Davy Fitz's face. His face reveals everything. When you saw his face before a match, you knew if everybody was up for the game or not. People outside judged by the way he came out onto the field. Whenever he bounced into the goals and drew a lash, you knew everyone was up for the game. After the League final in '95 I could see Davy was very down. He had lost another final by a big score. Would it ever be any different?'

Though players' passions would sway, Davy Fitzgerald was a pillar of rectitude throughout Loughnane's steward-ship of the Clare team. 'He has nerves of steel. He would never show the slightest fear in a competitive hurling situa-tion. He would have faced a pride of starving lions. His nerve in facing John Leahy right at the death in the All-Ireland final in '97 was something to behold. He had cat-like reflexes. His save from DJ Carey's penalty in the All-Ireland semi-final that year was the greatest save I've ever seen. When Kilkenny got the penalty I was right behind the goals, telling our lads that they were going to stop it. DJ Carey connected with it perfectly and hit it magnificently. Ninety-nine times out of 100 it would have been a goal but Davy Fitz made a stunning save. He wanted it and was defying DJ to hit it as hard as he could. In saving it he blocked it away from his own goal so that no in-rushing forward would score on the rebound.

'You never had to worry about his physical and mental preparation. He had his own goalkeeping routine. The greatest saves he ever made were in training. We'd line up twenty players who would bombard him with shots. The saves he made were absolutely breathtaking. Often the saves were so good that no goal would be scored out of the twenty shots. He's been very hard done by, by the All-Star selectors. He should have got a lot more.'

Loughnane is well placed to assess the man as well as the player: 'As a person he was the most charming and popular of all the players, especially with young people. He's a massive ambassador for the game. He doesn't drink but crowds gather around him and like him instantly. The contradiction is that he's totally self-centred like most goalies! His own performance was paramount.

'I used to give Fitzie a desperate time in training. The very odd time he'd let in a soft goal and I'd eat him, but I'd always be killing him about his puckouts. I would never say anything quietly to a player because I wasn't just giving a message to him, I was always giving a message to the whole team. I was always in the middle of the field so everyone would hear what I said and my criticism was always laced with outrageous language. There was one night in Cusack Park I gave him a particularly terrible time. He belted the goals and was seething.

'I went with him to Castlebar in June 2001 for a golf classic and he confessed that on that night he had called me every foul name under the sun. I told him I knew that because my son, Conor, was standing behind him all night and reported everything back to me. He went pale. All he could say was, "Oh, f**k."'

It is Loughane who provides the definitive summary of Davy: 'He manages the same as he played – in only one gear. Mad up for it.'

5

STRAIGHT SHOOTER

Pat Spillane: 1974–1991

Eight All-Ireland medals, nine All-Star awards, twice Footballer of the Year, chosen on both the Team of the Century and Team of the Millennium – by any standards Pat Spillane's record means he must be acknowledged as one of the greatest players of all time.

To get an objective appraisal of Pat's career, I spoke to someone who played against him on many occasions. In 1979 Dermot Earley cried openly when the Rossies beat Kerry in the National League quarter-final. After his five-star performance in the All-Ireland final the previous year, Spillane was widely seen as one player who needed constant watching. Against Roscommon, though, Gerry Fitzmaurice was having one of his greatest games and was giving Spillane a torrid time. When the half-time whistle went, Earley raced up to Fitzmaurice and told him that it was he who should have been the All-Star, he was playing so well. Spillane reacted badly to his intervention, as Dermot recalled years later. 'I was not "sledging" Pat. I was praising Gerry to the hilt to boost his confidence and to encourage him to continue to play well. In fact it was a backhanded compliment to Pat because he was so crucial to Kerry as one of the genuine greatest players of all time I wanted to see him curtailed and Gerry was doing just that. Pat, though, was very indignant at my comments. In fact, he was fuming. I didn't want to engage with him, so I ran into the dressing room. But he almost followed me in, shouting at me that I was "only an auld fella", that I was "past it" and that I was "over the hill". I was delighted because I knew we had them rattled and that was the moment when I knew we were going to win the match.

'Pat was a wholehearted, skilful, unselfish player for Kerry for seventeen years who thrilled crowds in Croke Park on so many occasions. He had the ability to cover the whole field. I can remember one occasion in the 1978 All-Ireland final when Kerry were temporarily without a goalie and the man who went in goal was Pat Spillane.

'He had the ability to take scores from difficult angles, mostly with his right foot. He was a quick thinker and his release of the ball was always excellent. Above all he was an inspiration to those around him. When things were going against Kerry, Spillane would be the man who would pull something special out of the bag, whether it would be a catch or a run, or a pass or a point. It would lift the team again and establish Kerry on top.

'One of the things you would have to remember about him during his long and fruitful career was that, although he had received a serious knee injury, his determination was so great that he was able to come back and perform at the highest level again, wearing that distinctive blue knee brace that everyone became familiar with. On one occasion I saw an opponent deliberately swiping at Spillane's knee with the obvious intention of re-injuring it, but nothing like that ever worked against him.

'No player on the great Kerry team bought more into the ethos that pain is temporary, glory is eternal than Pat Spillane. What can't be cured must be endured.'

In Roscommon, the Kerry ace is still remembered for one incident during the 1980 All-Ireland final. He and Gerry Fitzmaurice were involved in an incident off the ball. Pat was prostrate on the ground and took an age to get up. Time went by and many efforts were made to assist his recovery, to no avail. About four minutes later Pat staggered up. Roscommon had got off to a whirlwind start and were leading 1–2 to no score after eleven minutes. It did not escape the fans' attention that Roscommon were playing with a strong wind at the time. Within a minute, Pat was flying up the wing like a March hare.

In 2007 Earley and Spillane found themselves travelling to Roscommon for a celebrity version of questions and answers. As the star guests entered the premises a young Roscommon footballer who was there to attend the famous Rockfords nightclub made a beeline for Spillane. It amused Dermot that the Roscommon player was a bit miffed when Spillane didn't recognise him. The slightly humbled player sent one of his friends over a few minutes later to inform the Kerry man exactly who he was.

After the charity event was completed and the guests were making their way home they passed the young Roscommon player in the hotel corridor; he was well lubricated and made a very derogatory comment to Spillane. Having being brought up in the family pub in Templenoe, Spillane did not bat an eyelid and walked quickly past without offering any comment. Dermot, though, was visibly crestfallen at what he heard.

———————

'It should never have happened and I was mortified, but fair play to Pat – it was like water off a duck's back to him. Like many people, he has annoyed me at times with his comments on *The Sunday Game*, but I have to say he has really gone up in my estimation since he has spoken out so forcefully about the danger of young people abusing drink. He's also been a powerful advocate for people in rural Ireland.

'Pat grew up in the family bar and the interaction with customers from a young age sharpened his wits and prepared him for his subsequent career in the media, where he has to think quickly. However, in recent times he has decided that he must speak out about what he sees as "the sickness of Saturday-night Ireland", which sees so many young Irish people getting drunk, with a consequent increase in aggression and accidents.'

Becoming a teacher gave Spillane an extra dimension to his sense of the importance of responsible behaviour. 'When you are a parent, you realise how much an act of faith it is to leave your kids in somebody else's care. It's a huge responsibility. Naturally, you want the very best for your own kids and it helps you to understand how parents feel when they entrust their children to you as a coach of juvenile teams. As a result I worked hard when I became a teacher at helping young people to get the best out of themselves.'

6

GOLDEN GREAT

Pat Gilroy: 1992–2000

If Pat Gilroy was ever to star in a remake of a James Bond film, it would be *Goldfinger*. Why? He is the man with the Midas touch. He won an All-Ireland playing for Dublin as a player in 1995, he won an All-Ireland with Dublin as manager in 2011 – and he has become a leading figure in the corporate world as a CEO of a major company. His playing accomplishments are all the more impressive as he has a form of asthma. As a manager he believed in the creed of 'winning by inches', which led to meticulous planning.

Away from the game Gilroy is reflective about the sport he loves so well. His big frame gives him a huge physical presence but when he speaks he does so with gravitas. He is uncomfortable with some of the developments in Gaelic games: 'One of the most unethical things I see in the GAA is pushing young people into situations too early in life. Because if a manager wants to win an under-21 final, he plays a 15-year-old. Other things I see are pushing young people into a situation where they are playing with a top team and they are just not able for it; they are cut down because they don't make it and they are cast adrift.'

Gilroy feels that the GAA needs to confront the issue among its own members. 'Unfortunately some of our stars of the past, and indeed of the present, have struggled with addictions like gambling, but the biggest problem has been with drink. Status can become like a drug and people are often not prepared for the end of their career. There are some terribly sad stories in the GAA. We are great at talking about some character and saying, "He was some man to drink," but then he is dead at fifty. This is not good enough and we must work much harder to try and change that culture, though I know the GPA is already doing some good work in this area.

'There is no question that if induction to drinking at a young age continues, harms in later life will be inevitable, and I think ultimately the GAA will be the loser. I understand the financial imperatives for the Association but we also need to be mindful of our wider obligations to society.'

Being in the managerial hot seat forced Gilroy to examine his own conscience. 'When I was manager of Dublin, I was forced to reflect on my own role in terms of the instructions I was giving to the team and in particular when I was asking for more physicality. I did not want to be responsible for sending someone out to play for me if it was going to cause a serious injury. When I talked about more physicality, one player would take that to mean getting much tighter on his man and putting him under pressure when they lost the ball, but maybe one of the other lads would have taken it as incitement to go out and decapitate somebody. Yes, I wanted to win; but no, I did not want to win at all costs.'

Another social problem troubles Gilroy: 'We in Ireland are all experts in one area: the blame game. I am not just talking about the media here, but all of us in our clubs and talking in the pub – we all do it. I made mistakes as a manager and I know that I have to take criticism in those situations, but there has to be a line that we don't cross. When a team loses, there is always a rush to judgement and some poor unfortunate – the manager, or the referee, or the freetaker who has an off day and misses – will be slaughtered to bits. Since social media has come into prominence, players and managers are subject to the most savage criticism, but the people responsible for these often nasty and vicous comments do not have the guts to put their names to it.'

Media scrutiny also brings potential problems in Gilroy's eyes. 'The media spotlight has changed dramatically. There is certainly a fair bit of negativity in the media coverage. What particularly annoys me is what I consider the blight of radio phone-ins. It also creates a much more difficult environment for players and managers to operate in. You have to remember these players are amateurs but often people under the cloak of anonymity ring in and make very personalised comments about players. We can all have a view on a pundit's comments on TV, but at least they're putting their name to them. I don't have any time for radio stations who give credibility to callers who don't have the guts to put their names to their opinions. And of course on the internet you can say absolutely anything and sometimes these comments can be very destructive.'

Gilroy feels that the GAA would benefit from looking at the wider context. 'I think we could learn a lot from rugby because of the culture they have in relation to referees in particular. In rugby nobody dares to question the authority of the referee; that is far from the case in Gaelic games, where referees are often treated with nothing short of contempt.

The GAA is an incredible organisation, but the one thing we need more of at all levels is respect.

'I remember hearing Ireland's Olympic icon Ronnie Delany speaking one day. He said: "Respect is an enormous attribute for the younger athlete. Respect for the colours you wear, respect for your club, your county, your country, your province."'

Gilroy offers a parable about the way the game should be played: 'The 2013 All-Ireland football final did produce a great moment of sportsmanship. When the final whistle went, you would have expected Johnny Cooper to have celebrated but he did not. His first instinct was to run over and console Rob Hennelly, one of the Mayo players and a friend of his from college. They won a Sigerson together with DCU. There was a picture taken of Johnny trying to console Rob – whoever said a picture tells a thousand words could have been thinking of this photo. It speaks volumes about Johnny and the way the game should be played.'

7

THE FLYING DOCTOR

Pádraig Carney: 1945–1954

Sometimes star players do not get on together. Newstalk presenter and former lead singer with Something Happens Tom Dunne is an avid Manchester United fan and one of the highlights of his life came when he was invited to do a public interview with some of the United legends. One of them was Peter Schmeichel. He had heard that the great goalie did not get on well with Roy Keane and enquired how best to broach the subject. In response, he got a message saying that Schmeichel was no longer happy to do the interview and would stay in the dressing room. Eventually a compromise was agreed. Schmeichel said he'd do the interview as long as there were no questions about Keane.

Pádraig Carney was loved universally by his teammates. Such was his value to Mayo that they flew Pádraig home from his work as a doctor in the United States for the 1954 National League semi-final and final. They won, so the expense and his Homeric path was justified. Carney had established himself in the pantheon of the greats of the game because of his performances when Mayo won consecutive All-Irelands in 1950 and '51.

Leitrim great Packy McGarty acknowledges his debt to a larger-than-life figure: 'I will always remember sitting in the back of the car on the way to my first match with Connacht beside Pádraig Carney – the Flying Doctor – who was the greatest footballer I ever saw. I was only a young lad from Leitrim and I was going to be marking the Munster captain Jas Murphy, who captained Kerry to win the All-Ireland in 1953. He was six foot three and I was only a small lad in comparison. I was thinking about this and looking at Pádraig's massive legs when he said, "Junior, don't be afraid." It gave me great confidence.

'The only problem was that as we were getting ready to go out on the pitch Tull Dunne from Ballinasloe, who was in charge of the team, said, "Anyone that's not doing his stuff, we have good subs and we'll take him off." With respect to Tull, that didn't give me much confidence. I was thinking to myself, I shouldn't be on this team. As I looked around those great players with great reputations, all I could think was, *Here I am, a nobody from Leitrim.* Our captain, Mayo's Seán Flanagan, stepped in at that stage and said, "Stop. Ye had a night to pick the team and anybody who was good enough to be chosen that night is good enough to play unless they get injured." I grew in confidence again.

'A few days before the match I had got a splinter in my hand and I had a bandage on it and was wearing gloves. The first ball that came into me I caught but it fell out of my hand and I caught it again and kicked it over the bar. I got rid of my gloves and bandage straight away and as I was doing that Pádraig Carney clapped me on the back and said, "Well done, Junior." I got a goal and four points and had one of my best games ever. Those few words from Carney were critical, though, because I looked up to him so much; he gave me the confidence to take my place among some of the greats of the game.'

Carney's place in the GAA immortals rests in no small measure with his epic tussles with Seán Purcell. The Galway legend spoke to me about Carney in the context of a discussion of the characters of the game.

'Characters are good for sport. There were a lot of characters in the old days in Gaelic games, when there were no managers and players were individuals. Nowadays, with managers controlling players and not allowing them to talk to the media, characters are not as plentiful as they once were. Pádraig Carney, from the great Mayo team was a wonderful character. Sometimes he would even hold up the ball to show to the crowd and usually it went over the bar. He had a little bit of arrogance, but he also had the skill to match. He was one of the first players to bring glamour to the GAA. He had an aura about him and the fans related to that. He helped bring the game to a wider audience. Apart from his genius on the field the GAA owes him a debt because he was great box office at a time when Ireland needed glamour badly.'

8

JIMMY'S WINNING MATCHES

Jim McGuinness: 1992–2003

Although still a teenager Jim McGuiness was on the panel when Donegal won their first All-Ireland in 1992 and Anthony Molloy raised the Sam Maguire Cup. Twenty years later McGuinness was at the helm when Donegal were deservedly crowned All-Ireland champions following their four-point victory over Mayo in the first Ulster–Connacht final since 1948 when Cavan, captained by the Gallant John Joe O'Reilly, had defeated Mayo. In 2012 Michael Murphy, who, along with Colm McFadden, scored 1–4 in the final, had the honour of lifting the most coveted cup in Gaelic football. When the Glenswilly clubman sang a verse of the popular song of that summer, 'Jimmy's Winning Matches', it was an acknowledgement of the centrality of McGuinness in Donegal's victory.

When Jim had taken the job two years earlier, Donegal were in freefall, having lost by nine points to Armagh in Crossmaglen in a first-round qualifier in June 2010. It is a measure of McGuinness's skills as a manager that no fewer than thirteen of the players who featured in the Armagh game would play some part in the All-Ireland victory.

McGuinness created a managerial culture based on empowering his players: 'It wasn't just about taking a football team and doing the best you could do with the team. I wanted it to be a bit more than that. I wanted it to be a life experience for the people that were involved.'

He also dismisses the widely held notion of a win-at-all-costs mentality and admits that being second best in 2011 to Dublin gave plenty of food for thought: 'Obviously we wanted to win, we wanted to win more than anything in the world, but we wanted to give the best account of ourselves as possible. If you do that and you push yourself to the limit and you get the most out of yourself, you have to be happy with the result. If it's a win, or a loss, or a draw, that's what is involved in the process.

'There's nothing wrong with second place if the other team is better than you. All you have got to do then is re-evaluate where you are at, look at your weaknesses and see whether you can push on. That's what we did between 2011 and 2012. Dublin were better than us and we weren't developed to the level that we were good enough to win an All-Ireland.

'When we brought the support team together, a big part of the remit was that you need to be professional and really, really positive. Never talk down to a player – never talk behind a player's back to another member of the support team. Never disrespect somebody and you would hope you would get the same back. I think that's really, really important. The whole concept is about relationships. We were all there for the same goal.

'If you don't feel you are able to manage a task, people become demotivated. With the task and the challenge that you are being set you have got to be able to identify the fact that you are able to do it.'

Pat Spillane has been a persistent critic not of McGuiness personally but of the style of football he employed as Donegal manager. 'Fair play to Jim McGuinness. You have to give him credit for winning an All-Ireland with a team that were seen as no-hopers when he got the job. And no matter how much I disliked the style at times, he was an innovator of sorts. The pity is that he did so by shackling some of the talents of his players. In October 2015, I picked my forty greatest players of the day in my column in the *Sunday World* and my number one was Michael Murphy. Did we see all of his talents under Jim McGuinness's management? No way. That thought depresses me and it is an indictment of the modern game.'

McGuiness came close to winning a second All-Ireland in 2014, but Éamonn Fitzmaurice outfoxed him and Kerry emerged with a narrow victory. Kerry beat Donegal with both sides playing very negative styles and making multiple mistakes. Hence one fan's tweet after the match: 'In a game that both sides seemed to want to lose Donegal seemed to want to lose it more.'

Joe Brolly was characteristically understated: 'Kerry were like the little girl in *The Exorcist* whose head revolves as she machine-guns the walls with vomit.'

Former Kerry manager Jack O'Connor said of Donegal's style: 'If I tried to play football like that in Kerry, I'd get *bata agus bothar*.'

After that All-Ireland Final defeat at the hands of Kerry, McGuinness said that his time had come to a natural end but he created something of a sensation when he took a post as psychologist with Glasgow Celtic.

———

'There is only so long you can drive people,' he said. 'You need people to drive themselves.'

A few days before the final the GAA had its own 'spygate' when Donegal civil servant Patrick Roarty was rumbled up a tree apparently trying to spy on the Kerry training session. The Kerry background team heard the noise of rustling branches coming from the grounds of St Finan's Hospital, the now vacant psychiatric unit adjacent to Fitzgerald Stadium. When asked what he believed Roarty was doing up a tree overlooking the stadium, former Donegal star John Gildea calmly observed: 'Sure it's September. He was probably just looking for apples.'

9

YOU CAN ONLY DANCE WITH THE GIRLS IN THE HALL

John O'Mahony: 1982–2009

John O'Mahony led St Nathy's College to an All-Ireland title. Then, after twenty-eight years in the wilderness, he awakened the sleeping giant that was St Brigid's to lead them to a county title and set them on the trail to eventually become the first Roscommon team to win an All-Ireland club final. He also came within a whisker of leading Mayo to an All-Ireland title in 1989, then in 1994 he famously led Leitrim to an historic Connacht title. He went on to guide a Galway team that Eugene McGee had dismissed as 'fancy Dans' to All-Irelands in 1998 and 2001. What is the secret of his success?

'You can only dance with the girls in the hall. There's no use wishing for what you don't have. You have to work with what you have and find a way to get the best out of them.' O'Mahony is a disciple of the 'creating a squad' approach.

Before the 1989 All-Ireland final, Anthony Finnerty asked him, 'Where's the strength of the team?'

He replied, 'On the bench.'

O'Mahony believes in the culture of winning. 'One of the most impressive people I have met was the former captain of the All-Blacks Sean Fitzpatrick. His father was also an All-Black. In fact, he was on the first All-Blacks team to lose to Wales in 1953 and had to carry the stigma for the rest of his life. When he was on his deathbed, they tried to rally him by bringing his All-Blacks jersey to him, but he waved it away. Even as he was getting ready to take his dying breath he could not let go of the scar of that defeat. So it was a powerful reminder to me of the importance of winning – and I believe in winning, within the rules of decency, sportsmanship and ethics.'

O'Mahony was also taken by another rugby icon. 'I am sometimes asked who I think makes a good role model, and for me the ultimate role model for any young GAA player should be Dan Carter. I met him shortly after he starred in the All-Blacks World Cup win in 2015. What struck me most about him was his humility. My wife Ger is a big rugby fan and I wanted him to sign her jersey, and he could not have been more accommodating. Here was the biggest name in world rugby, but there was no hint of airs and graces, he was so down to earth and unaffected. I am sometimes disappointed by young GAA players who, once they get a small bit of profile, completely lose the run of themselves, even if they will never achieve a tiny fraction of what Dan Carter has achieved.'

Although he is a very mild-mannered man, there is a steel to John O'Mahony as was evident in his preparation for the 2001 All-Ireland final. 'I went to see Meath humiliate Kerry in the All-Ireland semi-final. I was going home on the train and I met a number of Kerry supporters at the station. They came over to shake my hand and were nearly sympathising with me. I remember thinking to myself that we were going to prove everyone wrong. Although Meath were favourites, I was determined that we were going to put it up to them. At the end of the Kerry game, the Meath players were almost showboating, but there was no way I was going to let that happen to us. I knew the week before that we were ready to push Meath all the way and basically we did to them what they did to Kerry.'

O'Mahony's famed diplomatic skills were called into action that year when his star player, Michael Donnellan, and his brother, John, sensationally left the squad. The story at the time was that John was not happy with the amount of game time he was getting on the team. 'The key thing was to resolve the issue behind closed doors,' said O'Mahony. 'If either of the lads had gone to the media or if I had said anything, the affair would never have been solved and we would have lost two vital members of the squad, including one of the finest players of his generation. So it was about getting people into the room and keeping everybody else out of it.'

In his famous interview with Roy Keane in 2002, Tommie Gorman contrasted what had happened between Keane and Mick McCarthy on the Japanese island Saipan, where the Ireland team were training for the World Cup, with the private and diplomatic way O'Mahony had handled the Donnellan situation.

Those same skills would come in very useful for O'Mahony when he entered the political arena. He served two terms as TD – for Mayo. He takes his heroes from the political world: 'Because I was in Fine Gael people expect that my hero is Michael Collins – and of course he is a hero – but my two greatest heroes are John Hume and Seamus Mallon of the SDLP. They were the ones that brought Sinn Féin into the fold in the Northern Ireland peace process. They probably knew that in the medium and long term it was going to be very damaging for their own party but they sacrificed their own party interest for the greater good. That spirit of sacrifice is what I most admire in any leader. A manager of a GAA team should be thinking always of what is in the best long-term interests of the team, even if the price is sometimes extreme unpopularity with the fans in the short term – especially in this age of social media. I wish county boards had more people like John Hume and Seamus Mallon, and would always set aside their own interests for the greater good. I was taken with something Dermot Earley once said: "There are teams that achieve success not because of their County Boards but in spite of them."'

O'Mahony has seen big changes in the game since he first made his mark as a manager when he steered Mayo to an under-21 All-Ireland. 'One of the biggest changes has been technology,' he says. 'I will never forget the first time mobile phones came in. A county secretary, who must remain nameless, received notification that he had a message in his mailbox. He spent the evening frantically combing through his post to find out what it was.'

What, then, is O'Mahony's philosophy of sport?

'A winner never quits. A quitter never wins.'

10

THE EARLEY YEARS

Dermot Earley: 1965–1985

The late Dermot Earley was often described as the greatest player never to win an-All-Ireland medal. Jimmy Magee, though, is keen to pay tribute in more positive terms.

'Dermot was kinda part of my life. He wasn't a close friend but he was a friend. He always seemed as if he was happy to see you and I am sure he was. He had an endearing smile and a great personal warmth.

'Men are not judged in my lifetime by the number of honours but by their behaviour in the pursuit of honours. He had the greatest medal of all. He had respect. Wouldn't that be great to have on your tombstone? "This man had great respect."'

A lost leader of exemplary virtues, Earley found himself embroiled in controversy in the All-Ireland semi-final against Armagh in 1977. With the score tied at Armagh 3–9 Roscommon 2–12, as Earley faced up to a long-distance free, the last kick of the game, Gerry O'Neill (brother of Irish manager Martin), the Armagh trainer, ran across the field in front of him and shouted something at him. The kick sailed high and wide.

There was much press comment on the 'O'Neill–Earley' incident in the following days. In his column in *The Evening Press* Con Houlihan offered two All-Ireland tickets to the person who could tell him what O'Neill had said. The Roscommon star was not unduly distracted. 'I had no idea what he said to me that time. I wasn't even aware that he was talking to me. All I wanted to do was drill the ball over the bar.'

What did bother him was the outcome of the game.

'We were seven points up with ten minutes to go in the All-Ireland semi-final against Armagh but we lost concentration and let them back to draw the game. You could feel the giddiness running through the team. We thought we had one foot in the All-Ireland final. We were shell-shocked in the dressing room afterwards. We had been much better than them but in the replay they beat us by a point.

'It was pretty much the same story two years later when we snatched defeat from the jaws of victory against Dublin in the semi-final to again lose by a point. If we had won either of those two semi-finals, the experience of having played an All-Ireland final would have been invaluable when we took on Kerry in the 1980 final.'

Away from the sporting fields Dermot rose to the top of the Defence Forces, where he was described as 'the most iconic Chief of Staff since Michael Collins'. He was also a leading diplomat on the international stage, spending four years in New York as Military Advisor to the Secretary-General of the United Nations.

Dermot's contacts in conflict zones would become very useful when Sharon Commins was taken hostage when working with a development agency in Sudan's war-torn region of Darfur in July 2009. She was held in captivity for days. A laybrinth of Irish government departments were involved.

'Sharon was released eventually. The nation was happy. Nobody knew anything about my role, which was as it should be, but it was a great thrill when we got the happy outcome. It was very satisfying but involved many hours of work behind the scenes.'

For her part Sharon Commins was keenly aware of Dermot's role in her release: 'When I went to Roscommon, one of the things I was keen to do was to publicly express my thanks for the role Dermot had played in securing my release from captivity.'

One thing that set Dermot apart was that he was a brilliant public speaker. Micheál O'Muircheartaigh said of his speeches, 'You'd sit back and listen to him and hope it would go on a little bit longer.'

Whenever he spoke in public, he invariably told a joke against himself. He turned self-deprecation into an art form. His favourite described one night as he was approaching Roscommon town. He saw a teenager thumbing a lift. As it was raining, he picked him up. As they got close to the football pitch, Dermot asked the youngster if he had ever played in Dr Hyde Park. The young man replied: 'Many times.'

Dermot said: 'I played a few good games here myself. In 1973 Roscommon were playing the All-Ireland champions of the time, Cork, here. The team were just a point ahead in the last minute when Cork mounted an attack and I made the saving clearance.'

The teenager replied: 'I know.'

Dermot continued: 'In 1977 I played on with a broken

finger and helped Roscommon beat Galway in the Connacht final.'

Again the young man responded: 'I know.'

Undeterred Dermot persisted: 'I once kicked a fifty against a gale-force wind and landed it over the bar in a match against Down.'

Yet again the young man's reply was: 'I know.'

By now Dermot was puzzled and asked his companion what age he was. When his guest replied that he was only sixteen, Dermot asked: 'All those matches were over twenty years ago, before you were even born. How could you possibly know about them?'

The teenager sighed deeply before saying: 'You gave me a lift two weeks ago and you told me the exact same things then.'

Dermot's dream team from his playing days, excluding Roscommon players, was:

1. Billy Morgan
(*Cork*)

2. Enda Colleran   **3. Jack Quinn**   **4. Tom O'Hare**
(*Galway*)   (*Meath*)   (*Down*)

5. Paídí Ó Sé   **6. Nicholas Clavin**   **7. Martin Newell**
(*Kerry*)   (*Offaly*)   (*Galway*)

8. Jimmy Duggan   **9. Jack O'Shea**
(*Galway*)   (*Kerry*)

10. Matt Connor   **11. Denis 'Oige' Moran**   **12. Pat Spillane**
(*Offaly*)   (*Kerry*)   (*Kerry*)

13. Mike Sheehy   **14. Seán O'Neill**   **15. John Egan**
(*Kerry*)   (*Down*)   (*Kerry*)

11

IN THE NAME OF THE FATHER

Dermot Earley, Jnr: 1997–2013

From almost his first breath, Dermot Earley, Jnr was immersed in football.

'I was born in 1978, two days before Roscommon played Galway in the Connacht final in Pearse Stadium. Dad always said he got the family–football balance just right: 70 per cent football, 30 per cent family.

'At the time, a member of the clergy threw in the ball. So when the midfielders gathered for the throw-in, there waiting for them was Bishop Eamon Casey. He said: "Well, lads, are ye nervous?"

'Thankfully Roscommon won. The next day the cup was smuggled out of Roscommon and brought up to my mother and I in Mount Carmel Hospital. I was placed in it. It was my first taste of inter-county football.'

Dermot Jnr looks back on the biggest game of his career, the 1998 All-Ireland final, with surprising detachment. 'There was a huge amount of hype in Kildare in the build-up and Galway kind of slipped in under the radar. There were posters saying: *There's going to be a wedding: Sam Maguire is going to marry Lily White.*

'We were three points up at half-time and I can remember thinking: we're in a good place. Glen Ryan had kept Ja Fallon quiet in the first half and in the second it wasn't that Glen didn't play well but that Ja started scoring the most inspirational points, including that famous one from the sideline, and of course they got the goal so the momentum was with them. It was only then that the country fully appreciated the great job John O'Mahony had done, bringing together such a collection of great players and giving them the freedom to play free-flowing, attacking football. They proved they were a great team by winning a second All-Ireland in 2001.'

When I asked him about which of his son's games for the Lilywhites had he most enjoyed, Dermot Snr immediately went for Saturday, 12 August 2000. 'It was the Leinster final replay. The Dubs were on fire in the first half and led by 0–11 to 0–5. Pat Spillane was writing Kildare's obituary. But ninety seconds into the second half Dermot got a goal back and then Tadhg Fennin got an equalising goal. The pendulum swung completely in Kildare's direction and Willie McCreery was mighty in midfield. Any Kildare fan who was there that day will never forget it. Kildare ran out comfortable winners by 2–11 to 0–12. It was a great day for the Lilywhites and another proud moment for a dad of one of the players. It was like a moment of grace, but a moment of grace that is granted only rarely.'

Like his father before him Dermot Jnr had a glittering career, but unlike his dad he was forced to retire prematurely, in 2013, after a lengthy struggle with injury – or more accurately, injuries. 'In 2010 I jarred my knee in an early season training and turned on it in a league game against Laois, a moment that caused me to tear 90 per cent of the cruciate ligament. I was told I'd need an operation eventually, but I may be able to keep playing. It depended on how strong my quads and other muscles were to stabilise the knee. So I kept going.

'The doctor said I would have to tone it down about 10 per cent, but in championship instinct takes over. I remember thinking against Leitrim, when I came down from the throw-in at the start of the second half, the last bit of the ligament is gone and it's completely torn. I played on for a while that day and in the rest of the qualifiers I had no problems. There were times when I would get a dart of pain but it went away again. If you were in the same boat, then you'd do the same thing. Any footballer would keep going unless his leg was hanging off. I don't want it to sound like I'm delighted I came through some pain barrier and it makes me unique. I'm not.

'My knee had little holding it together. And I knew the minute I went to launch a long ball into the Kildare full-forward line early on in the quarter-final against Meath that I was in big trouble. I got up, thinking, "I've been down before and carried on." But this time I just couldn't play with a snapped cruciate. Tests later revealed my knee bones had slid out of place, as they had in the games against Derry and Monaghan, but this time they never slid back. The real pain came from missing the games themselves.'

Like his father before him, Dermot won two All-Star awards (his sister Noelle and his uncle Paul also won All-Stars) and his displays in the Kildare jersey and in the Compromise Rules were a source of immense pride for his father. There was one time, though, when Dermot Snr was not happy to see his son wearing the green jersey, as his brother Paul witnessed first hand.

———

'Dermot was irate about what happened in 2006 in the Second Test because he considered what the Aussies did was nothing less than thuggery. Many people will remember Kieran McGeeney's comments after the match: "If you wanna box, say you wanna box and we'll box. If you wanna play football, say you wanna play football and we'll play football."

'There was a dinner afterwards and Dermot was one of the guests. I was talking to one of the most high-profile members of the Aussie delegation and he was trying to tell me what happened was no big deal – despite the fact that Graham Geraghty was left unconscious and required hospitalisation. I told him to stop talking through his arse.

'The atmosphere was very tense. Then Nickey Brennan, who was GAA president at the time, stood up to speak. He pointedly said before he started he wanted to wish Graham Geraghty well because he was in hospital. You could feel the tension go up another notch immediately.

'The Aussie coach that year was Kevin Sheedy and he came over to our table and was trying to be placatory and said that it would be very different the next time and said there would be a dinner for both teams first and that would sort everything out. It was so out of character for Dermot, who was always so diplomatic, but he asked him, "Will you have the fight before, during or after the dinner?" Talk about an awkward silence afterwards.'

Dermot has inherited his father's quick wit and flair for public speaking. In 2014 Enda Kenny launched his father's authorised biography. In his address as a proud Mayo fan, the Taoiseach drew attention to the fact that Dermot had been born in Castlebar. Dermot Earley, Jnr quipped: 'And the reason he left Mayo and moved to Roscommon was that he knew it was going to take so long for Mayo to win the All-Ireland.'

When I asked Dermot to pick his dream team, he prefaced his selection with the following comments: 'I know I'm missing a few all-time greats, but I picked it on players from my experience in my era that I played with (Kildare, Leinster and Ireland) and against. The only exception is Rory O'Carroll, but having watched him in recent years and worked with him with the International Rules management team in 2015 I think he is one of the toughest and best full-backs to play the game. He has a brilliant attitude as well. Centre back and my captain was a tough one, but Glen gets the nod because he was inspirational to play with, Kieran McGeeney another brilliant leader and brilliant player is at seven. Not a bad half-back line. Niall Buckley was the greatest player I ever played with – he had it all.'

Dermot Earley, Jnr's dream team is:

1. Stephen Cluxton
(Dublin)

2. Marc Ó Sé　　**3. Rory O'Carroll**　　**4. Keith Higgins**
(Kerry)　　　　　*(Dublin)*　　　　　*(Mayo)*

5. Tomás Ó Sé　**6. Glen Ryan (capt.)**　**7. Kieran McGeeney**
(Kerry)　　　　　*(Kildare)*　　　　　*(Armagh)*

8. Darragh Ó Sé　　　**9. Niall Buckley**
(Kerry)　　　　　　*(Kildare)*

10. Michael Donnellan　**11. Trevor Giles**　**12. Seán Cavanagh**
(Tyrone)　　　　　*(Meath)*　　　　　*(Tyrone)*

13. Colm Cooper　**14. Pádraic Joyce**　**15. Peter Canavan**
(Kerry)　　　　　*(Galway)*　　　　　*(Tyrone)*

12

THE KING OF THE KINGDOM

Mick O'Connell: 1956–1974

The first media spat of 2017 came at the start of January. To mark the occasion of Mick O'Connell's eightieth birthday, Ger Gilroy and Joe Molloy interviewed him on Newstalk's popular *Off the Ball*. However, in his newspaper column Joe Brolly was openly scornful about the pair's efforts because he felt that they did not have a true appreciation for Gaelic football's legend of legends.

The acerbic exchange did prompt a revealing insight from Joe about O'Connell in his column in the *Sunday Independent* about his time in Trinity College, when he played on the Sigerson team with the O'Sullivan brothers from Cahirciveen, Seanie and Diarmuid.

Sigerson was hot and heavy in those days, and attrition was the name of the game,' Joe wrote. 'Both boys were purists when they arrived in Dublin and quickly had to be schooled in the dark arts ... When they were in their third year, they went home to play a South Kerry championship match for St Mary's against Valentia Island. Seanie was corner back, and from the first whistle tucked into his man with a vengeance, thumping, pulling and trash talking.

Mick O'Connell was standing behind the goals watching on in horror, and after fifteen minutes the great man could take no more. He stepped onto the field of play and told Seanie his behaviour was disgraceful and that whatever he had learned in Dublin there was no place for it in the Kingdom. 'Stop that nonsense immediately, son, and play like a Kerryman.'

Seanie, who is only 5 ft 7in., looked him straight in the eye and said: 'Would you ever f**k off?' It was too late for redemption. Seanie had been converted to the dark side.

In 2016 the Association of Irish Journalists chose to honour Mick O'Connell on the eve of the Dublin–Kerry All-Ireland semi-final. As the AIJ's president Peter Byrne noted on the day, the very first live televised game of Gaelic football on RTÉ was the 1962 All-Ireland semi-final. Kerry–Dublin. In a clash among two footballing superpowers, Mick O'Connell's high fielding literally elevated him above all others. That day he would not only become Gaelic football's first-ever TV star but also an ambassador of the game at its most skilful and pure.

O'Connell is the most iconic name in Gaelic football – the game's first superstar. He was the catch and kick footballer par excellence and played the game as if his motto was 'Catch it like you love it and kick it like you hate it.' He is the yardstick by which all subsequent midfielders with aspirations to greatness are judged and not surprisingly he was chosen in that position on both the Team of the Century and Team of the Millennium.

At the beginning of every year Kerry footballers put two dates in their diary: the Munster final and the All-Ireland final. Mick O'Connell knew this phenomenon better than most. He won four All-Ireland medals (in 1959, '62, '69 and '70) and six National Leagues. In 1962 he was chosen as Footballer of the Year and in that year's All-Ireland final O'Connell was the driving force when Kerry beat the men in primrose and blue from Roscommon by 1–12 to 1–6.

While no one has ever questioned his extraordinary skills, there are those who questioned O'Connell's ability when he was tightly marked. Maurice Hayes, in an indictment of the modern game rather than a criticism of a legend, observed: 'Mick O'Connell would not last five minutes today with the blanket defence.'

The fact that he lived on the island of Valentia and rowed himself on his boat to the Kerry coastline for training and games added to his aura as a man apart. Although the game's most public figure because of his wonders on the field, he remained an intensely private man off it. Experience had taught him that for someone in his position reserve is an indispensable virtue. Those who have penetrated his inner circle testify that he has the gentle nature typical of country people.

13

CAMOGIE'S QUEEN

Angela Downey: 1970–1995

Cáit Ní Dhonnchadha, a camogie player, wrote in 1911 that the game was important and its sole object 'under that of national emancipation, would be the raising of the sex from the slough of a false and foreign civilisation'.

Camogie's most famous star, Kilkenny's Angela Downey, would probably look at the game somewhat differently. As a girl Angela always had a hurley stick in her hand and her theatre of dreams was her backyard. As a teenager there was not much to do other than camogie – no discos, no cinemas locally, although she did cross-country running for Kilkenny City Harriers – so she practised by hitting stones on the roof of the slaughterhouse in her father's butcher shop. Her heroes included Liz Neary and Helen O'Neill. She made the senior county team when she was fifteen and won her first All-Ireland when she was seventeen. The Kilkenny team were trained by Tom Ryan, who often came to training in his wellingtons.

Not surprisingly she has been immortalised in folklore and is to camogie what Christy Ring is to hurling. Hurling was in her genes. Her father was the legendary Shem Downey, who starred for the black and amber in the 1940s and '50s, winning an All-Ireland medal in 1947 in Kilkenny's classic triumph over Cork. Shem brought the passion he exhibited in the black and amber onto the sidelines when he watched his daughters on the camogie field.

Angela played in her first senior All-Ireland final with Kilkenny in 1972 against Cork. It was to be a rare reversal for the young player, but all present that day remember their first acquaintance with Angela and knew intuitively that something special had arrived on the sporting scene. In the coming years they were destined to often see her glide through bedraggled defenders, making a feast from a famine of poor possession. She appealed to the finer side of the imagination, with memory cherishing not only what she did in Croke Park and elsewhere but also how she did it – with panache and elegance. She went on to win seven consecutive All-Irelands for Kilkenny from 1985 to 1991. In total she would win twelve All-Irelands; the first would come after a replay against Cork in 1974. Only Dublin's Úna O'Connor, with thirteen, and the late Dublin star Kathleen Mills, with fifteen, have surpassed that achievement. She captained the county to All-Ireland successes in 1977, 1988 and 1991.

To add to Angela's joy, all her All-Ireland medals were won with her twin sister, Ann. In 2010 both were jointly presented with the Lifetime Achievement Award in the *Irish Times* Sportswoman of the Year awards.

Angela was also keenly appreciative of the importance of the club, in her case St Paul's and later Lisdowney. To add to Angela's medal haul, she won an incredible twenty-two county titles and six All-Ireland club titles.

A lot of strange things happen in club games in camogie.

The strangest story must be about a camogie club match in Westmeath when Cullion had a man on their team in the 1970s. What was stranger was that nobody noticed the difference until after the match. The headline in the local paper was: 'When is a girl not a girl?'

Angela sees the club as the heart of camogie. 'Our game is not just about the winning. It's about the experience. As you get older you start to appreciate the real power of both camogie and the GAA: the sense of togetherness and community and the importance of the club. The pride of the parish is critical to what players do. There's also a great community involvement behind it. I think the GAA is so important when you are away from home. I saw in the United States the one place the community gathered was to watch a match. It is then you really see how important the GAA is for our identity of being Irish. Camogie and the GAA bring people together.'

A geography teacher at Grennan College in Thomastown, Angela's career witnessed two controversies. In 1988 just before her club faced Glenamaddy in the All-Ireland final, Angela was sensationally suspended for six months. Appropriately St Paul's united in the face of what they saw as an injustice against Angela and won by a point with the last puck of the ball.

In February 2004 Angela boycotted the presentation of the Team of the Century in protest at the absence of her twin sister, Ann, from the team. When asked to clarify her absence, Angela said: 'I don't like singling out individuals because Gaelic games are team-based and it is teams who win and lose matches, and being part of a team always appealed to me. Ann gave twenty-five years to camogie, has twelve All-Irelands and actually one more club title than me because I was suspended for one final.'

During an All-Ireland final against Cork, Angela was goal-bound when her opponent, Liz O'Neill, made a desperate lunge at her which caused Angela's skirt to end up on the ground. Undeterred Angela kept on running, and even when the Cork goalie Marian McCarthy whisked the hurley from her hands she palmed the ball into the net and then calmly returned to collect her skirt. Even more telling was her subsequent comment: 'Even if she had pulled off all my clothes I was going to score a goal first!' The following morning the picture of her without her skirt appeared on the front page of the *Irish Times*. It encapsulated a career that lived by the Spartan motto that a warrior should leave the battle only if carried on their shield.

14

THE MAN IN THE MIDDLE

Peter McDermott: 1940–1954

It was a different time. Only thirteen Meath men paraded before the 1949 Leinster final. Brian Smyth and his brother-in-law Michael O'Brien from the Skryne club, who were county champions at the time, stayed behind in the dressing room to decide who should be Meath captain. Smyth was chosen and a few months later became the first Meath man to raise the Sam Maguire Cup.

It was also the era of the most celebrated headgear in the history of the GAA – that of Peter McDermott, famously christened by the voice of Gaelic games, Michael O'Hehir, as 'the man in the cap'. The cap was to control what Peter modestly described as 'my fabulous head of long hair'. He was the driving force behind a mighty Meath team that won two All-Irelands, two League titles and six Leinster triumphs between 1940 and 1954. He has the unique distinction of being the only man to referee an All-Ireland final both before and after winning one as a player.

He also made his mark as an official. He was county secretary when he captained Meath to the All-Ireland in 1954. He was a key advisor to Down when they won their first All-Ireland in 1960. He coached his native county when they won the All-Ireland in 1967. The following year he initiated the link between Ireland and Australia Rules by lining up games for the county's tour of Australia.

The late Mick Dunne was a big admirer of the man in the cap:

'As a referee he was probably as good as we've seen. It was much harder in his day to keep control. At that time you couldn't pick a ball off the ground. If you dived on the ball, you had to get up and put your toe under it and lift it. There was little chance of that in a goalmouth. There was way more body contact then, which Peter relished, as it made the game very exciting. Mind you, if you lost possession, you couldn't always use it well because the game was so crowded. So you needed eyes in the back of your head. You couldn't be a shrinking violet if you were a referee.

'As a naive young journalist I found myself standing alone with him on the sideline at a match when a shemozzle broke out that would leave the toughest contest today look like a harmless tiff between two little girls in a playground. Think Mayo versus Meath in 1996 and multiply by four, with the spectators bunched so close together on the centre of the pitch that they could hear each other's inner thoughts. The referee was not having a good day and Peter gently said to me: "The advantage law is the best because it lets you ignore all the others for the good of the game."

'Attention to detail was important to him. For all his planning, there was one factor he would have no control over. Luck. For whom the bell tolls is often a case for whom the ball rolls. Napoleon always wanted lucky generals. He would have wanted the man in the cap.'

———————

15

DUAL STAR

Jimmy Barry-Murphy: 1973–1986

Jimmy Barry-Murphy exploded onto the GAA scene when at the age of nineteen he scored two fine goals in Cork's All-Ireland football final triumph over Galway in 1973. In his commentary, Michael O'Hehir said, 'He may be nineteen but today he's joined the ranks of the football immortals.'

Galway defender Johnny Hughes still recalls the day vividly: 'We scored 2–13 and lost the All-Ireland by seven points. I have no cribs about losing in 1973 because we were comprehensively beaten. We couldn't match their firepower. Jimmy Barry-Murphy and Jimmy Barrett caused us untold trouble. Jimmy Barry-Murphy even then was a most difficult opponent. He was both very confident and very skilfull, and he could take you to the cleaners. He had two great feet, but above all he had a great head. Had he stuck to football, he would have gone on to become one of the all-time greats.'

Donegal great Martin Carney saw the more relaxed side of the legend of JBM. 'I played for Ulster in 1975 and remember it as Seán O'Neill's last game for Ulster. Jimmy Barry-Murphy had played the day before in a senior hurling club final for the Barrs against Johnstown. I remember meeting him that night and, let's put it this way, he was enjoying himself. Yet the next day he produced a devastating performance. Jimmy scored 4–1 in that game from five kicks of the ball.'

Having won All-Stars in 1973 and 1974 in football, Barry-Murphy's talents were most often seen on the national stage in hurling because Kerry ruled supreme in Munster. In full flight JBM lit up the stage like a flash of forked lightning: thrilling and, from the opposition's point of view, frightening. He is probably the greatest dual star of all time, winning five All-Ireland hurling medals and five hurling All-Stars.

With characteristic modesty, he downplays his role in Cork's three-in-a row winning side of 1976–78: 'There are those who will say that we were in the right place at the right time because other teams like Kilkenny were not as strong as they usually were, but look at the players we had at the time – Martin O'Doherty, John Horgan, Gerald McCarthy, Charlie McCarthy, Ray Cummins and Seánie O'Leary. The fact that we won those All-Irelands had much more to do with their brilliance than anything I ever did.'

He also had the honour of winning an All-Ireland medal during the centenary year on the hallowed sod of Semple Stadium against Offaly.

JBM's sublime overheard flick against Galway in the 1983 All-Ireland semi-final was voted as the greatest hurling goal of all time in 2009.

Eileen Dunne sums up JBM's place in the pantheon of greats: 'Gaelic games provide an unending theatre of drama and very often a spectacle that is unique to this country. My late father, Mick Dunne, had a deep love of all things GAA. Growing up, my sisters and I acquired some of his passion for hurling, Gaelic football, handball and camogie. We remember trips to the Grand Hotel in Malahide on All-Ireland Sunday mornings in the '60s, trips to the Munster final in Thurles to watch the likes of JBM and Ray Cummins in action, or Clones, to meet the McCartans and the O'Neills on Ulster final day. Now we have our own heroes – the whole Dublin team (hurling and football!) – but of course still JBM.'

16

Raising the Banner

Ger Loughnane: 1972–1987

Ger Loughnane lives in Anecdote Central. In his sixteen years as a player with Clare he won the county's first All-Star in 1974, then another followed in 1977. He won two League medals, in 1977 and '78. Having made five Munster final losing appearances, he was determined to break that record when he started managing the team.

After losing the 1995 League final, his prediction that Clare would win the Munster final was widely quoted in the media the next day. 'That was one of the greatest flukes of all time. When we got back into the dressing room, Liam Horan of the *Irish Independent* must have been there, but I didn't see him. I didn't want any journalist to hear what I had to say.

'The Clare players had lost a Munster final in '93, a Munster final in '94 and a League final in '95. Even the most optimistic had their head down. Even county board officers and all others present in the room seem to be drowned in a sea of despair. Instinctively, I decided that something different had to be done.

'I jumped up on the table and I spoke for two minutes. I said, "Listen, ye're all very down, but this is only the League. Everyone look up at me now." I held up my finger and pointed around the room and said, "This year we're going to win the Munster championship. Get that into yer heads. This year we're going to win the Munster championship." They all looked at me aghast! I think they picked up on the conviction in my voice, but I never suspected there was a journalist in the room.'

But the march to glory would not come without sacrifice. 'The training sessions in Ennis are part of legend. One of the reasons they are part of legend is that nobody ever saw them! There would be at least two matches played a week with an intensity that you would not see in most championship matches. There were no lineballs. If there was ever a game when the pace was slack, I stopped it straightaway. I'd rather an eight-minute game at lightning pace than a forty-five-minute game at average pace.

'All that people thought we were really interested in was fitness. Much of that we orchestrated ourselves. But that was also sending a message to our own players that their physical well-being could never be better. There was no reason for them to fail, except a mental one. If you believe that you've done everything possible on the physical and mental side, that every facet is covered, it reassures your conscious mind that you've done everything. The players just had to switch themselves on in the match and let it happen.'

Loughnane's tonsils took great punishment during his stewardship of Clare, as he exhorted and screamed his team to victory. For all the intensity of his passion and desire to win, he nonetheless could stay calm and focused during a match, which enabled him to offer a penetrating analysis of the team's performance at half-time. Never was this talent more needed than the 1995 Munster championship, when Clare trailed Cork by four points and faced the wind in the second half. Loughnane defiantly told his team, 'The ship has sprung a leak but we are not going down!

'The show looked really over, especially as we had been beaten badly in the League final. I was praying for half-time. It couldn't come quick enough. I clearly remember as I spoke, Mike O'Halloran, who was as mentally tough as anyone on the team, looked at me for the first time straight in the eye. He knew immediately it wasn't the normal half-time speech, the "Come on now, lads" variety. It struck a chord, even though we went seven points down in the second half. It was as if something magic had occurred – never mind that we were playing against the wind and Seánie [McMahon] broke his shoulder.

'The half-time speech was central to our revival but, important as it was, going in on the pitch to drive them on was equally crucial. That was the first time the players ever saw me doing that. I can still see the look of surprise on Liam Doyle's face when he saw me coming on. I could almost see him thinking, "Christ, there's something big going on here."'

Loughnane had an uncanny ability to turn the most unlikely scenario into a motivational ploy. 'Morale was at an all-time low when we took over in September '94. Clare had been hammered in two consecutive Munster finals. Partly to build up morale we went for a weekend to Kerry at the end of the following March just before the real hurling began. We had four training sessions and a match against Kerry and a bit of fun as well. We found a corner in a small pub in Killarney on the Saturday night. Everyone was drinking away and eventually a sing-song started. A night like that is so enlightening because you see another side to people's personalities. Dalo and Fergal Hegarty are brilliant singers. At about one o'clock in the morning I was press-ganged into singing a song. They all expected me to sing a silly song, but I had just done a poem with the kids in school, 'The Band Played Waltzing Matilda'. I'd heard it sung by Ralph McTell and I knew the air of it, but it wasn't for the quality of the song I chose it but because of the message I wanted to get across.

'I started the song and, coming to the end, I stopped and said, "Now listen carefully to the next bit. These lines are about ye coming home for the last two years after the Munster final, but it'll never happen again.

And the band played Waltzing Matilda
as they carried us down the gangway
Nobody cheered.
They just stood there and stared and turned their faces away.

'Then I said, "Do you recognise that situation? That's never going to happen again." You could hear a pin drop. They never forgot it. It had such an effect on them. You could see the goose pimples rising. It happened by fluke, but it was a defining moment for us.'

Loughnane was always looking for an opportunity to stress that this team were not for turning or rolling over. 'The morning of the All-Ireland in '95 we were driving out for the airport from the Oakwood Hotel in Shannon. We had met there as usual at 8 a.m. Instead of turning in the yard, the bus driver decided to drive right around the hotel and come out via the back exit. When we arrived there, we found the gate was locked. The bus driver said he would turn around.

77

I told him no. Tony, Mike Mac and one of the players got off the bus with me and we lifted the gate off its hinges. A clear message was being sent out to the team. Unlike Clare sides in the past, we were never going to turn back and no obstacle was going to stand in our way. That was the message.'

My favourite sound is Ger Loughnane's great laugh. He can find humour in the most difficult situation. A number of years ago a national newsparer reported that he had died while he was undergoing treatment for leukemia. His neighgbour in Feakle was distraught when he read it and although it was in the early morning he woke up his son. The two of them drank the two bottles of wine they had been saving for a special occasion. When they woke up at noon the next day with massive hangovers they found out that the reports of Ger's demise were greatly exaggerated. Rather than celebrating, to Ger's amusement the father said with real feeling, 'F**k you, Loughnane, you ruined my two best bottles of wine!'

17

THE STAR OF THE COUNTY DOWN

Seán O'Neill: 1959–1975

Seán O'Neill was Footballer of the Year in 1968 (when he scored twelve goals and sixty-five points for the county), on the inaugural All-Star team in 1971 and the following year, and above all was included at right half-forward on both the Team of the Century and the Team of the Millennium. He was the first Down man to captain Ulster to Railway Cup victory in 1960.

The explosion of O'Neill's Down team on the national stage had a unique appeal in the 1960s, winning three All-Irelands ('60, '61 and '68).

On a September day in 1968 O'Neill wrote himself into immortality when Down beat Kerry in the All-Ireland final and he scored one of the most talked-about goals of all time. 'We were 0–2 to 0–1 ahead. Peter Rooney cut in and shot over my head for a score. Now, I have always made the point of following the ball when it went anyway towards the opponent's goal. Ninety-nine times out of a hundred it will be a waste of energy, however always expect the unexpected. And on that occasion the unexpected happened. The ball hit the post about five feet above the crossbar and it rebounded very fast back towards me.

'Now I was in full stride and I realised in that split second that the ball was going to hit me below the knee, and if that happened I would not connect properly. Automatically I leaned my body forward and that is why it appeared as if I was falling forward. I connected perfectly as the ball came off the pitch and, as if using the drop kick, I stabbed at the ball and in an instant it was in the net. I never before or after scored a goal like this; I was lucky – it all happened in split second.'

All-Ireland winner with Armagh and Ireland's leading sports psychologist Enda McNulty is a huge fan of O'Neill. 'When I was studying psychology in Queens University, Seán O'Neill was a mentor of the Sigerson team. Seán was a great role model for all young players like me back then because of his philosophy of playing the game – where his focus was solely on beating his opponent through skill. That Down team he won three All-Irelands with were a breath of fresh air to Gaelic football.

'I wanted to win the Sigerson more than concentrate on my studies, but my greatest education as a psychologist came from men like Seán O'Neill, who taught me so much about being a team player and a leader. I can illustrate this with an example of winning the Sigerson over a horribly wet weekend in Galway. Because the conditions were so bad Queens were physically drained and when we drew the final with UCD we thought we had nothing more to give, but Seán was great in that situation. He told us that UCD wanted not to play extra time but to hold out for a replay. At that stage our heads lifted and suddenly we were ready to go out and play extra time and we knew then there was no way we were going to be beaten.'

––––––––––

In conversation with this writer, O'Neill expressed his concerns with the way the game has developed. 'I do think we need to talk more about ethics in the GAA. I especially would like to see the cyncial fouls that were so apparent in recent championships cut out. Gaelic football has such a rich tradition and we can't have that tradition scarred by the cyncisim – sometimes nothing less than thuggery – that has cast a dark shadow on our games. This is not a new thing, but since I have retired I have been disappointed by what some teams have been prepared to do to win an All-Ireland. I sometimes shake my head when I see some of the greats of the game when they have done so much to change the culture from playing positive football to one of stopping the opposition.'

18

HEALING HANDS

Seán Boylan: 1982–2005

Seán Boylan's diplomatic skills were honed while he worked with a giant at his shoulder: his father. A military man, a friend of Michael Collins and above all a healer, to this day Boylan still refers to the man as 'the Boss'. When asked how his father influenced him, he jokes: 'My father married a woman twenty-seven years younger than him and I married Tina, who is eighteen years younger than me. Can you see a pattern there?'

Boylan became Meath manager in the early 1980s at a time when nobody else wanted the job. His own background was as a hurler: 'I went to Belvedere College and played rugby. Somebody told me that if I stuck at it I could become an Irish international, but hurling was my passion and that is where my energies went.'

The proof is in Boylan's 22-year career as Meath manager and the four All-Irelands he won with essentially three different teams. But you don't get this far on passion alone. Creating a sense of family within the squad and even within their family members is also vital.

'I suppose one of the things people remember most is the four-game saga against Dublin in 1991, and of course nobody will ever forget Kevin Foley's goal in the last game. I decided that we needed a break after the third match and I thought about taking the team for a break in a beautiful, quiet spot in Scotland. Before I made the arrangements, though, I rang all the wives and girlfriends of the players and asked them if they were OK with me doing it. Pretty much to a woman they all said, "Sean, whatever it takes to beat the Dubs."'

He lights up at one memory from the trip: 'On the Sunday morning we went to Mass in the local church, which was a tiny, tiny chapel. We had seventy-six people in the group, including wives and girlfriends. The priest nearly wept for joy because he'd never got such a big collection!

'We did very little physical training; the only thing we did do was practise that move again and again, which was replicated with Kevin's goal. The only thing was that I'd not expected it would be Kevin who finished the move.'

There was an interesting postscript to the game: 'My abiding memory of the dressing room was of the journalist Donal Healy interviewing Kevin. He basically asked him ten thousand different ways if he had ever scored a goal before and Kevin kept answering that he had never, ever scored a goal before in any match he'd ever played. Eventually he got so frustrated, he said to Donal: "Look, you are standing on my towel and I need my shower." And he walked away.'

Boylan had come up with an unusual strategy at the start of the year. 'The boys had a lot of miles on the clock by 1991 and I knew they would not be able for the wear and tear of brutal physical training again. I met one of my key players Gerry McEntee for training one night at the start of the year and I told him we were going training in the pool. I had got the county board to splash out three and a half grand for buoyancy aids for the lads. I told the squad that we would be training for most of that year in the pool. After that first session, though, when I was giving Gerry a lift home, he turned to me and said, "Sean, what are you going to tell everyone when we lose the first round of the Leinster championship?"'

Meath's 1996 All-Ireland final win is best remembered for the brawl in the replay, but Boylan's memories are more gentle. 'They were building a bypass on our normal route and I knew that would cause a problem for us, so we stayed in the Davenport Hotel in the city centre for the game. That meant we had to find a new venue to have a training session and I got permission to have one in Trinity College. Who came to watch it but one of Ireland's favourite poets and one of Trinity's most famous lecturers, Brendan Kennelly, who himself had played for Kerry. He had a lovely chat with us after the session. When the match was a draw, I made the same arrangements for the replay. In the meantime, though, Brendan had had a major coronary incident and had been rushed to hospital. While we were training the second day, I got a message from Brendan: "Seán, sorry I had to miss your session today. Am on the bypass."'

19

THE ORANGE REVOLUTION

Kieran McGeeney: 1992–2007

Kieran McGeeney achieved the impossible. He reduced Joe Brolly to silence.

After the sad death of their All-Ireland-winning manager Eamonn Coleman, the former Derry players gathered for the funeral in 2007. They went for a mini-reunion afterwards. Kieran McGeeney also attended the funeral and his friend Anthony Tohill asked him to join the Derry lads. As the players had not got together for a number of years, they were busy catching up. Suddenly McGeeney said to Brolly, 'Joe, you really wasted your talent. You could have accomplished so much more in the game if you had been serious about it.'

Joe Brolly was lost for words.

A loser makes hard things impossible. A winner makes impossible things hard. Kieran McGeeney proved his credentials as a winner when he captained his county to their first All-Ireland in 2002. To complete an unforgettable season for him, he was selected as Footballer of the Year.

Armagh corner-back that day, Enda McNulty, is keenly

aware that McGeeney was crucial to the 'orange revolution'. 'Kieran is a leader. When he walks into a dressing room and talks about dedication, players know that nobody is more dedicated than him. But Kieran would be the first to admit that there are other leaders, men such as Paul McGrane, Diarmaid Marsden and the McEntees, and guys who got very little credit, like Andrew McCann, who drove to training every single night from Armagh to Dublin on his own. Andy was a leader in actions rather than words.

'Kieran is a great friend, but more than anything he has a desire for excellence and is unwilling to settle for mediocrity in anything he does, from weight training and nutrition to skills training, and you always know that even when a game looks as if it's gone he's not going to throw in the towel.

'We were trailing by seven points to nil against Galway in 2001 and they were on fire. I remember I was out of breath and Kieran was out of breath as we were both trying to dam the waves of Galway attacks. I can still hear in my ears Kieran saying, "Weather the storm, weather the storm, weather the storm." I'm sure he said it to the other boys too, and we did, and very nearly hauled them back.

'We fancied ourselves, not in a joking way, as a band of brothers. We knew each other better than some of our own brothers, we spent so much time together. One of the things that encapsulate Kieran is that in every one of the big games, when he talked to us in the circle before the game, he'd be nearly crying and that's how emotional he would be. He was very focused. After we won the Ulster finals, he'd say, "Boys, take a good look at the cup. That's the last time ye're going to look at it. The next cup we want to see is the All-Ireland." He was very good at bringing guys down to earth. He would be very good at calling a spade a spade. If one of the guys was not pulling his weight, he'd say, "What the f**k is going on here? You're dossing, Enda," or "Oisín, you're not up to your own high standards. I'm disappointed in you." Because he was able to walk the walk, you could never argue with that.'

McGeeney also brought his formidable presence to bear on the international stage, captaining Ireland against Australia in the International Rules series. John Kavanagh says of McGeeney: 'He often says that you need to have a darkness inside you to compete at a high level in any sport. If you can't tap into that dark side, you'll quickly come unstuck.'

Given his leadership qualities on the field, there were high hopes that McGeeney would bring the same success he had as a player to management when he was appointed manager of the Kildare team. He showed things were going to be different when he dropped star forward Johnny Doyle. When Doyle complained – 'But, Kieran, I am one of the six best forwards in Kildare' – McGeeney's riposte was immediate: 'I don't want you to be one of the best six forwards in Kildare. I want you to be one of the best six forwards in the country.'

To the acute disappointment of many of the players, the romance between the Geezer and the Kildare County Board ended prematurely. Not surprisingly his next job was with Armagh. Further chapters in McGeeney's management career are yet to be written as the circle of victory spins incessantly, beckoning him like an irresistible force. It can be safely predicted that he will replicate the same ethos he displayed as a player: ask not what your teammates can do for you, ask what you can do for your teammates.

20

TRUE BLUE

Stephen Cluxton: 2001–2017

It is said that sport is meditation in motion. Stephen Cluxton is probably confirmation of this, given the way he has revolutionised the role of the goalkeeper in Gaelic football by shaping the Dublin attack through his kickouts. As he could place the ball so accurately he could seemingly always find his man and as a consequence put them in more attacking positions.

Dermot Earley was a big admirer of Cluxon: 'The blanket defence, used first by Armagh and then taken even further by Tyrone, meant that the retention of possession became paramount. Cluxon, though, changed all of this and ensured that there was no longer a contest for the ball from most kickouts. The days of the goalie aiming it for the big men in the centre field to fight over died with Stephen. He started off targeting Ciaran Whelan but Pat Gilroy saw his potential and exploited it to the fullest. In 2009 the Dubs were hammered by Kerry and Pat went back to the drawing board and came up with a defence-oriented game plan that had Cluxton as the key man, and he started to hit their dangerous players and set up wave after wave of Dublin tactics. The Down team of the 1960s changed Gaelic football forever. Stephen is one of that elite group to do the same.'

Of course Cluxon will never be forgotten for kicking the winning point from a thirty-five-metre free into the Hill 16 end to beat the favourites Kerry in the 2011 All-Ireland final. Kerry had led by four points with just seven minutes to go at a time when a generation of Dublin players (notably the teriffically talented, towering midfielder Ciarán Whelan) had missed out on an All-Ireland medal.

Cluxton was involved in a controversy in 2003 when he was sent off in an All-Ireland semi-final against Armagh, leading some to claim that he cost Dublin the game.

Pat Spillane has firm views on the issue: 'The Dublin manager Tommy Lyons was not swallowing anything after the defeat to Armagh in 2003 and came out in front of the media and had a go at his own player, Stephen Cluxton, who had been sent off.

'Tommy's critics will say that he hung Cluxton out to dry, that he humiliated him, and that he broke the golden rule because he had spoken out about a player outside the dressing room. Tommy will maintain otherwise. He would say that if Cluxton deserved to be sent off he should have been and he hadn't seen the video evidence when he gave his now infamous interview to Jim Carney. I thought it was a good interview, but I genuinely don't think Tommy hung Cluxton out to dry. When you interview a losing manager immediately after such a big game, when the stakes are so high, he isn't thinking rationally. Instead he's wounded and emotional and you can't expect a detached, clinical analysis with total objectivity.

———————

'One thing always puzzled me about that affair. Before the sending off Dublin were in the ascendancy and they seemed likely to win, but after the sending off the wheels came off the Dublin wagon. Afterwards Tommy was vilified. Cluxton got away scot-free in terms of public criticism, even though his sending off cost Dublin in all probability an All-Ireland appearance. Yet Cluxton became the victim and Tommy Lyons the villain. It's GAA logic.'

Cluxton enjoys the strong sense of collegiality within the Dublin squad. As a ritual after a big match they meet up on the Monday for some liquid refreshment. This proved problematic one night for one of the team who was intent on attending the drinking session. He worked as a van driver and his company monitored where the vans went from their office every day on their computers, so he had to pay a student to drive his van all around the city for him!

In 2016, Cluxton became the first man in history to captain a team to three Sam Maguire cups. Alan Brogan paid Cluxton the ultimate compliment: 'In my eyes he is the greatest player ever to play for Dublin.'

Cluxton is his own man. In a television documentary on Dublin's 2005 championship before it became a matter of routine for them to win Leinster titles, the Dubs were celebrating wildly after beating Laois in the final. Cluxton just walked into the dressing room. He explained on camera, 'This is not really for me. I'm out to play football and that's really all it is. It's nothing else.'

21

THE SHANNONSIDE SUPREMO

Éamonn Cregan: 1964–1983

In his twenty-year career with Limerick, Éamonn Cregan's finest hour was at centre half-back in the 1973 All-Ireland final. In a tactical masterstoke the Limerick mentors switched him to curb the menace of Kilkenny's ace centre forward Pat Delaney.

'There was no way I was going to let Pat Delaney pass me and hop the ball on the ground and thunder through for scores as he had done so often for Kilkenny. Switching me to centre back for the final gave me a certain psychological advantage in the position. Kilkenny had never seen me line-out at centre back and were not used to my style of play, at least in that position. I had the major advantage, though, of playing in that role for my club, Claughaun.'

Cregan would miss out on another All-Ireland medal in 1980, when Galway made the breakthrough. He scored 2–7 against Galway, but his team lost by 2–15 to 3–9.

Noel Lane starred on that Galway team. 'We won that day because our leaders, especially Joe Connolly, stood up and were counted. We were a powerful team and that side should have won more than one All-Ireland. It suited us that day that we were playing Limerick rather than Cork or Kilkenny, and that gave us confidence. It felt like it was for us that day, though Limerick could have considered themselves unlucky. Éamonn Cregan gave a star performance on that day and did not deserve to lose. His goal was a clinical finish and he got a particularly brilliant point from out the field. He was a very versatile player. To play senior hurling for Limerick with such distinction from 1964 to 1983 was a major achievement.'

Cregan won three All-Star awards – in 1971, '72 and '80. In 1994 he tasted All-Ireland glory again when he coached Offaly to beat his native Limerick in the final, with two late goals in one of the most dramatic comebacks in living memory. It was a bittersweet day for Cregan: 'I had to separate my personal affiliation from my role of planning for an Offaly success.'

That Offaly team were a unique mix of characters and greatness. Liam Griffin described them as 'the Harlem Globetrotters of hurling' because of their skill. Of John Troy, Cregan remarked: 'If he had speed, he would be the greatest player in the history of the game.' They also had the great Johnny Pilkington.

The day before that All-Ireland Cregan was asked, 'What will it mean if ye win the All-Ireland?'

He replied, 'It will mean we will be drinking till Christmas.'

The following year Cregan led Offaly back to another All-Ireland final only to lose to Clare. One of Offaly's stars on the day, Daithí Regan, has spoken on Newstalk radio about Cregan's sense of the occasion. 'He warned us to be prepared for the roar once the Clare team ran onto the pitch because they had not been in a final for so long. He was right. Croke

Park seemed to shake with the roar. As I walked around in the parade and looked into the stands and saw the place teeming with Clare people, I thought to myself: "Is there anybody from Offaly here at all?"

'I had played poorly the previous year, even though we won. I was determined to redeem myself against Clare and I was going to be ruthless to do it. I "did" Ollie Baker at the start of the match and scored a point after sixteen seconds. I was flying.

'Although we lost, there was an amusing end to the games. Not surprisingly the banquet that night was a bit flat in our team hotel. That was not to Johnny Pilkington's liking and he dragged a few of us to what he said would be the best party in town. Where did he bring us? Only to the Clare Hotel! The chairman of the Clare County Board, Robert Frost, invited Johnny to say a few words. Typical of Johnny, he said, "We'll keep those Kilkenny f**kers down and ye keep those f**kers down in Cork and Tipperary, and we'll have a few great years together."

'I was sorry that Éamonn Cregan was not around when we won the All-Ireland in 1998 because he did a great job with us. He got very few things wrong when he worked with us.'

22

DUB-LE TROUBLE

Tommy Carr: 1986–2010

Tommy Carr starred for Dublin in the famous 'four games saga' against Meath which enthralled the nation in the first round of the Leinster Championship in 1991. At a time when Ireland was going through soccer mania after Italia 1990 and when the nation was under the spell of Jack Charlton, the series of games showed that reports of the GAA's demise were premature. Territorially, Dublin were dominant in all matches but still ended up as the losing side.

Losing the final game was a bitter pill for Carr. 'There were stages in each of the four games when I thought we had won. The memory of the games is all blurred into one apart from the last fifteen minutes of the final match which is frozen in my mind forever. I was watching the game from the sideline, having gone off injured at that stage, and it was literally sickening to see the way we snatched defeat from the jaws of victory.

'It's not being dramatic to say that it was a very traumatic defeat – and profoundly depressing for Dublin. I was shattered after the defeat. I am not sure which was worse – 1991 or 1992. Although I was very, very down after the Meath saga, to miss out on captaining Dublin to an All-Ireland in '92 was devastating. That was a once-in-my-life opportunity.'

Why did Dublin not live up to expectations in the decider?

'You always think you are preparing properly for a game – you always like to think that anyway – and that you will be right for the game, but subconsciously things are playing on your mind, telling you things are not as they should be. We didn't play well on the day. Everybody knows that. Psychologists have tried for years to figure out why an individual or team does not give their normal performance on a particular day but have never come up with a proper answer. It's not a physical thing – it must be mental.

'I personally feel it had a lot to do with what the Americans call "focusing". We weren't properly focused. There were just too many distractions and external activities – guys modelling clothes and going on radio shows and so on. In isolation there was nothing wrong with any of them, but when you added them all up the focus was badly distracted. They all mounted up. You judge a player by the way he plays and we weren't up to it on the day. They were up to it and we weren't. It was that simple.'

One of the first casualties of Dublin's defeat was their coach Paddy Cullen. Was the Dublin camp really driven apart by strife, as the media suggested?

'You'd have to be a blind man not to know there were major differences in the Dublin camp in 1992, but if we had won all that would have been glossed over. Defeat brought the cracks and divisions more closely to the surface. Without saying too much, Pat O'Neill would have taken a very different approach to Paddy.

———

'The bad reaction to the defeat would not have happened in the '70s because everybody realised that Kerry were an exceptional team and that there was normally only a bounce of a ball between the two teams. In 1992 it was different because 99 per cent of the population thought that Dublin would win. I thought we were the form team that year and should have – and would have – won, but Donegal performed out of their skins that day. We did the opposite.'

Carr went chasing an All-Ireland title as Dublin manager. Declan Darcy played under him on that Dublin team. 'We came very close in 2002, when Ray Cosgrove almost equalised against Armagh, but to be honest I believe Tommy Carr had a better team. John Bailey, then the county chairman, told us after the drawn game against Kerry in the All-Ireland quarter-final in 2001 that no matter what happened Tommy Carr would be staying for the next year. He actually cried with emotion as he said that, but less than a month later Tommy was gone. Players would have done anything for Tommy, but we didn't do enough for him. I felt sorry for him because he was very unlucky, never more so than with the Maurice Fitzgerald sideline that drew the match for Kerry the first day. Tommy was as honest as the day was long and was fiercely driven. There was nothing he wouldn't have done for Dublin. He was probably a better manager at the end, but had more to learn and I think it's a shame he didn't get the chance.'

Pat Spillane offers his appraisal of Carr: 'He got very close as Dublin manager to the Holy Grail, but I believe he got an incredibly raw deal from the Dublin County Board. I think he did well with Roscommon in 2003, but it was probably downhill from then on and his time in Cavan will not feature prominently in the annals of the GAA.

'In a way he is quite similar in character to his friend John Maughan because fitness and discipline seem to be the hallmarks of their managerial style. The fact that both have an army background may have something to do with it. There is a general rule of thumb that I believe carries a fair amount of weight: teachers, priests, army men and guards do not in the long run make great managers because they are used to getting their own way – they are disciplinarians, like the sound of their own voice and are not the greatest of communicators. I was a teacher myself and I know I would not make it as a manager for those reasons.

'Like Maughan, I think Tommy mellowed and that he improved his man-management skills and become sharper tactically and more astute in his switches from the sideline.'

23

THE COMEBACK KID

Brian Corcoran: 1991–2006

Brian Corcoran exploded onto the Gaelic games scene in 1992. A series of masterful performances in the Cork colours saw him crowned as hurler of that year. In 1999 he reclaimed that honour. Not long after that the cumulative wear and tear of unending training sessions and games took their toll. Corcoran retired prematurely from inter-county football and hurling at the tender age of twenty-nine.

The arrival of a young family also played a major factor in his decision to quit at the top of his game, as he recalls: 'To be honest, hurling had become a chore. I'd be on my way home from work and all I wanted to do was play with the baby; instead, I was being dragged away to do something that I didn't want to do. By the time I came home from training she was asleep. It got to the stage where I was getting up in the morning and saying, "Oh no, I've got training tonight."'

Initially he did not miss the game. For a time it seemed as if Cork could get on without him too, and it seemed as if Cork hurlers were more interested in off-the-pitch activities than on-the-pitch stuff as they famously went on strike to get better facilities and conditions from the county board.

In 2004, the time was right for Corcoran's second coming, not least because the expectation of a success-starved county awaiting retrieval of its oldest sporting prize demanded another All-Ireland. Setanta Ó hAilpín had departed to Australia and after a relatively unconvincing league campaign Cork were ready for the return of the legend:

'It was a big gamble to come out of retirement. I could have fallen flat on my face and Cork could have struggled. Some people told me that I had twice been Hurler of the Year and I had nothing to prove. But you make decisions and you live by them. To be honest, I was half-afraid of going back. I wasn't sure if the lads would welcome me back with me being out so long.

'When I returned to the inter-county scene after a break of a couple of years, it showed me just how professional Gaelic games had become. When we came into training, our gear was up on a hook for us. All we needed to bring in were our boots and hurlies. After the training was over we just left the gear behind us and someone washed it. In terms of fitness, the drills that had been in vogue three years previously were considered obsolete. The biggest change I found, though, was that when the manager came into training, he brought his laptop and could pull out clips from any of the Cork games. That in a nutshell sums up the modern game.'

A Hollywood scriptwriter could not have written such a fairy tale for Corcoran's championship story in 2004. It began and ended with him on his knees. On his return in his opening match of the Munster championship against Limerick he scored a wonder point while still on his knees. In the dying seconds of the All-Ireland final he sprinted onto the ball, rode a tackle, turned on his left, shot and scored the insurance score. He fell on his knees just as the final whistle went and roared in triumph. It was nice to be back. Yet there had been a few anxious moments on the way.

'Waterford were the form team in the Munster championship and had an excellent League campaign, apart from the final, when they flopped against Galway. They beat us in the final, but I hadn't come back to the game to win a Munster medal. I'd come back for an All-Ireland and after that game we put things right and achieved our goal.'

Corcoran found himself unexpectedly embroiled in controversy before the All-Ireland quarter-final. The Antrim manager, Dinny Cahill, adopted an unusual strategy before the match when he publicly rubbished Cork's chances. Corcoran was singled out for special criticism. 'Cork have to have a problem when they recall Brian Corcoran,' Cahill said. 'They have to have problems. They've had a dreadful inside-forward line all season, couldn't get the scores, so they had to recall a man who'd finished playing. Well, he will be finished after Sunday, there's no doubt about that. If you look at their games, they had a dreadful centre forward but got away with it. We have a class centre back; we know how to stop that man from hurling. We are going to win the All-Ireland this year. We can win the All-Ireland. After getting over this game, anything can happen.'

Corcoran responded in the best way possible and scored the two goals that obliterated Antrim's chances and helped Cork beat Kilkenny by 0–17 to 0–9 in the All-Ireland final.

In 2005 he was at the centre of perhaps the defining moment of the championship – with his wonder goal against Waterford in the All-Ireland quarter-final. He remembers that magic moment with characteristic modesty.

'A hit and hope high ball was brilliantly rescued by Joe Deane on the endline and he sent it back to me. I took two steps back while turning, dropped the ball and let it bounce, held my backswing in case I was hooked and skimmed the sliotar off the top of the ground and it ended up in the net.'

He retired finally in 2006 after old rivals Kilkenny deprived the team of a three-in-a-row.

24

FROM LONGFORD TO OFFALY

Eugene McGee: 1973–

As a manager Longford native McGee first came to prominence in the 1970s with UCD. Legendary Roscommon
footballer Tony McManus's happiest memories in the game
are from the period between 1976 and 1980 with UCD under
McGee's stewardship. 'In 1979 I was captain and Colm
O'Rourke was vice-captain. Eugene McGee produced a
newsletter about the fortunes of the team and he named the
player who never shut up as the mouth of the team, but he
added that Colm was a strong contender!

'From our Freshers' year Eugene had taken Colm and
myself under his wing. He was a complex character, but it
was very enjoyable working with him. He certainly had a
way with him. He commanded respect and had great ideas
and was able to communicate them. There were lots of
county players around at that time but he had no qualms
about dropping them. Reputations meant nothing to him.
You never knew what to expect from him. Days you thought
you played well he might lacerate you. Days you thought

you didn't play well, he would encourage you and compliment you.

'My lasting memory of him came the day we had to play Queens. The night before I'd gone to the Veterinary Ball. The next morning he heard about it and was not happy. He made me travel with him in his car and never said a word to me all the way up to Belfast. In the circumstances I was really keen to do well and I scored 2–3. He said nothing to me after the match. Eventually, when all the lads were gone and I was behind waiting for him in the dressing room to make the journey home, he turned to the caretaker and said in his typically gruff accent: "Would you have a jackhammer to widen the door a bit more? This fella's head is so big he won't be able to get out through it."'

McGee's finest hour came in 1982 when he guided Offaly to the All-Ireland. He identifies the critical part of the game: 'The first half was open and it was a very good game of football. The second half it started raining fairly heavily and the game deteriorated a good bit. Kerry dominated for a long time and we were lucky enough to stay with them. Martin Furlong's penalty save was very important. If they had scored that, I don't think we would have come back. The rest is history. We were four points down and we got two frees to put us two points behind. Then a long ball came to Séamus Darby and he banged it into the net. It was a super shot. All Croke Park went wild, but there was still a minute and a half left in the game and we had to hold on with all our might.

'The magnificent players on that team personified not only their own accomplishments but the sacrifices of generations of Offaly people who made that moment possible. I was very conscious of all the people who organised games and travelling arrangements down through the years, regardless of personal inconvenience or harsh weather. Without those people, the sequence which led to Offaly's historic success would not have started. The fact that the years of disappointment have been wiped out with that win gave me a certain amount of pleasure. It was a unique occasion.'

Dublin took Offaly's Leinster crown in 1983 and McGee's team were unable to reach those dizzy heights ever again. McGee continues to be one of the most influential voices in Gaelic football as a pundit. He chaired the GAA's Football Review Committee, which recommended the introduction of the black card. He is not afraid to take on his critics. When Jim McGuinness challenged the validity of the black-card system, McGee replied, 'He thinks because he won one All-Ireland he is the high priest of football. If he is that good why didn't he win a second or third All-Ireland.'

25

Six of the Best

Seánie McMahon: 1994–2006

There had been a moment in the championship in 1994 when Ger Loughnane came to realise that Seánie McMahon had a fire burning deeply within him.

'We had a team meeting to discuss our plans in the Clare Inn. Seánie had just come onto the panel that year. At the time I would have seen him as one of those quiet lads who plays away and never says anything but who wouldn't be half-aggressive enough for inter-county hurling. The meeting was nearly over and Seánie got up. Well, you could hear a pin drop. Here was a young lad of twenty and he gave a speech of such viciousness that it left everybody absolutely stunned! The gist of it was: Look at what those Tipp f**kers have done to Clare and by Jesus this year we're going to put them down. When he was finished, I said, "Stop it, now." There was no need to say another word. We beat Tipp.'

As Clare marched on to glory, Seánie established himself as the finest centre half-back in modern times, doubling up as a lethal attacking weapon with the accuracy of his long distance frees, winning three All-Stars, being chosen as Hurler of the Year and winning an All-Ireland club title with St Joseph's Doora Barefield in 1999.

Ger Loughnane tops his list of admirers. 'There are men and there are men, and then there's Seánie McMahon. You just couldn't have greater regard for a person than you'd have for Seánie. If you had a daughter and she brought Seánie home, you'd be really, really delighted. You'd think, rightly, here comes the nicest, most sociable, most humble and intelligent person you could ever meet. Put him on a field and that is his demeanour but inside is the mind of a killer! He was the Bertie Ahern of hurling, "the most cunning and most ruthless of them all".

'He'd do anything to win,' Ger claims. 'That doesn't mean that he'd cut anybody's head off, but he would do what had to be done, coolly and calmly. If Seánie had been in the mafia, he would have been a killer. He'd be a babyface killer. He's a fantastic person above all else and in spite of what I said he's a very ethical person, a terrific hurler and a real leader. The substance and depth in Seánie is such that you meet in very few people in life. That is the really, really great thing to admire about him. Whenever things were at their worst, Seánie always did something to redress the situation. In the All-Ireland final in '95, who got Clare's first two points? Seánie McMahon. When chances were going astray, he showed the way with a 65 and one from play. Look at all the vital scores he got from frees in the most pressurised of situations. If you were listing all the best qualities you would want in a person, you'd find them in Seánie, but when you want a job done Seánie is the man. For his skill, his character, the inspiration he gave in the dressing room, his loyalty and his mental toughness, I admire him as much as I admire any person in the world. He was a leader behind the scenes off the pitch and a Colossus on it.

'If there is one example of Seánie's mental toughness, it has to be the Munster semi-final against Cork in '95,' Ger recalls. 'He broke his collarbone and we'd already used three subs. I said, "F**k it, Seánie, you're going to have to come off." He replied, "I can't go off. We can't play with fourteen. I'll go corner-forward." All I could say was, "Fine." Up he went to corner-forward, holding his shoulder. With a few minutes to go, Timmy Kelleher got the ball in the Cork backline. Seánie went towards him to put him under pressure and Kelleher sent the ball over the sideline. Fergie Tuohy, who I'd never seen in my life taking a line ball, took the perfect line ball and Ollie Baker put it into the net. From the puckout, Alan Browne got the ball out near the sideline and went for a point. His shot hit the post and fell straight into the hands of a Cork forward with a goal at his mercy. As he threw up the ball, out of the corner of my eye I saw Frank Lohan coming out of nowhere and he flicked the ball away and cleared it out. It came to Fergie Tuohy and the final whistle blew. Clare had won by a point and that set us off to win the All-Ireland. Without that win, would anyone have ever taken notice of us?'

Given the absolute centrality of McMahon to the Clare team, Loughnane resorted to unusual tactics to conceal his injury: 'In the week leading up to the Munster final in '95 there was a debate about whether Seánie McMahon should play after his shoulder injury. Opinion in our group was divided. Their job was to advise me. My job was to make the decision. I decided that we'd do something I never did, which was to have a match between backs and forwards for five minutes. Nobody was trying too hard, but Seánie seemed fine.

'The problem was that we knew that the first thing that would happen was that Limerick would hit him on the shoulder, so we decided to strap him up on the wrong shoulder. Practically the first thing that happened was that a Limerick forward crashed into Seánie's shoulder. There was a terrific outcry from the crowd, but it was the wrong shoulder! Seánie was outstanding in the Munster final.'

In his distinctive soft-spoken manner, Seánie McMahon plays down all talk of his greatness but when prompted reflects on his day of days: 'Personally the memory that will stand out was when we won the first Munster final in 1995. I never dreamt of All-Irelands, just the Munster final, and I remember when we won I just went down on my knees and said thank you to God. It was such a relief. There were lots of tears shed – but for once Clare people were crying tears of joy. It was hugely uplifting for them.'

26

PRIMROSE AND BLUE

Gerry O'Malley: 1947–1964

Two Roscommon players, Aidan Brady and Gerry O'Malley, were chosen on the official GAA team of players who never won an All-Ireland medal.

As Aidan Brady shook my hand a few months before his death and stared me deep in the face I knew I was being evaluated with surgical precision. He recalled the magnitude of the disappointment for Gerry O'Malley and Roscommon of losing the 1962 All-Ireland.

'Of course it was a big comedown. The match itself was forgettable. We were badly hamstrung when O'Malley had to leave the field injured. He was the mainstay of our team for so long and at that stage a Roscommon team without Gerry was like *Hamlet* without the prince.

'What a lot of people forget is that he had an even bigger influence on the team that year because he had taken charge of collective training before the All-Ireland final. I couldn't swear to this, but I think if Gerry could live his life again he wouldn't do it that way a second time. Up to then he had always trained on his own. I'd guess he found it to be a great pressure to be responsible for all of us.

'Gerry was one of the very best players ever to grace Croke Park and it was tragic that he never won an All-Ireland final. In 1965, though, he finally won an All-Ireland medal – when Roscommon won the Junior hurling All-Ireland championship. An administrative cock-up meant that he was presented with an All-Ireland Under-21 medal, which should have gone to a Wexford man, though the Central Council intervened and the right medal finally made its way to him. Gerry was a great servant of his club, St Brigid's, and I'd say it was one of the joys of his life when he won a county title with them.'

Leitrim great Packy McGarty laughs heartily at the memory of an incident from his playing days. 'I went to America for the Kennedy games in 1964 with the late Gerry O'Malley and Charlie Gallagher. They were chalk and cheese but became amazingly close on the trip. O'Malley was very serious, religious and quiet; Charlie was devil-may-care. Every match he played he had to win. I played once with him in a veterans' match and he had to win that too! Gallagher was always winding Gerry up and saying that if they ever met in a match he would destroy him – which drove O'Malley mad. They were a pantomime. In private, Charlie admitted that he would have hated to have to play O'Malley.

'Down's Joe Lennon was on that trip, too. He had written a book about Gaelic football at the time and he brought loads of them out with him and sold them wherever he went. One day Charlie went up to O'Malley and said, "You know what. I'm going to write my own book about football."

'"Really? And I suppose we're going to see Gallagher on the front cover in full flight with the ball?"

'"You will in my barney. You'll see a big, juicy blonde!"'

27

THE TUAM STAR

Seán Purcell: 1947–1962

Jack Mangan made history by becoming the first goalkeeper to lift the Sam Maguire Cup when he captained Galway in 1956. When I asked him about the greatest player he ever saw his answer came with lightning speed.

'Seán Purcell was the best. We were from the same street in Tuam. I took the captaincy off him after a vote. Although I felt bad for him, he didn't hold it against me and we remained the best of friends. He was a natural, with a wonderful temperament. If we were behind, we would always rely on him to do something special. The next best I would have seen was another Tuam man, Frank Stockwell. The two of them didn't even have to look for each other on the field of play, they knew each other so well.'

The illustrious GAA writer Pádraig Puirseál described Purcell as 'the most complete Gaelic footballer of all time'. My only meeting with Seán Purcell is a memory that will stay with me forever. He transmitted vitality and enthusiasm like electricity. In his early days in the maroon of Galway, he was in the right place at the wrong time as he told me.

'I came on the inter-county scene in the late '40s. Mayo had a wonderful team and overshadowed us for years. I will never forget one day they beat us very badly in Tuam. I happened to be in Galway that night and I met a great old friend of mine, Mayo's greatest-ever forward, Tom Langan. Tom was a very quiet man who didn't have much to say. But he had a few pints that night and he came over to me and he said: "Don't let that worry you. I played in six Connacht finals before I won one." I think that gave me heart. Before we played Mayo in the Connacht championship in '54 we decided we had to give it everything, that we had a chance. We beat them against all the odds and, after that, we took off. From there on, things fell into position easily enough.'

The 1956 All-Ireland final was the apex of the team's achievement when they beat Cork by 2–13 to 3–7.

'We had a great lead at half-time and Cork came back to us in a big way. They really put it up to us and they got back within a point or so. We were lucky enough to get back one or two points at the end.

'We got a wonderful reception at home. I remember that quite well, coming from Dublin into Tuam. By present day standards the crowd was not huge but it was a great night. The match was broadcast around the town that day and there would have been a great spirit of victory around the place. When we arrived in Tuam, I think the crowd met us and we were carried shoulder-high or on the lorry down to the town.'

Another national honour came the following year when Galway beat Kerry by 1–8 to 0–7 in the League final. Kerry, captained by Mick O'Connell, got their revenge in the All-

Ireland final in 1959, when they beat the Westerners by 3–7 to 1–4, as he reminded me.

'I made a stupid mistake early on. I was playing full-forward. My opponent, Niall Sheehy, was a big, strong man and the ball was going wide. I could have let it go, but I saw Niall coming towards me. I said I'd get my retaliation in first and I did. I hit him an almighty crack with my forearm across the head and he got in under me and he put me up in the air. I really thought I had killed him, but when I looked up all he did was shake his head a few times and trot away. It was a bad start, a foolish mistake, and after that we were well beaten. We didn't really make much of a show. The lads did their best, all right, but we just weren't good enough that day.'

Seán Purcell's name, good nature and face lives on in his son John, who himself played championship football for Galway in 1985. With a twinkle in his eye, John recalls his father's mischievous nature.

'Daddy had a great capacity to become friends with a large section of people. Seán Óg Ó hAilpín was just one of the people who visited him in hospital. He became very friendly with the Dublin team of the 1970s through his role in managing the All-Stars, especially with Tony Hanahoe. They have a charity function every year and present Hall of Fame style awards. The night before Dad died they were presenting Martin O'Neill and himself with an award and I was accepting it on his behalf. I asked him, had he any message for them? He replied: "Tell them before I got to know them I thought they were a crowd of f**kers but once I got to know them I didn't think they were too bad!" I said a softer version of that on the night!

'One time he was collecting an award himself up north and

113

the MC was going on and on about how great a player Daddy had been,' he says. 'Daddy grabbed the microphone off him in midflow and said, "Don't think I'm that famous. I ran for election once. Both John Donnellan and I were running for Fine Gael for the one seat in 1965. I barely got my deposit back and was lucky to get even that. John was easily elected. As I was leaving the count centre crestfallen, a woman called me over and said, "Don't worry, Seánin, there'll be another day. Isn't it a pity you didn't play a bit of football!"'

I asked Seán to select the greatest team of players he had seen since he retired from the game. Here is his team.

1. Johnny Geraghty
(*Galway*)

2. Enda Colleran **3. Noel Tierney** **4. Tom O'Hare**
(*Galway*) (*Galway*) (*Down*)

5. John Donnellan **6. Gerry O'Malley** **7. Martin Newell**
(*Galway*) (*Roscommon*) (*Galway*)

8. Mick O'Connell **9. Jack O'Shea**
(*Kerry*) (*Kerry*)

10. Dermot Earley **11. Micheál Kearins** **12. Pat Spillane**
(*Roscommon*) (*Sligo*) (*Kerry*)

13. Tony McTague **14. Seán O'Neill** **15. Mike Sheehy**
(*Kerry*) (*Down*) (*Kerry*)

28

TYRONE'S TRIUMPHS

Mickey Harte: 2003–

Some managers are unorthodox. When he managed Nottingham Forest, Brian Clough once watched his team play a five-a-side in training as he walked his dog. He called over his full-back Brian Laws and said, 'You're wasting your time doing this – take my dog for a walk.' Laws did – twice around the training ground.

Mickey Harte has rewritten the manual for GAA management. His record as a manager at minor and under-21 is unrivalled and the final part of his CV came when he delivered Sam Maguire three times to Tyrone.

The Tyrone manager has showed himself as a genius, a tactical master. He innovated a new style of football that nobody had seen before. His towering gifts as a manager have never been better exemplified than in his icily patient delivery of the injured Peter Canavan in the 2003 All-Ireland final.

Harte guided Tyrone to glory that year using controversial new tactics. In this approach nothing was left to chance.

Tyrone's success was based on a platform of defence and safety first: keep possession, keep mistakes to a minimum, and play in a manner that allows skilful players only the smallest bit of room and the shortest time to do their thing. It appeared that Tyrone football subscribed to the belief that victory is based on getting defences right, players funnelling back and slowly but surely choking individuality.

After Kerry lost to Tyrone in 2003 in the All-Ireland semi-final, Seamus Moynihan incisively observed: 'The midfield area was like New York City, going down Times Square, crazy.' While such a tactical approach was in the eyes of many ugly and horrible to look at, it was both deadly effective and legal.

Pat Spillane was its most vocal critic and famously called it 'puke football': 'I am not going to use the P-word again but at its worst Gaelic football is like watching Tyrone beat Kerry in the 2003 All-Ireland semi-final. A perversion of the beautiful game like that is like measles; it is something you should get over young, not at my stage of life. Football should leave you looking frenzied, looking mad with joy. That type of football simply left me looking mad. It is watching muck like this that is causing me to grow old disgracefully.

'Having said that, Harte brought a more expansive style to Tyrone in 2005 when they deservedly beat Kerry to win the All-Ireland playing some great football. Before Tyrone played Dublin in the All-Ireland quarter-final in 2008 I was ready to write their obituary, but they produced the performance of the year and came out and totally demolished the much-hyped Dubs. They played with composure, class, total commitment, teamwork, flair and skill. They put up a great score in the most atrocious conditions. I know many people will be surprised to hear me saying this but in short they played football the way it should be played. Even my beloved Kerry could learn from them on that performance and they would prove that when they beat the Kingdom in the final that year. Although they have some great players, a lot of the credit for Tyrone's success must go to Mickey Harte, but I was still glad when Kerry won the All-Ireland in 2009 and pipped Tyrone as team of the decade.'

Harte has also experienced the most devastating tragedy. His daughter Michaela had become a well-known face in the GAA because of her devotion to the Tyrone team and because of her frequent appearances in the media. In 2004 she was a finalist in the Rose of Tralee competition. She shared her father's strong faith and had a great devotion to Padre Pio in particular. Before the historic 2003 All-Ireland she presented each member of the Tyrone team with Padre Pio medals and rosary beads. To the horror of the entire nation, she was shockingly murdered while she was on honeymoon.

Dermot Earley, Jnr was struck at the speed at which dreams can be shattered and how close the veil between life and death is, as tragedy swoops like a hawk flying down from the sky, a fearsome beast, ferocious as it ripped and shredded and tore, attacking all it saw.

'On the morning of Dad's removal, as we were having our breakfast, Mickey Harte called to express his sympathies. As he shared tea and toast with us I never dreamt that just seven months later my mother would end up making the journey to Tyrone to offer words of condolence to him after the horrific murder of his much loved daughter Michaela.'

Joe Brolly admired Harte's achievements as a manager in 2005 in particular: 'In 2005 Mickey Harte had been working on the team for three years and had a harmonious blend between defence and attack. Although Kerry got off to a great start in the All-Ireland final that year, Tyrone wiped the floor with them, playing beautiful football and showing they had some great players. Harte's tactical genius was again showcased in 2008 when against the odds he led Tyrone to another All-Ireland at the expense of red-hot favourites Kerry, having earlier crushed the highly fancied Dublin side in the All-Ireland quarter-final. Nobody can take that achievement off him.'

29

THE RIVERDANCE OF SPORT

Liam Griffin: 1995–1996

Peter Shilton was one of the most celebrated players in the history of English soccer. It was natural when he stepped down that some clubs would want to see if he could translate that into management. First up was Plymouth Argyle. It did not go well and relegation was staring the team in the face. Shilton decided that a Churchillian speech was needed before the next match. He gave an impassioned oration and the energy level was visibly rising in the dressing room. His final line was: 'Lads, we will rise like a pheasant.'

There was a silence and he knew that somehow he had said something wrong but he was not sure what. He asked the players what the problem was. After an uncomfortable silence one of them finally said, 'It's actually the phoenix that rises from the ashes, gaffer.'

A long pause.

Eventually Shilton said, 'Sh*t, I knew it began with an F.'

A small parable that a great player does not necessarily a great manager make.

Liam Griffin is proof that you do not need to have been a top-class player to be a top-class manager. In 1996 the charismatic Griffin made Wexford the home of 'the Riverdance of Sport' and the story of paradise regained, steering them to their first All-Ireland since 1968 when, captained by Martin Storey, they beat Limerick by 1–13 to 0–14. Griffin brought inspired management to one of the sleeping giants of hurling with innovative new techniques, such as camping out with the team as a bonding exercise – and of course his masterstroke of having the team walk across the county border between Wexford and Wicklow on the way to the All-Ireland final.

Griffin believes that hurling is a game for warriors, and if his Wexford team were going to win the All-Ireland he wanted them to do it the hard way. After the Leinster final he said, 'If we're going to win the All-Ireland, I want to do it in a year when we beat Kilkenny, Dublin, Offaly, Galway and Limerick.' His dream came true.

Griffin often said that he had not the best fifteen hurlers in Wexford but he had the fifteen who most wanted to win. He believed that previous Wexford teams had lost because of lack of belief. He devised a training programme that would cater for the psychological and emotional elements as well as the fitness. Before the All-Ireland in '96 he told the team to believe in the game plan and to believe in each other and keep working – even if the team were fifteen points down. His man-management of the team is probably best illustrated in his dealings with one of the veterans of the team, Tom Dempsey. Griffin asked him if he was prepared to 'shed 500 beads of sweat to win the All-Ireland for Wexford'. When Dempsey answered in the affirmative, Griffin's response was, 'Make that 1,000 beads.' Dempsey went on to score a

120

critical goal and three points in the final and won an All-Star.

Former Wexford star Martin Quigley is ideally placed to explain why the yellow bellies won the All-Ireland that year and not earlier: 'Expectations were low in 1996 because we had been beaten in the League semi-final. To me the key match in 1996 was not the All-Ireland final but beating Offaly in the Leinster final. That really set them up as a team of winners. I think the supporters played a huge part in Wexford's win – almost as much as the team itself. It was fascinating to see the way the support snowballed in the county throughout the championship. It was said there were 8,000 Wexford fans at the Kilkenny match, but there were 40,000 there for the final.

'I think there were two crucial factors to explain why Wexford won that year. Firstly, there was Liam Griffin and the passion, motivation, organisation and leadership he gave to the team. Secondly, there was Damien Fitzhenry. I don't want to cast any aspersions on anybody but Wexford had been waiting for a long time for a goalie up to that standard. He was the best goalie in Ireland, in my opinion. If I had to pinpoint one player on the pitch who meant the difference between victory and defeat in 1996, it would be him combined with Griffin's influence off the pitch. When the history of hurling in Wexford is written, there will be a special place for Liam.'

Griffin is imbued with the ethos of Gaelic games. At grass-roots level the games are based far more on giving than taking, though whether time and the corporate boxes in Croke Park will sustain that remains open to question. They are rooted in a sense of community which enables so many to give so much, in purely material terms, for so little.

In the last twenty years Liam Griffin has become hurling's greatest evangelist. With his extraordinary passion for

---

the game, he is a one-off. One of the media's rituals every Christmas is to publish the sports quotes of the year. Liam Griffin stole the honours in 2000 with his comments on the GAA: 'I have never seen an organisation so hidebound by bullshit.' Not content just to talk the talk, Griffin became one of the leading lights of the Hurling Development Committee and was determined to bring a stubbornly conservative sporting organisation face to face with the realities of its current situation. It often seems to him that the most important things in the GAA, like underage coaching, are those that are least talked about. In the process, his deep passion for the game won the admiration of fellow committee members like Ger Loughnane.

30

DALY PLEASURES

Anthony Daly: 1987–2003

In 1995, after eighty-one years wandering in the hurling wilderness, Clare finally reached the Promised Land. In one of the greatest All-Ireland final acceptance speeches Anthony Daly spoke for a whole county when he said: 'There's been a missing person in Clare for eighty-one long years – well, today that person has been found and his name is Liam McCarthy.'

During a game communication is almost impossible on the field because of the noise. The Clare manager Ger Loughnane had to rely on his players for leadership on the field. Anthony Daly was the natural choice to be the team's spokesman and captain. Daly had to be an excellent craftsman with a superb fighting spirit and the stamina of body and mind to cope with the long haul. While his famous speeches and innate media skills might have seemed to be his obvious credentials, Loughnane chose him for his ability in the dressing room, given his flair for helping players cope with frustration and disappointment.

'Dalo knew moves before everybody else. I'd say there was

never an occasion when Dalo didn't know who was really playing when we needed dummy teams. He was never told but he always knew. Dalo was adept at deflecting any anger by giving his teammates a chance to air their complaints. If there ever was a grievance, Dalo would come to me. It was sorted out immediately. The players were treated exceptionally well, which was the best way to prevent grievances from arising, but if they did come up we dealt with them straight away. The fact that we had a holiday-fund committee meant that we could do things for them that other counties couldn't do.'

For the first half of 1995 Clare fans were anything but optimistic. Even when one major disappointment followed another, hope and dream always lived side by side in Clare. In 1995, as Daly recalls, his team was poised to react hungrily to a disappointing first half of the year: 'I think after the League final in 1995, 90 per cent of Clare followers felt, *This is it – we can't take any more trouncings*. You couldn't blame them. Although we hadn't been trounced on the scoreboard, in hurling terms we were. Coming out after the game, one supporter said, "Kilkenny were a different class." This massacre came on the back of major defeats in the two previous years in Munster finals. When Ger Loughnane spoke about us winning the Munster final, none of the fans believed him.

'There were less than 15,000 fans at our first game in the Championship and most of them were from Cork. Even when we beat Cork and the Munster final was jammed, it was mostly filled with Limerick people.'

Ger Loughnane believes that never was Daly's role as captain more clearly illustrated than before the Munster final in '95: 'Everybody in Clare was convinced that we had no chance of winning that game because two weeks before we had played Galway in a challenge match in Shannon and we bombed. It was on a glorious, sunny day and the previous day had been the very same. When we were inside in the dressing room, I noticed that some of our players were sunburnt and I said, "What the f**k were ye doing? Two weeks before the Munster final and ye come here sunburnt." Most of the crowd that were there went home at half-time thinking we hadn't a chance in the Munster final. When the team came into the dressing room, I gave them a fierce lambasting. We trained very well after that. On the day of the final we stopped in the hotel in Cashel for a cup of tea. You could tell that morale was very good and that they were in terrific form.

'We were on the way into Thurles and, just when we came to the bridge, the place was crowded with supporters wearing the Limerick colours. A few of them shouted at us, "What a waste of time." They were sure they were going back to the All-Ireland final. Straightaway, Daly said, "We'll f**king show ye whether it's a waste of time or not." That had a crucial bearing. It was just the sort of little spark that the players really needed to liven them up. As everybody got off the bus, there wasn't a word. As the players went out of the dressing room, I said, "If Clare don't win today, we're never going to win anything." I was sure we were going to win. Everything was just right. The rest is history but the incident on the bus showed Daly's sharpness of mind. Top marks to him for picking it up. A small thing like that can make a big difference.

'There was a brilliant photo taken during the All-Ireland of Brian Lohan and John Troy going for the ball. Instead of looking at the two of them Anthony Daly was in shot looking for the loose man. It was driven home again and again it's not the man in possession you watch but the loose man. That was how we kept Offaly down to 2–8 in that match. Daly's role was critical.'

The turning point in the All-Ireland final that year came with minutes to go. With the clock ticking, Anthony Daly, a master at the height of his powers, lobbed the sliotar into the square. Éamonn Taaffe connected and the umpire was reaching for the green flag. Another long-range free from Daly gave them the crucial lead that Clare held onto in defeating Offaly. Two years later he captained Clare to his second All-Ireland. His exceptional gifts as a player were recognised in the three All-Stars he won.

After he retired from playing he turned his attention to management and was an unlucky manager with Clare, particularly in 2005, when they lost out narrowly to eventual All-Ireland champions Cork. In 2008 he gave a massive lift to Dublin hurling when he agreed to manage the county team and in his first year brought them to an All-Ireland quarter-final.

One memory from his playing days gives him the most contentment: 'It was great going to the schools after we won the All-Ireland in 1995, just to witness the magic, the awe and the wonder, but to me the most special part was meeting the older people. I remember meeting my brother's father-in-law crying in Thurles after we won. He could remember back to '55 and the catalogue of Clare's heartbreaks. At the time I was so wound up and drained from games that I didn't fully appreciate it till later.'

Asked to pick one vignette which summed up Dalo, Ger Loughnane chose a critical incident in the 1995 All-Ireland: 'After Offaly equalised, Baker forced a 65. Dalo was facing up to it, though Seánie should have been taking it. Dalo had made up his mind. There was somebody injured and the game was delayed. I ran into Dalo and said to him, "Give it a right lash." I'd say he never even heard me. He was looking at the posts the same as if it was Cusack Park. I was standing on the sideline and was shouting a point before it had gone halfway.'

31

CAPTAIN MARVEL

Enda Colleran: 1961–1971

Enda Colleran was the first chief football analyst on *The Sunday Game*. He used the knowledge he acquired thorughout his career to telling effect as an analyst and blazed the trail for the rest to follow. A key part of the Galway three-in-a-row All-Ireland winning side of 1964, 1965 and 1966, and captaining the side in the latter two years, he was selected at right full-back on both the Team of the Century and the Team of the Millennium. He certainly had top credentials for the job.

Enda had no hesitation when I asked him which was his outstanding personal memory from the three-in-a-row triumph. 'It was the All-Ireland semi-final against Down in 1965, my best ever game. The ironic thing was that I had a terrible start to the match. I was marking Brian Johnson and he scored two points off me in the first few minutes. I felt that if I didn't get my act together, he would end up as man of the match and decided to change my tactics. Down were storming our goal for most of the second half and I found that no matter where I went, the ball seemed to land into my hands. I seemed to be in the right place all the time and made all the right decisions. Often I took terrible decisions and went forward and left my man and still the ball came to me. I was so thankful that a thing like that happened to me in an All-Ireland semi-final rather than in a challenge game with two men and a dog watching.

'At one stage Seán O'Neill had the ball around the midfield and Paddy Doherty, completely unmarked, came at speed to the full-forward position. I had two options: one was to stay on my own man, and the other was that Seán O'Neill would pass the ball to Paddy Doherty. I took the chance and ran for Doherty, and Seán passed the ball to him and I actually remember coming behind Paddy, trying not to make any noise, so that he wouldn't hear me coming towards him. At the last second I nipped in front of him and got possession. I felt he had a certain goal, only for that. It's amazing, with 60,000 people present, that I still thought my approach had to be as quiet as possible.'

A more tense occasion came the following year when Galway were to face the favourites Meath in the All-Ireland. Colleran was due to mark sprint champion Ollie Shanley, who had given a top-class performance in the semi-final.

'Everybody was saying to me, "You've an awful job in the final to mark him, you'll never mark him." Martin Newell and I went out to the Aran Islands for a few days, just before we started training for the All-Ireland final, and we were sleeping in the one room; he was on one side and I on the other. He woke up at one stage of the night and I was standing over him. I was sleepwalking! Martin told me the next day that I had said: "By Jaysus, if I can keep up with Shanley, I'll mark him." It just shows you the pressure I was under.'

What was the secret of Galway's success?

'We had great belief, which meant that we would always believe we would win a game when it was tight at the end. Other teams choked in that position. We also had that vital ingredient you need if you are to win anything – a bit of luck.

'I think back especially to the Connacht championship in 1965. Both Sligo and Mayo should have beaten us. It was there for them, if they'd kept their heads. We were in terrible trouble against Sligo after they got two early goals, but we sneaked victory by three points. Against Mayo we were losing by a point in the dying minutes when they got a fifty. Three Mayo players were fighting over who should take it when one of them rushed up and kicked it straight to one of our half-backs. He cleared it up the field and we got the equalising point. And then we got the winning point almost immediately. Mayo were all over us that day and without doubt should have won. It's amazing how a tiny incident can make all the difference in deciding who gets their hands on the Sam Maguire Cup.'

Enda has since moved on to the playing fields of Heaven. Even God needs a great number two.

The dream team Enda selected for me was:

1. Johnny Geraghty
(Galway)

2. Donie O'Sullivan **3. Noel Tierney** **4. Paddy McCormack**
(Kerry) *(Galway)* *(Offaly)*

5. John Donnellan **6. Kevin Moran** **7. Martin Newell**
(Galway) *(Dublin)* *(Galway)*

8. Mick O'Connell **9. Mattie McDonagh**
(Kerry) *(Galway)*

———

130

10. Matt Connor
(*Offaly*)

11. Seán Purcell
(*Galway*)

12. Pat Spillane
(*Kerry*)

13. Mike Sheehy
(*Kerry*)

14. Seán O'Neill
(*Down*)

15. Liam Sammon
(*Galway*)

32

DOWN BUT NOT OUT

Ross Carr: 1986–2000

Ross Carr played a pivotal role in one of the most stylish teams in the modern game. He helped Down become a team that was a godsend for the purists – the epitome of skill, strength and scoring power.

For much of the 1970s and '80s Ulster football was in the doldrums. Down's All-Ireland triumph in 1991 would change that. Their All-Ireland victory was the fullfilment of a promise of a life as it was meant to be lived for an entire province. The unthinkable had become the thinkable. The memory lingered long into the night only to be stopped gently by sleep, like a candle flickering faintly in the breeze. Yet a flame had been lit that day which would fuel an entire generation. The next morning the football worlds settled into the rhythms of a new life. Without the scoring feats of Ross Carr that season the football landscape would have looked very different.

Haunting echoes of failure were finally banished from an

entire province and would usher in an era of unprecedented success, as Joe Brolly recognises. 'If Down hadn't won that All-Ireland, you could have forgotten about Derry winning an All-Ireland, you could absolutely forget about Donegal winning an All-Ireland, and there wouldn't be Tyrone or Armagh All-Irelands. All of those titles were grafted on the back of Down's 1991 win. Donegal realised they could win an All-Ireland and there was a sense of inevitability that Derry would win in '93, and Down came back to win another final in '94.

'Derry had nearly beaten them in '91 in a titanic game in the Athletic Grounds. We were a point up at the end when they got a free 60 yards out. I was close to the ball at the time and I heard Ross Carr saying to Enda Gormley: "I'm going to drive this over the bar." Enda told him: "Wise up, you f**king eejit." But Ross sent it over the bar and they went through instead of us, but when they won the All-Ireland it inspired us because it made us realise how close we were. It was a class score from a class forward. I doubt if anybody else could have done what he did under that kind of pressure in that kind of cauldron.'

Ross Carr was at the heart of that Down team. Carr is universally recognised as one of the great forwards in the modern game. He starred in Down's 1–16 to 1–14 All-Ireland victory over Meath in 1991 and again in their 1–12 to 0–13 win over Dublin in the 1994 All-Ireland final. His performance in that match would secure his selection on the All-Star team in 1994.

The widespread admiration for that Down team is shared by Armagh's Enda McNulty. 'I would be a massive fan of Greg Blaney. The amount of balls he put into Mickey Linden's hands was incredible. I would be a big fan of James McCartan too, who I would say was one of the greatest players of all time because of his ability to lose a player, his ability to tackle, his ability to score and his ability to catch a high ball, even though he was only five foot six or seven. And then of course there was Ross Carr, who would always be relied on for the big scores in the biggest matches – which is the ultimate test of a great player.'

As Ireland's best-known sports psychologist Enda McNulty was also interested in Carr from a psychological perspective. 'The will to win is easy, but the will to prepare to win is more problematic. What singles out the great players like Ross Carr is their willingness to give everything for the cause and to prepare in every way possible. By having adversity in life we can see in others and in ourselves who quits and those who won't quit, and in the end adversity will make winners of those who won't quit. Early in his career, Ross Carr, like most players in Ulster, went through many a dark day, but that did not stop him from thinking he could reverse that trend and bring the Sam Maguire back over the border. Ross and his colleagues were the trailblazers. They were an inspiration and a call for all Ulster teams to raise their game and believe we could win an All-Ireland. It was guys like Ross who inspired guys like me, and I am sure boys in Tyrone, to bring the All-Ireland to our counties for the first time.'

Carr brings a keen intellect to bear on the issues that confront the GAA today. He believes that the GAA must not just consider the games themselves but the wider ethical and social issues it is confronted with. The experience of the widespread abuse that took place in Irish swimming prompted Carr to encourage the GAA to increase its measures in the area of child protection. 'My church has been badly tainted by the scandals in child abuse. The GAA has had its own scandals in this area too, though on a much smaller scale. I know from the people in charge of our juvenile coaching that certainly we are trying to get our act together.'

Ross Carr has a nice line in self-deprecation. One of the stories he tells against himself goes back to 1980, when he was just sixteen and was playing senior club in one of the biggest games in the club's history and he was incredibly nervous because he had not reached the highest standards of play at all levels. His poor mother prepared a great breakfast before the match that morning but he was just pushing the bacon after the egg on the plate because he couldn't concieve of keeping it down. He got up and went to the bathroom and on the way his mother drenched him in holy water to help him play well.

He came back and this time pushed the egg after the bacon, but again he could not take anything. His mother got out her rosary beads and blessed him. His late father was quietly reading the paper and was seemingly oblivious to his plight, but eventually he peered over the paper and asked, 'What's wrong, son?'

'I'm too nervous about the match to eat anything,' he answerd sadly.

His father then uttered the immortal words: 'Don't worry, son. You're sh*te. There's nothing you can do about that, but there's no need to be hungry as well.'

When I asked Ross to pick his dream team, he excluded Down players as 'that might be perceived as biased towards my own'.

1. Stephen Cluxton
(*Dublin*)

2. Robbie O'Malley **3. Mick Lyons** **4. Tony Scullion**
(*Meath*) (*Meath*) (*Derry*)

5. Tomás O'Sé **6. Seamus Moynihan** **7. Philip Jordan**
(*Kerry*) (*Kerry*) (*Tyrone*)

8. Anthony Tohill **9. Jack O'Shea**
(*Derry*) (*Kerry*)

10. Diarmuid Connolly 11. Larry Thompkins 12. Maurice Fitzgerald
(*Dublin*) (*Cork*) (*Kerry*)

13. Colm Cooper **14. Michael Murphy** **15. Peter Canavan**
(*Kerry*) (*Donegal*) (*Tyrone*)

33

Quinn's Worth

Mickey Quinn: 1978–1997

Leitrim for Croke Park. Mayo for Croagh Patrick.
(Sign outside a church in Leitrim after their Connacht title in 1994.)

Gaelic football needs every nostalgic prop it can muster and, when many of the controversies of today are forgotten, the powerful grip Leitrim's Connacht final triumph exerted on the popular imagination will never vanish. At the centre of that famous victory was Mickey Quinn who played under-age football for Leitrim for five years, twenty years for the senior team (1978–1997) and nine years with the over-40s. He made his senior inter-county debut in 1978. Although he was under six feet he could hold his own with giants like Liam McHale but his toughest battles were with Willie Joe Padden.

Glamour was alien to much of Quinn's own career.

'One day we were playing Mayo in Charlestown and there was such a gale blowing that at one stage when the Mayo goalie kicked out the ball it got caught in the wind and blew back over the inline for a 45.'

Throughout the 1980s, Leitrim experienced nothing but disappointment.

'In 1983 Galway beat us by a point in injury time. I was sick the night before the All-Ireland final when Galway were preparing to meet Dublin knowing we could have and should have beaten them but we hadn't the confidence and lacked quality in the full-forward line.'

Things changed for the better for Quinn personally and Leitrim when P. J. Carroll became manager.

'We went on a fourteen or fifteen unbeaten game run which was very unusual for Leitrim and won an All-Ireland B final in 1990. I won an All-Star that year and being the first one in Leitrim, it caused a lot of excitement in the county and gave me a new lease of life even though I had two or three trips with them as replacements at that stage. It meant everything to me because it was always my burning ambition. Winning an All-Ireland with Leitrim was too much to hope for. We were playing Leinster in the 1984 Railway Cup in Ballinasloe when the journalist David Walsh told me that I had missed out on an All-Star the year before by just one vote.'

A major catalyst for Leitrim's taste of glory was the management of John O'Mahony.

'He is a very tough trainer. He took everbody back because he drove us so hard. There were evenings that we would turn up for training in Kells that would be so wet that you wouldn't let your dog out in it. We'd be wondering if he would send us out in the absolute deluge but he would be out just in a T-shirt and track-suit setting up the bollards. We'd be thinking: "This guy is off his rocker," but he was setting us an example.'

———————

Quinn admits to playing a leading role in the infamous 'battle of the fog'.

'My club Aughawillian were playing Roscommon's Clann na Gael in the Connacht club championship but the match shouldn't have gone ahead. The fog was so bad you couldn't see the goalie kicking out the ball. Things heated up when two of our players were hit. I think it was me who really started it off! I "had a go" at Jimmy McManus and soon the whole set of players, subs and supporters were involved. The referee had a hard time getting law and order back but the game was a great battle in every sense.'

The match did have an amusing postscript though.

'Jerome Quinn played for Aughawillian against Clann na Gael that day and really dished it out to some of the Clann lads and developed a reputation as a hard nut. That was one of the reasons why Aughawillian versus Clann was renamed "the Provos versus the Guards". We were playing Roscommon in the Connacht Championship in 1990 and before the match P. J. Carroll had an unusual mind game planned. He said: "Jerome Quinn, they all think you're fu*king mad in Roscommon, what you need to do is pick up a clump of grass, stick it in your mouth and eat it in front of your marker's face. He'll sh*t himself." Jerome was wing half-back and was marking a lovely, skillful player. Sure enough Jerome did as he was told and you could see the Roscommon player's legs turn to jelly!'

Quinn picked a dream team of Connacht players.

1. Johnny Geraghty
(*Galway*)

2. Martin Carney   **3. Seamus Quinn**   **4. Dermot Flanagan**
(*Mayo*)   (*Leitrim*)   (*Mayo*)

---

5. Declan Meehan   **6. Barnes Murphy**   **7. Declan Darcy**
(Galway)   *(Sligo)*   *(Leitrim)*

8. Dermot Earley   **9. Willie Joe Padden**
(Roscommon)   *(Mayo)*

10. Paddy Dolan   **11. Seán Purcell**   **12. Mickey Martin**
(Leitrim)   *(Galway)*   *(Leitrim)*

13. Packy McGarty   **14. Micheál Kearins**   **15. Tony McManus**
(Leitrim)   *(Sligo)*   *(Roscommon)*

34

Star Forward

Mick Bermingham: 1961–1977

Mick Bermingham's career with Dublin spanned four decades. He first played senior inter-county hurling with Dublin as a sixteen-year-old in 1959 and his last game for Dublin in 1982 was at Intermediate level. He enjoyed great success with Leinster, winning six Railway Cup medals, including a four-in-a-row between 1971 and 1974. In 1971 Mick was selected at right-corner forward in the inaugural All-Stars. In 1984 he was chosen at left-corner forward on the centenary team of greatest players never to have won an All-Ireland final. Additional achievements include ten senior club championship medals. The highlight was when he captained Kilmacud Crokes to win the Dublin title. Mick considers that side unlucky not to have won a Leinster club title. He was also a prolific scorer for Kilmacud Crokes in the All-Ireland sevens competition. He had an impressive family lineage.

'I had hurling on both sides of the family. My mother's brother, Paddy Ford, played full-back in the 1947 Connacht Railway Cup side that beat Munster. My father's first cousin,

"Young" Mick Gill, was on the 1938 Dublin side that won the All-Ireland.'

However, Bermingham was denied the same opportunity to perform on the highest stage. 'In 1961 I broke a few fingers in a club match and I missed out on the chance to play for Dublin in the All-Ireland. It was agonising to watch the Leinster final, let alone the All-Ireland final. Dublin could have won. We lost to Tipperary on a scoreline of 1–12 to 0–16. We had a lean year in 1962 and qualified for the Leinster finals in both '63 and '64, only to lose to an emerging Kilkenny side who went on to have fifteen years of great success. The consolation for me came in the Railway Cups, which were massive back then.'

One of his best moments came in 1964 when Dublin scored a shock win over Kilkenny in the Walsh Cup final in Nowlan Park by 5–4 to 2–12. Bermingham was the winner's hero, scoring 4–3 of his side's total despite receiving an injury which forced him to retire for a spell. He had the ball in the Kilkenny net twice in the opening two minutes: the first coming from a free and the second in a melee from which he received his injury. The corner-forward was back before time and he went on to score two further goals and three points. His last point proved to be the winner. The match had a comical sequel.

'I didn't know it at the time but I had dislocated my shoulder,' he remembered. 'Des Ferguson was over the team and asked me if I could go back. I was patched up again and took my place. The circulation went out of my arms, and my shoulder was paralyzed after the match. There was great jubilation in the dressing room. It was like winning the Leinster final because we had beaten Kilkenny. I was having great, great difficulty changing my clothes. When I came back from having a shower, our dressing room was empty. As I finished dressing I found out that some so and so had tied my shoelaces together!'

However, his best match was for Leinster. 'When we beat Munster in the Railway Cup final for my first medal, I couldn't believe how excited the great Kilkenny and Wexford players were, legends of the game and multiple All-Ireland medal winners but they were like children because they hadn't won the Railway Cup before. I had an exceptional day. I was on John Doyle, a giant of the game, and who was I – only a nipper from Dublin. Coming out of the dressing room, another of the hurling immortals, Jimmy Langton of Kilkenny, came up to me and congratulated me on how well I played. It meant a lot.

'I resumed my career with Dublin when I came back in 1970. We won the Leinster Intermediate championship, beating Kilkenny, which was a great boost. The following year was a particularly good one for me in the scoring stakes. Dublin had won the minor All-Ireland in 1965 and seven or eight of them had come through. Things started to move with the senior team. Kilkenny beat us in the Leinster semi-final two years. They were at their peak then. In 1974 we got to the League semi-final but Cork beat us by a point. They went on to hammer the reigning All-Ireland champions, Limerick, in the final and that Cork team went on to win three All-Irelands. So although we never got there we were thereabouts.'

One of the impediments to Bermingham's hurling career was his work in the bar business, which caused him to constantly work antisocial hours. There was one memorable moment, though, when his job came back to haunt him on the hurling field.

'I played in the 1963 Leinster final against Kilkenny. It was a lovely sunny day and I was the free taker. At the time a friend of mine was working on a luxury liner, so he asked the captain if he could listen to the match on whatever frequency it was available. In fact he talked my skills up so much that the captain decided to listen in with him. Micheál O'Hehir had been praising me in his commentary, so my friend was feeling totally vindicated. Then we got a free into the Canal End goal and Micheál said something like, "The diminutive Mick Berminghan is about to take a free for Dublin and this will surely be a point." When I was lifting the ball, it tilted away from me and I put it wide. The captain turned to my friend and said, "He wasn't much of a hero there."

Bermingham's dream team is as follows:

1. Ollie Walsh
(*Kilkenny*)

2. Fan Larkin   **3. Nick O'Donnell**   **4. Tom Neville**
(*Kilkenny*)   (*Wexford*)   (*Wexford*)

5. Mick Roche   **6. Pat Henderson**   **7. Martin Coogan**
(*Tipperary*)   (*Kilkenny*)   (*Kilkenny*)

8. John Connolly   **9. Frank Cummins**
(*Galway*)   (*Kilkenny*)

10. Jimmy Doyle   **11. Des Foley**   **12. Eddie Keher**
(*Tipperary*)   (*Dublin*)   (*Kilkenny*)

13. Christy Ring   **14. Tony Doran**   **15. Eamonn Cregan**
(*Cork*)   (*Wexford*)   (*Limerick*)

35

OVER THE BARR

Ciaran Barr: 1984–1994

Ciaran Barr had gone bravely where no one had gone before as Antrim's first All-Star hurler in 1988. Later in his career the former Irish international water-polo player would transfer to Dublin and give outstanding service in the blue jersey. The high point of his career came in 1989 when he captained Antrim to a memorable All-Ireland semi-final win over Offaly. It was the first time that Antrim had qualified for the All-Ireland final since 1943. The match is fondly remembered by all sports fans because of the way the Offaly players made a guard of honour for the Antrim team as they left the pitch, as Barr recalls.

'It was a strange situation. We were confident we could beat Offaly as we had beaten them twice that year. Although it was an All-Ireland semi-final we didn't think of it like that, we just thought we were playing Offaly. Although Offaly were the form team in Leinster in the '80s, we would have been a lot more scared if we had been playing Kilkenny. It was only after we had beaten them that we thought – gosh, we're in the All-Ireland final now.

'Although we started off slow enough it was a day every-thing went right for us. Things we had planned in training just came off for us unbelievably well. We were lucky in the sense that we had five or six players who could turn things around for us when the going got tough.'

If Barr was ecstatic after that victory, the emotions were very different after the All-Ireland final. He has no doubts where the game was won and lost.

'We didn't focus properly on the occasion. We were slightly naïve and didn't know the pitfalls. Chiefly we were flattered and distracted by too much media attention. The organisation of all our efforts fell onto the shoulders of our manager Jim Nelson. A lot of the energies of our backroom team were dissipated with the result that the players' energies were deflected. It was crazy that the likes of Jim should be worrying about tracksuits and team blazers and shoes when they should have been focusing just on playing matters. Our playing population is so small that there was nobody to come in and take the administrative load off them. In any other county a committee would have rushed into place to help them out.

'We found the whole occasion very daunting. We were determined to enjoy the day but we made far too many mistakes in the build-up. We arrived far too early and were talking to people so we got caught up in the atmosphere. We were all new to the experience, the management as much as the players, and were naturally very inquisitive. So determined were we to enjoy the experience we were on the pitch far too early and were wasting a lot of energy running around with the result that physically and emotionally it felt as if we had played half a match. We just couldn't relax.'

Barr's memories of the match are surprisingly sparse in some respects:

'I don't remember much about the whole game. It was not as intimidating as I thought it would be but it passes by so fast. I was right under the Hogan Stand at the start of the match and I could hear individual voices I recognised shouting encouragement to me. I didn't think that would happen.

'We kept it 50-50 with Tipperary on the day for the first fifteen minutes or so. We had chances but drove a lot of wides. Then they got a soft goal which really deflated us. It took a lot out of our play. I remember how deflated the crowd were after the goal. It was as if they were expecting it. As a team we were very naïve.'

Barr feels that 1991 was another lost opportunity.

'We were taken by surprise in '89. If we had beaten Kilkenny in the semi-final in '91 when we gave them a great battle we would have been much better prepared and would not have repeated our mistakes and really got on with the job in hand.'

Time though has healed the wounds of those defeats for Barr.

'Our preparation for that game was absolutely superb. I've never played in a game where the team was so well prepared and focused on the job of winning although our '91 semi-final preparations against Kilkenny came pretty close. If the preparation is absolutely right things happen for you that wouldn't normally and you can react well to the various incidents that turn a game – though you always need the element of luck.'

36

Boyle's Law

Eddie Boyle: 1932–1952

At the top of the list of Louth immortals is the late Eddie Boyle, an outstanding full-back for Louth and Leinster. He played for Leinster between 1935 and 1948 and won five Railway Cup medals during that period. He won Louth senior championship medals with Cooley Kickhams in 1935 and 1939, and a Dublin senior championship medal with Seán McDermotts in 1947.

In 1932 he made his debut in a Louth jersey with the county minor side. In 1934, he was a member of the Louth junior team that reached the All-Ireland final, but after the semi-final he was promoted to the senior team and was therefore ineligible for junior grade when Louth won the final. However, he was awarded a junior medal. In 1990 he became Louth's first All-Star, when he received the All-time All-Star award.

The highlight of his inter-county career came in 1943, when he won his first Leinster senior championship medal. Boyle was the spine of the team, along with Jim Thornton at midfield and the classy Peter Corr in the forwards. In the Leinster semi-final Louth trailed Offaly by four points but with his bucket-like hands repelling virtually everything Offaly could throw at him, Boyle and his fellow backs kept them to a solitary point in the second half while the Louth forwards notched up 1–7 to win comfortably. In the actual Leinster final, Laois could only manage two points in the second half, while such was the service to the forwards that the final margin in Louth's favour was fifteen points. His second Leinster medal came in 1948, when Cavan thwarted their hopes in the All-Ireland semi-final.

Surprisingly, though, neither victory ranked as his most memorable match. 'I will always remember a National Football League match against Cavan in the Athletic Grounds in Dundalk. The Grounds were packed, as Cavan were All-Ireland champions and it was their first game after they won the title in New York. Cavan were hot favourites to win, as we were having a bad time, but it was a sizzler of a match and we played some inspired football, and we won by two points. The town was talking about the match for days afterwards.'

Boyle commanded great respect among his peers. When he retired, his Louth colleagues presented him with a magnificent gold watch. On its back were the words, 'To a great player from all Louth footballers'.

Louth goalkeeper Sean Thornton once said that when playing with Eddie Boyle he often felt like bringing a chair to relax in, because so commanding were Boyle's performances he had nothing to do!

While Eddie Boyle was chosen on the centenary team of players who never won an All-Ireland, Meath's Paddy O'Brien was chosen on the Team of the Century in the full-back position. Coincidentally both had played club football with Seán McDermotts. Asked once how he compared them, O'Brien said, 'Eddie was undoubtedly the greatest and you could put me somewhere in the bottom of the League table.'

The late Paddy Kennedy of Kerry was a close friend of Eddie. Boyle told me that he also retained a particularly close friendship with Peter McDermott. 'I really liked playing against Meath; there was always great football between us.'

How big a disappointment was it for Boyle not to have won an All-Ireland medal?

'I was always playing to get into an All-Ireland final and if I had succeeded in getting to it, I would certainly have been playing for a medal. But I always enjoyed the game so much that was what was important. Yet, while saying that, I don't mean that I wasn't always all out to win.'

Eddie Boyle was a very reflective man and gave a lot of thought to the secret of his success as a player.

'I loved being in the action. When the ball was up at the other goal, I was longing for it to be at my end, even if it meant danger. There is one thing you need in any position and that's anticipation. My intention was always to close down all traffic to the goal. You cannot afford to allow anything to develop in the play, otherwise anything can happen and you are in trouble. I was always blessed with good anticipation, but in playing full-back I was never relaxed. I was always on my toes, even when the ball was way up the field.

'My biggest asset was my ability to read the game. I never knew how I knew where the ball was going but I did. I'd be going out to the ball like a bullet. If you waited, the other fella had as good a chance as you of getting it. That's why I never looked for my man at any time; the ball was always all I was interested in. When the ball came in, my man was looking for me, but I was already clearing the ball.'

When I asked him to pick his dream team he selected the following players.

1. Danno Keeffe
(*Kerry*)

2. Enda Colleran   **3. Paddy O'Brien**   **4. Seán Flanagan**
(*Galway*)   (*Meath*)   (*Mayo*)

5. Seán Murphy   **6. John Joe Reilly**   **7. Stephen White**
(*Kerry*)   (*Cavan*)   (*Louth*)

8. Mick O'Connell   **9. Padraig Carney**
(*Kerry*)   (*Mayo*)

10. Seán O'Neill   **11. Seán Purcell**   **12. Peter Doherty**
(*Down*)   (*Galway*)   (*Down*)

13. Maurice Fitzgerald   **14. Tom Langan**   **15. Kevin Heffernan**
(*Kerry*)   (*Mayo*)   (*Dublin*)

37

BRAIN AND BAWN

Paddy Bawn Brosnan: 1937–1952

Paddy Bawn Brosnan played senior football for Kerry, winning thirteen Munster medals, three Railway Cups, and All-Irelands in 1940, '41 and '46. He captained the team in the 1944 All-Ireland, only to lose to Jimmy Murray's Roscommon.

One player who never forgot his encounter with 'the Bawn' that day was Roscommon's Brendan Lynch: 'You have to remember it was a very different time because of the war years. Some people listened to the news on the battery set radio, which was the only programme we were allowed to listen to because of the Emergency, but then they kept it on to hear Seán Óg Ó Ceallacháin reading the sports news. Most people heard that either Roscommon had won or Kerry had lost on the radio. The belief then was that you hadn't really won an All-Ireland until you beat Kerry in a final, so we were all keen to do that. I was marking the famous Paddy Bawn Brosnan. He was a fisherman and fond of the women, fond of the porter and fond of the rough and tumble!'

For his part, the Bawn believed that the pivotal incident in that final was when Lynch had a head collision with Kerry's great midfielder Paddy Kennedy, who had to be stretchered off. Kennedy asked Lynch, 'Jaysus, what did you do to me?'

Early in his career Paddy Bawn played in the forwards but then switched back to the defence. As a defender his most famous encounters were with the late Mayo great Tom Langan. One player had the inside story on their most memorable exchange. Some context is necessary first. Seán Freyne captained the Mayo minors in 1953 but missed out on playing in the final because he had entered the seminary in Maynooth and was precluded from playing because of the rules of the Catholic Church at the time. He finally got the opportunity to play for Mayo seniors in 1956 against Galway. Before the match Tom Langan told him that he would send him in the perfect ball. Uncharacteristically he did not. Ten years later Seán was walking into Croke Park and met Langan for the first time since that match: 'I got a very revealing insight into Langan's perfectionism. Tom's immediate response was to say to me: "Jaysus, that was an awful ball I sent you."'

Seán recalled: 'Langan had a rare off day in the 1951 All-Ireland final. Kerry were leading with moments to go and Paddy Bawn Brosnan, described by Langan as a "strong fella who was very butty", had dominated him. Brosnan took a kick out and a high ball was sent in and Langan flicked into the net. Paddy Bawn's verdict was: "He stood inside me while I was taking a kick out. It was probably illegal but it was very effective." The goal secured Mayo the replay they needed and they went on to reclaim the title.'

One of the stars of that Mayo team, Paddy Prendergast, went to work as a garda in Kerry, where he formed a close friendship with one of the icons of Kerry football.

———————

'Kerry had such wonderful players. I always felt that Paddy Kennedy was the prince of footballers. He was majestic. But Paddy Bawn Brosnan was something else – a great player and an exceptional man. He was a lovely human being and at that stage had a pub in Dingle. He had a great feeling for Mayo and I spent a lot of time with him. One time Seán Flanagan came down to visit me. I brought him to see the Bawn. We went into a quiet nook of the pub and chatted for hours. What I most remember about it, though, was over the course of the evening thirty people must have peered into the nook just to get a glimpse of Paddy Bawn, such was his legendary status. It was like going to Lourdes.'

38

THERE'S NO SHOW LIKE A JOE SHOW

Joe Canning: 2008–

In 2017 Trinity College Dublin awarded Galway hurling icon Joe Canning their Fair Play: Legend in Sport Award as part of their annual ethics in sport conference. The citation described him as: 'Hurler, Gentleman and Sportsman'. It is a small snapshot into the esteem with which the Prince of Portumuna is held amongst the hurling fraternity – as a player and as a man.

It is often said that sport builds character but the real function of sport is to expose character. Never was Joe Canning's character more exposed than deep into injury time in Galway's epic 2017 All-Ireland semi-final against Tipperary when he conjured up a sensational winning score from the sideline in the face of marauding Tipp defence. If Carlsberg did sporting heroes, they would create Joe Canning.

A teenage sensation with club and county, Joe Canning seemed certain to be suppering at hurling's top table but the expected deluge of national honours were not forthcoming because people just don't know which Galway is going to show up from one game to the next. He is happy to address this question.

'We're trying to get the consistency – that's the big thing for us. Over the last number of years, we've always had one big performance and then the next day it's a little bit flatter so that consistency is the big thing for us. We do believe in ourselves and in our own ability but it's about getting that consistency and backing up a good game with another.'

Canning's skills adorn countless sites on YouTube; epic sideline scores, stunning goals, deft flicks – each bearing his signature stamp of genius. Yet perhaps he does not get enough credit for his courage. He played in the 2012 All-Ireland final against Kilkenny although he had ligament damage on the side of the knee and he had not been able to train for the game.

There are two types of hurlers: those on the field who shift the piano and those rare few who play it. Joe Canning is firmly in the latter camp. The rich history of the GAA is studded with personalities who have retained forever a niche in the memory of those who have had the good fortune to see them in action. Yet Canning and his Galway team have been the subject of some strong criticism, notably from Ger Loughnane. When I raised this with Jimmy Magee, he chose to respond in a parable.

'I am sure Joe is keenly aware of the moral of the GAA star, the donkey and the bridge. A man and his son were bringing their donkey to the fair. The man was walking with the donkey and his son was up on the animal's back. A passer-by said: 'Isn't it a disgrace to see that poor man walking and the young fella up on the donkey having an easy time? He should walk and let his poor father have a rest.'

So the boy dismounted and the father took his place. A

mile later they met another man who said: 'Isn't it a disgrace to have that boy walking while his father takes it easy? You should both get up on the donkey's back.'

They duly did but a short time later they met an enraged woman who screamed: 'How cruel it is to have two healthy men up on that poor donkey's back. The two of you should get down and carry the donkey.' Again they did as they were told but the donkey fell, as they walked over the bridge, into the river and drowned.

'The moral is that if you are a top-class hurler and you are trying to please everyone you might as well kiss your ass goodbye. Joe should continue to be the very best he can be and continue to showcase his astonishing skills without worrying about what anybody else says, writes or tweets. He is one of the best we have seen and hopefully there is more to come. He is one of the few people around at the moment that I would pay good money to see because he can just take your breath away with those silken skills. The phrase national treasure is overused but he is as deserving of it as anybody I can think of at the moment.'

Having worked with him in Africa on behalf of the charity UNICEF, Dermot Earley is a massive fan of Joe Canning. 'Everyone admires Joe for what he does on the pitch, but having been fortunate enough to see him in action, he is even more impressive off it. He is a great guy, a wonderful ambassador for the GAA and a great role model.'

39

KING OF THE CATS

D. J. Carey: 1989–2006

D. J. Carey's roll of honour includes nine All-Stars, five All-Ireland medals and four National League medals. He was the supreme sportsman; he was never booked in a club or inter-county game. When he announced his retirement in 1998, it was a major news story, but Carey came back and played on until 2005.

For Carey the main rewards of the game were spiritual.

'A lot of people think we do what we do for the medals and the glory. It's not about that. It's about fun and pride in one's parish and county.'

Ger Loughnane has radically revised his views on the mental toughness of the master executioner of hurling. 'There was a lot of talk before the 2000 All-Ireland when D. J. Carey wasn't on the Team of the Millennium. I was of the opinion that he didn't deserve it because he hadn't proved himself in an All-Ireland final. The test of a really good player is to produce the goods against a top-class player on the really big occasion.

'In '97 before we played Kilkenny in the All-Ireland semi-final, I was asked in an interview what I thought of D. J. He had been absolutely brilliant in the All-Ireland quarter-final in a thrilling game against Galway in Thurles. He practically beat the westerners all on his own. I said, "D. J. will prove himself to be an outstanding player when he plays really well against one of the best players in the country in a big match. Next Sunday he will be playing in a really big match against Brian Lohan, and if he plays really well against Brian Lohan, he will prove himself to be a really great player. But I won't regard him as a great player until he does it against somebody like Brian on the big day."

'Nickey Brennan was Kilkenny manager then and he taped the interview and played it on the bus on the way to the match. According to the version I heard, and how true this is I don't know, he said, "Listen to what that c**t Loughnane said about one of our best players." Eddie O'Connor is supposed to have piped up, "He's f**king right!"

'In 2000 we went to play Kilkenny down in Gowran on his home pitch. D. J. put on an exhibition. I never realised he had the skill, the pace and the wit to the degree he showed that night. All that night he was like somebody on a different plane. He left Brian Lohan totally and utterly stranded. I met Brian Cody coming off the field and he said, "He's something else." I answered, "He's a wizard." In 2000 I was delighted that he played a great game in the All-Ireland. What people underestimate about him is his courage. Down the years he collected many injuries. Yet his nerve remained as good as ever. His one instinct was to go for goal, no matter what kind of punishment he was going to be subjected to. Under every category of defining a great player, he is without doubt the finest player of his generation, if not ever.'

Brian Cody's description is equally fullsome: 'He brought everything to hurling. He's a great tackler, he's a great player, he's a great winner of a ball. His skills – he just had them all. He's been the most exciting player in hurling for a long time.'

40

TYRONE'S TERRIFIC TALENT

Peter Canavan: 1989–2005

Some players resort to unorthodox methods to put off an opponent. In the 1974 FA Cup final Liverpool's Phil Thompson did not give Newcastle star forward Malcolm Macdonald a kick of the ball. Afterwards Macdonald discovered that Thompson couldn't stand the smell of garlic. After that Macdonald would eat cloves of the stuff before every match against Liverpool and breathe on Thompson the moment he got near.

Some players rely on more old-fashioned methods. In 1996 after the All-Ireland semi-final two irate Tyrone fans were loud in their condemnation of the Meath team, particularly of their alleged ill-treatment of their star player Peter Canavan. A Meath fan made an interesting and revealing slip of the tongue in response: 'You can't make an omelette without breaking legs.' Having almost won the All-Ireland final against Dublin for the county on his own, scoring eleven of his team's twelve points when they lost by a single point, it was a backhanded compliment to Canavan that he was singled out for 'special attention' by the Meath men.

The match was, to use a classic GAA euphemism, 'a robust affair'. The Meath team were criticised for their aggressive treatment of Peter Canavan and some of the Tyrone players. Discretion precludes me from naming the very earnest Meath legend who afterwards apologised in a team meeting for losing his man momentarily in the match. One of his colleagues had the dressing room in stitches – though not the player in question – when he quipped: 'Not to worry. The only reason you couldn't see him was that you had your boot on his throat at the time.'

A great player's career is like a rose on a bush: it blooms brilliantly only to fade away. Peter Canavan's fame is destined to endure for many years. He captained the county to All-Ireland under-21 glory in both 1991 and '92, and in 2003, despite struggling with injury, captained them to their first senior All-Ireland and won a second All-Ireland in 2005.

As he lifted the Sam Maguire Cup, Canavan said: 'They said we were like the British Army – that we lose our power when we cross the border – but we've proved we have power today.'

Canavan is very aware of the spiritual importance of the victory. 'To take the Sam Maguire trophy to Tyrone for the first time meant so much to so many and we were very aware of that. The memory of the celebrations will live with me forever. However, what I really appreciate now is going around Tyrone and seeing young children wearing their county jerseys or displaying the flag of their county team with pride. You really can't put a price on that.'

Although he played with a very serious manner, Canavan also has a light side. In 2003 he was speaking at a reception to launch his book. All the Tyrone team were there apart from the delayed Eoin Mulligan. Canavan explained to the crowd that Mulligan was late because his mother had bought him a new mirror and he was still admiring his reflection.

Few people had the opportunity in their careers to see Canavan up close and personal more regularly than Armagh's Enda McNulty. 'Against Tyrone in 2003 we decided we were going to show the whole country that we could win by playing nice football. We tried to play less tough football and more champagne football. We needed to marry the skills with the physical dimension, which we failed to do in that final. We could also have been more intelligent on the day on the pitch – I'm not talking about management. For example, I was marking Peter Canavan and he wasn't fit to walk and I marked him man to man. I should have come out in front of him and covered off Eoin Mulligan as well. So I am taking the blame for my own performance when we lost a final I still believe we should have won. The player I always knew I had to be unbelievably focused on when I was marking him was Peter Canavan. You knew you had to be incredibly switched on for every single ball because if you even blinked he would stick the ball in the net. He has to rank up there as one of the greatest forwards of the game.'

41

THE WESTMEATH WARRIOR

Mick Carley: 1957–1977

Mick Carley's inter-county career, which began in 1957, spanned twenty years. Carley quickly established a reputation as a top-class player, which led to his selection in 1961, '62 and '63 on the Leinster Railway Cup team. At that time, Railway Cup football and hurling were prestigious events: to be selected to play was the highest accolade of recognition for a player of exceptional talent. By then Carley had blossomed as a midfielder and it was in this position that he scaled his greatest heights. Leinster won this competition in 1961 and '62, and were beaten in the final in '63. In 1961 he was selected on the Rest of Ireland team in the annual fixture with the Combined Universities. This remains one of Mick's cherished memories because of the privilege of lining out with and against the cream of footballing talent in the country. In 1966 he was chosen to tour America for the Cardinal Cushing Games.

He believes there were two crushing disappointments in his career. 'The first that stands out was not beating Kerry in

1969 in the league final in Croke Park, a game we could have won. The second was the day Laois beat us in the championship in Tullamore. At half-time we were leading by ten points and when Noel Delaney scored his second goal in as many minutes, and in the dying seconds of the game, I could feel the hair literally standing on my head. I just could not believe it.'

Although he never won medals with Westmeath, one of the rewards of his career was to meet so many characters.

'My favourite character in Gaelic games was Tipperary's John Doyle. We were roommates in the Cardinal Cushing Games in America. He was some operator.

'Meath's Patsy [Red] Collier was another. I went with Red to the Cushing Games. He was great craic. We were walking down Washington one day and we passed what we thought was just a public house. Red looked in and called us back and said, "Jaysus, come back here, lads. Ye never saw anything like this." We went back to see what he was so excited about. There was a woman up on the bar doing a striptease!'

Offaly great Willie Nolan was a big admirer of Mick Carley. 'He was a great player. I won two Railway Cups with him. It was a great competition then because it didn't matter whether you were from a weak county or a strong one. All that mattered was talent, and a good player always stood out because the cream always rose to the top. Mick was more than a match for the star players from Down or Kerry.'

Club football provided Carley with the most memorable incidents of his career. 'I was marking Seán Heavin, who I played with for Westmeath, in a club match. I was playing centre-forward and I was at the end of my career, so my legs were going. At one stage the ball came in to us and was about ten foot in the air. Seán was younger and much quicker than

───────────

me, so there was no way I was going to beat him. Just as he was about to jump and claim the ball I let out a roar: "Let it go, Seán." He stopped and let down his hands and the ball fell into my arms. The whole field opened up for me and I just ran through and tapped it over the bar.

'I once was playing a club match in Offaly against Walsh Island, a club most people will know about because of Matt Connor. After the game was over I togged in and was about to go home when a fella called me over and told me I should stay for a junior match between Clonbullogue and Bracknagh. I didn't really want to, but he was adamant that I should. I agreed to stay for five minutes. There was nothing special for the first couple of minutes but then suddenly a fracas developed and all hell broke loose. Everyone was swinging and punching. I found out later that they were all intermarried and there was a lot of history there. It took about five minutes for the referee to sort things out and get order back. He sent one of the lads off, but your man didn't do the usual thing and go back to the dressing room and take a shower. Instead he stood on the sideline waiting for things to boil over again so he could get back into the thick of the fighting. He didn't have long to wait! Another melee broke out and they went at it again, only twice as hard. The referee finally restored order. But almost as soon as he threw the ball back in another scrap broke out. I swear that there was no more than five minutes' football in the first half. In fact things were so bad that at half-time the priests from the two parishes went in to try and calm things down. Things went fine for the first twenty minutes of the second half and then another scrap broke out. I thought the fights in the first half were bad, but this one was really, really bad and the match had to be abandoned. Obviously the man who told me to stay knew what to expect. My only regret is that nobody made a video of the game. I would love to watch the match again. It would have made a great comedy.'

Carley's dream team is as follows.

1. Andy Phillips
(Wicklow)

2. John McDermott **3. Paddy O'Brien** **4. Johnny Egan**
(Galway) *(Meath)* *(Offaly)*

5. Mick O'Dwyer **6. Paddy Holden** **7. Martin Newell**
(Kerry) *(Dublin)* *(Galway)*

8. Seánie Walsh **9. Mick O'Connell**
(Kerry) *(Kerry)*

10. Tony McTague **11. Paddy Doherty** **12. Pat Spillane**
(Offaly) *(Down)* *(Kerry)*

13. Seán O'Neill **14. Seán Purcell** **15. Kevin Heffernan**
(Down) *(Galway)* *(Dublin)*

42

THE MAGNIFICENT SEVEN

Iggy Clarke: 1972–1984

Iggy Clarke was part of the new era in Galway hurling when he captained the county to their first All-Ireland under-21 title against Dublin in 1972. Three years later a National League medal came to Clarke.

'The watershed and one of my hurling highlights was beating Tipperary in that final. In those days the blue and gold jersey of Tipp had for us a hue of invincibility attached to it.'

There would be disappointment, though, later that year when Galway lost the All-Ireland final to Kilkenny.

'We beat Cork by two points in the '75 semi-final. After that, euphoria in Galway was unbelievable. The county was on a rollercoaster. But the expectations weren't based on reality. We were still unready to face a team of the calibre of Kilkenny and learned that in the final.'

Clarke had been ordained to the priesthood in 1979 when Galway played Kilkenny again in the final, only to make a present of two soft goals to the men in amber and black.

'We wasted a lot in the first half. I don't think the rain suited us. Kilkenny were spurred on by the defeat at the hands of Cork the previous year and didn't want a second successive defeat. There is a photograph as I'm walking off the field disconsolate and downhearted, with Eddie Keher saying to me: "You'll be there again next year." But I was not even looking at him. I was just thinking to myself that we could have and should have won that game.'

Unfortunately injury prevented Clarke from lining out in Galway's historic All-Ireland triumph over Limerick in 1980. However, his presence was publicly acknowledged following Joe Connolly's tour de force in his acceptance speech.

'In the All-Ireland semi-final against Offaly I was flying it. A high ball came in, falling between the half-back and full-back line, which I retreated to gather. I gained possession from Mark Corrigan and dodged his tackle. Out of the corner of my eye I saw Pádraig Horan coming to tackle me and I avoided him, but I failed to see Johnny Flaherty, whose tackle from behind drove up my shoulder blade and broke the cavicle. As I went down I could feel the heat of the rush of blood. I knew I was in trouble. I waited for the free that never came. Seán Silke was behind me saying, "Iggy, let go of the ball." I opened my hand and he cleared it down the field. I was removed on a stretcher and faintly heard the applause of the crowd in my ears, but in my mind I clearly saw my prospects of playing in the All-Ireland disappearing fast.

'The pain was unreal. I was placed against the X-ray machine in the Mater Hospital and I was afraid I was going to faint. A nurse tried to take off my jersey but it was agony, so I told her: "For God's sake, cut it off." I suppose I kept half-hoping for a while that I might be back for the final, but it was not realistic.

'During the second half I came out from the dugout and went up to the Hogan Stand. I had to mind my shoulder and didn't want to be crushed by people at the presentation. I had an inner feeling, you might say a premonition, that the lads were going to win, even though the game wasn't over. On the way people kept asking me if we were going to win and if I was praying. After his wonderful speech Joe Connolly handed me the cup, which enabled me to feel part of the whole victory. It was such a beautiful moment to hold it up in front of the crowd. We all felt that we were part of a turning point, a special moment in hurling history when Galway would take its rightful place at hurling's top table.'

There was further disappointment for Clarke in 1981.

'We were coasting in the All-Ireland final at half-time despite John Connolly's disallowed goal. We looked like winning until Johnny Flaherty's goal, and even then I thought we were good enough to come back. It was a bitter pill to lose, but the defeat didn't hurt me as much as in '79. That year we hadn't won an All-Ireland and I was very aware of the so-called curse on Galway hurlers, which said we would never win an All-Ireland. As a priest I wanted to disprove that rubbish and we had achieved that in 1980. I often wonder about priest's curses. I wish somebody had used them for positive things. I often think of the peasant who refused to hold a priest's dancing horse. The priest said to him: "I'll put a curse on you that will stick you to the ground." The peasant replied perfectly reasonably: "If you can do that, why don't you do it to the horse?"'

Having won four All-Star awards, Clarke retired at the tender age of thirty-two in Centenary Year. 'At that stage I didn't have the passion for it any longer.'

In 1997 Clarke left the priesthood and is now married to Mariel. He forged a new career as a deputy principal in a school in Galway and also on a part-time basis as a professional counsellor. However, it was his experiences in the priesthood that provided him with his most amusing memory from his career.

'The morning of the All-Ireland final in 1981 I was saying Mass for the team in the hotel. The gospel that day was about the parable of the mustard seed: the smallest grows into the biggest seed. In my sermon I gave a very eloquent philosophical presentation on how the story of the mustard seed equated with our journey as a team. In '75 we were a tiny seed but in '81 it would really grow to fruition. That night at the meal we were all down because we felt we had left another All-Ireland behind us. Joe Connolly turned to me and said: "Jaysus, whatever happened to that f**king mustard seed!"'

Iggy's Galway team was made up of great characters, none more so than Brendan Lynskey. When Galway played Offaly in 1988, Lynskey was marking a very young Michael Duignan. As Duignan ran up to him, Lynskey had a classic put-down: "A mhacin, the minor match is over.'

The dream team that Clarke would have liked to have played on from his playing days is as follows.

1. Noel Skehan
(*Kilkenny*)

| **2. Fan Larkin** | **3. Pat Hartigan** | **4. John Horgan** |
| (*Kilkenny*) | (*Limerick*) | (*Cork*) |

---

5. Joe McDonagh
(Galway)

6. Seán Silke
(Galway)

7. Iggy Clarke
(Galway)

8. John Connolly
(Galway)

9. Frank Cummins
(Kilkenny)

10. J. Barry-Murphy
(Cork)

11. Pat Delaney
(Kilkenny)

12. Martin Quigley
(Wexford)

13. Noel Lane
(Galway)

14. Ray Cummins
(Cork)

15. Eddie Keher
(Kilkenny)

43

MAKING THE CATS LAUGH

Brian Cody: 1973–

Tony Mowbray brought a no-nonsense style to management. He told his former Celtic teammate John Hartson: 'You are the only striker I know who puts on weight during a game.' Likewise Brian Cody does not do sentiment. Giants of the ash like Charlie Carter have found to their cost that Cody is an ardent believer that the ugly truth is preferable to the beautiful lie.

Cody does not do the obvious. In 2012 he sprung Walter Walsh from obscurity to give him his first start in an All-Ireland final. Walsh responded by winning the Man of the Match award and Kilkenny won another All-Ireland.

A member of the great Kilkenny team of the 1970s, Cody won four All-Irelands as a player and captained the county to All-Ireland success in 1982. He won two All-Star awards. He also won an All-Ireland club medal with his beloved James Stephens in 1976.

He won his first All-Ireland in 2000, back-to-back titles in 2002 and '03, and completed a memorable four-in-a-row in

2009 in an epic tussle with Tipperary. The basis of his success is that not only is he a proven judge of players but he also has the extra invaluable ability to recognise exactly where, how and in which onfield allowances they can best serve his teams. Moreover, he brings an analytical assessment, passion and a talent for motivating players individually to transcend their former limitations. A side's self-belief soars when the manager's methods work and in the history of hurling, no manager's methods have worked as well as Cody's.

Of course he has occasionally disappointed himself and others. In fairness, the perfect talent has never existed. As rabbits and hedgehogs quickly learn not to become transfixed by the headlights of oncoming cars, Cody learned speedily from his rare failures, notably the defeat to Galway in 2001. Yet with Cody, seeming to get his bearing from signs known only to him, the ratio of success to failure is incredible. After the loss to Galway, Cody introduced a more robust style of play to Kilkenny hurling. Nobody was going to push them around any more.

Apart from Cody's great achievements as a manager, Nicky English believes his legacy will be profound. 'I don't believe in the cult of a manager. The way I see it, a bad manager will stop you from winning an All-Ireland but a decent manager will win the All-Ireland for you, if he has the players, and that's the key. It is players who win the All-Ireland, not managers. The one exception I would make is that I rate Brian Cody very highly. He has achieved so much over such a long period, but above all he has changed the tradition of Kilkenny hurling. He brought in a new system and a way of playing that has become part of the hurling culture in Kilkenny now.'

Although best known as a twice world cross-country

champion and for his silver medal in the marathon at the 1984 Olympics, John Treacy, the head of the Irish Sports Council, is a keen hurling fan and a big admirer of Cody. 'I think of Brian as the Alex Ferguson of Irish sport. He is an incredible manager. He sets the bar very high and demands and gets the highest standards from his players. If you don't reach them, you have no future as a Kilkenny hurler, no matter how much skill you have. He knows everything about every promising player in every corner of the county. He is always looking for ways to improve the team. He leaves nothing to chance and everything about his preparation is always well thought through.'

With coaches, as with players, the cream rises to the top and good coaches tend to have success follow them. With the obvious exception of his memorable lynching of Marty Morrissey after the 2009 All-Ireland final, Cody's answers at press conferences may not be entertaining in the style of Babs Keating but players would follow him over the trenches. He is without doubt hurling's greatest ever manager.

For many years Ger Loughnane has witnessed Cody's performance on and off the pitch. 'Brian was a year behind me in St Pat's teacher-training college and lived in the room opposite me. We got on really well and when we played together in college he could do things with the ball that'd make you look completely stupid. His level of skill was a delight. He wouldn't say much, but when he spoke everybody listened. After he retired from playing I thought he'd be managing Kilkenny minors or under-21s because I remember that when he came on the field at Pat's he had a very strong presence. I really admire him as a man and as a manager. When he was appointed manager of the Kilkenny team, I said, "Everybody's in trouble now."'

44

SKY HIGH

Jamesie O'Connor: 1992–2004

Jamesie O'Connor was poetry in motion. He was almost a professional player in terms of his diet, training and attention to detail, which helped him to become one of the greatest hurling forwards in the modern era and Clare to win two All-Irelands. His speed of foot, of thought and of wrist were his hallmark, and his never-to-be-forgotten winning point in the 1997 All-Ireland final epitomised this.

His abiding memories of 1995 remain very vivid. 'People were in euphoria after we won the Munster final. Sixty-three years was a long wait. People couldn't believe it was actually happening. I remember towards the end of the game, as people started climbing in towards the pitch, thinking, "Jesus, get off the pitch or he'll abandon it." I thought some catastrophe was in store for us.

'With that win, a massive weight was lifted off the county. Clare people had travelled to so many Munster finals – minor, under-21 and senior – and always come home with their tail between their legs. I had the cup the next week and I brought it to Don Ryan, who lived just around the corner from my parents' shop in Ennis and who was a diehard Clare fan. He had been the first fan to every match for years and years. I said that he might like to take a look at it. He just broke down in tears and I said, "I will call back later." That's what it meant to the guy.'

Jamesie retains vivid memories of both his All-Ireland final wins.

'The second half was tense. We were going well and then Johnny Pilkington scored a second Offaly goal. With the clock ticking, Anthony Daly and Éamonn Taaffe combined to get us the goal we needed. Offaly came down the field again. They hit the post, but the ever reliable Frank Lohan was there to relieve the danger. The ball was cleared and we got a 21-yard free, which I pointed. Then the crowds descended on us. Every inch of Croke Park was covered with Clare people. Winning that All-Ireland was great and it meant so much to the county, but in many ways for the team the second All-Ireland was more important because it showed that we were no flash in the pan: Clare were a force to be reckoned with. The first win was for the county; the second one was for the team.'

Ger Loughnane's relationship with Jamesie was a microcosm of his curious relationship with his team – a fascinating combination of closeness and distance. Yet few people are better placed to furnish a glimpse of what stirred silently in Jamesie's cool, dark waters.

'Jamesie always said to me that he never knew who the real me was. Once he was asked, "What's Loughnane really like?" Jamesie replied, "Sure I don't know!" There was always a bit of distance, that bit of a gap.

'Jamesie was often shocked by things I'd say to him or other players, and they never knew when I was going to rear-up on them, but when they went out on the field there was an incredible bond between us. You'd need a great psychologist to explain the links between us. In the Munster final in '95, with four or five minutes to go, we scored a point. I was walking up the sideline and he put up his fist to me. No word was said, yet the message was clear.'

With a characteristic smile, Loughnane recalls, 'Jamesie is a most unusual man! After the '95 All-Ireland was over, to escape the crowd on the pitch, we went up into the VIP section in the Hogan Stand and had a cup of tea. Albert Reynolds and all the VIPs were there. Neither Albert nor any of the others were interested in us. We were just a sideshow.

'Jamesie came over to me and said, "Jesus, I'm sorry I let you down today."

'I replied, "What?"

'"I was sh*t. I let you down."

'"But, Jamesie, we wouldn't be here with the McCarthy Cup if it wasn't for you."

'"I know, but I was useless today."

'He was so self-critical. That he came along at that time was such a dream. Without him we would have won nothing. He was a pleasure to have in training. What he would do with the ball was spellbinding. He was always a huge test for the player he was marking in training, even though they often did very well on him. He had this great self-belief – as had the other Doora Barefield lads, Seánie [McMahon] and [Ollie] Baker – that no matter how badly he was doing in training, he would always do it on the big day. He's a brilliant, brilliant man. The best thing I'd say about Jamesie is that if you ever heard anybody saying anything bad about him you should be really suspicious of that person. He was always extremely popular and well-liked by fellow players. At his best he sent a kind of current through everybody watching.'

45

OFFALY GOOD

Matt Connor: 1977–1984

Matt Connor is forever imprinted into GAA history because of his scoring feats. Ireland's top marksman for five consecutive years, from 1979 to 1983, he scored a remarkable eighty-two goals and 606 points in 161 matches for Offaly. His silken skills, his free-taking ability, his power on the ball and his speed of movement and thought made him stand out from everybody else. He scored a stunning 2–9 (2–3 from play) in the All-Ireland semi-final in 1980 against Kerry, when the final score was 4–15 to 4–10 in Kerry's favour.

Dublin's status as kingpins of Leinster was abruptly ended by Offaly in the 1980 Leinster final. Offaly's manager, Eugene McGee, was to mastermind one of the biggest upsets in football history when his Offaly side beat a Kerry team seeking five-in-a-row in the 1982 All-Ireland final. The undisputed star of that team was Matt Connor, who scored seven points that day. His points when Offaly were under pressure enabled the team to claw their way back.

Connor is a very private man living a public life. Given

his exalted place in football's elite, he is in much too strong a position to go rushing wide-eyed and eager towards the beacons of welcome. Even those journalists closest to him have never quite penetrated the reserve that masks his rich wellspring of humanity. His is a protective spirit, raising a moat against the outside world. Though the pitch of his conversation is undramatic, almost downbeat, the depth and authenticity of his experience fills my mind with images of a score of summer afternoons in Tullamore and beyond, and of poorly attended league fixtures when the sound of thunder cracked the air and rain spilled down onto the stand roof, rattling like applause on metal slats. Anyone interviewing him is unlikely to be offered a stream of cosy reminiscences, but there are one or two. As we spoke, his talk came initially as a trickle then, as he cast away his inhibitions, swelled into a flood.

'The build-up in 1982 suited us very well because all the pressure was on Kerry. They were probably the best football team ever. They had a lethal forward line, an extremely good back line and a great midfield. They really had no weakness. We had to work hard on the day and never give up. One very important thing was that our manager, Eugene McGee, put my brother Richie in at centre-forward. That was a key decision because the year before Tim Kennelly had absolutely cleaned up at centre-back. He was going to make sure that the main reason we were beaten in 1981 wasn't going to happen again. He put Richie as a kind of stopper and a play-maker at centre-forward and that worked a treat. Another thing was that Eoin Liston was the key man in the Kerry forward line and we had to stop him and stop the supply of ball to him. Liam [O'Connor – Matt's cousin] did quite a good job in that sense on the day and the players out in the

180

field did a lot of hard grafting to stop the ball going into the Kerry full-forward line.'

A sadness so deep that no tears would come fell over football fans everywhere two years later with the news that at the age of twenty-five Matt Connor's career had come to a premature end.

'I was going home from Tullamore on Christmas Day to my Christmas dinner. My car went out of control and I was thrown out of the car and landed on my back. I damaged my spine and I suffered paraplegia from that accident. That finished my football career. When I had the accident, I suppose football wasn't the main priority at that stage. It was just a complete change of life that I was not able to walk again.'

Seldom has one man brought so much pleasure to so many.

46

THE NOBEL LAUREATE OF SKILL

Colm 'the Gooch' Cooper: 2002–2016

When Martin McHugh dismissed Colm Cooper as a two-trick pony, Pat Spillane responded by saying, 'It was a bit like saying the Pope isn't Catholic, the Earth isn't round, and Neil Armstrong didn't walk on the moon. It ranks with those three.'

Cooper was chosen as Footballer of the Year in 2004. Kerry followers focus on the team and the bigger picture rather than the individual, but fans of all ages have heroes. From the start, Cooper was one of them because of his supreme skills and his attitude – it is about doing everything as well as you can and no acceptance of second best, whether it be on or off the field. It is about the commitment to excellence. Cooper on the ball is as dangerous as a lion with a thorn in its paw.

Incredibly before Kerry's 2009 All-Ireland quarter-final with favourites Dublin, Cooper was being written off in some quarters. His early-season form had not been vintage and he made front-page news by getting dropped for the qualifier against Antrim after being caught drinking after a narrow victory over Sligo. Cooper responded in the best way possible with a goal in the opening minute and a five-star performance in Kerry's demolition of the Dubs by seventeen points. A new joke was born: What's the difference between Dublin and a school uniform? The school uniform will be seen in September.

Cooper kicked six points in Kerry's thirty-sixth All-Ireland final victory when they beat old rivals Cork and finished the year as top scorer in the championship.

The highlight of his career so far is no surprise: 'The first time that something great happens is special because there can never be another first time – so winning my first All-Ireland title in 2004 against Mayo is probably the greatest highlight, especially because we lost my first All-Ireland final in 2002 to Armagh. It was very emotional when the full-time whistle went.'

Cooper also played for Ireland against Australia. 'From my point of view, it was a tremendous honour to be invited to play for my country and I was delighted with the chance to be part of the experiment to give an international outlet to Gaelic football. Of course it did come as a shock when you were on the ball that an Aussie player could come up and knock you to the ground by any means necessary – and keep you pinned down. I do think we could learn from them. There is a very high emphasis on the basic skills, but as Kerry showed in 2004 in their defeat of Armagh there is still a major place for "catch and kick" in Gaelic football.'

Despite winning All-Irelands in 2004, 2006 and 2007, disappointment was to follow in the All-Ireland final against Tyrone in 2008.

Joe Brolly was concerned that we did not see the best of

the Gooch in recent years because of the way the game has gone. Brolly's frustration is that Gaelic football has become a 'demolition derby', with the emphasis on physicality, and he points to the number of serious injuries that players are suffering today as a by-product of this trend. He used the case study of 'our Nobel Laureate of skill,' Colm Cooper, who has endured a spate of injuries and consequently in recent times has had 'negligible impact on the big stage, either toiling against blanket defences or limping through Killarney on crutches'. Brolly uses the example of the 2015 All-Ireland final when Cooper 'spent most of his time in his own half, tracking Dublin's counter-attacking corner-back. The fact that the corner-back scored and Gooch didn't tells you all you need to know about modern county football.'

Then Brolly examined the transformation in Gooch's physique: 'At first, a lithe, supremely supple footballer running riot in his first final against Mayo. In the end, a muscled, tight gymnastic physique.' He also quoted Darragh Ó Sé's observation about Cooper: 'You used to see Gooch swigging a bottle of Coca-Cola and eating a bag of crisps. Now he walks down the main street in Killarney sipping spring water and eating a banana.'

47

THE PURPLE AND GOLD

Tony Doran: 1967–1986

Tony Doran played for Wexford from 1967 to 1984, winning an All-Ireland with the county in 1968. One of his biggest admirers, the late Mick Dunne, former Gaelic games correspondent with RTÉ, spoke to me about this legend of the ash.

'Although Tony had the good fortune to win an All-Ireland early on in his career, he and that Wexford team were unlucky in many ways. Having said that, they beat old rivals Kilkenny in a Leinster final by seventeen points in the 1970s and that made up for a lot of disappointments. Wexford played well in the 1976 All-Ireland final, but they lost to Cork by four points.'

Galway's Iggy Clarke had a unique insight into Wexford's performance on that day. 'We drew with Wexford in a great semi-final game and lost the replay by a goal. It was an extremely hot summer. The two games were played within a week of each other and the replay was within two weeks of the All-Ireland final. The game burned a lot of stamina. I believe if either ourselves or Wexford had won the first day Cork would have been defeated in the final. As it was, Wexford came close that year, but I think the two games against us took a lot out of them. They were not as fresh in the final as Cork were and that cost them dearly. I felt a bit sorry for them that day because they had some great players at that stage, none more so than Tony Doran. The fact that he was chosen as Hurler of the Year in 1976 is testimony to that because it is rare for the hurler of the year to be chosen from a county that does not win the All-Ireland.

'Waterford's Tony Browne would be one of the few others that spring to mind in that category in 1998 and only an elite few like Christy Ring, Brian Corcoran and Dan Shanahan have ever emulated that achievement.'

Further disappointment lay in store for Doran in 1977, as Mick Dunne recalled: 'Wexford were probably in the right place at the wrong time. They had the misfortune to come up in both years against a truly great team – the Cork three-in-a-row side. How rare is it for a team to win the three-in-a-row in either football or hurling in the modern era? There is a lot of truth in the old adage that if you win one All-Ireland you must be a good team but to be considered a great team you need to win a second one. In '77 Wexford played well, but probably not to their very best, and you can't hope to win an All-Ireland against a side like Cork without being at the very top of your form. Having said that, it was only a great save by Martin Coleman against Christy Keogh in the dying moments that denied Wexford that year.

'The problem for great players like Tony Doran was that it was so difficult for them to be seen in Croke Park on All-Ireland final day because every year they had to face the most formidable opposition of all in the Leinster champion-ship: Kilkenny. True to form after "loaning" their Leinster crown to Wexford for two years, as they would have seen it, Kilkenny were back in '78 and went on to win the All-Ireland in 1979 against an emerging Galway side.

'I know Tony would feel that the All-Ireland that really got away from Wexford was in 1974, even though they lost to Kilkenny at the Leinster final stage. Wexford were going toe to toe with them but had to play the entire second half with only fourteen players after Phil Wilson was sent off. Yet true to form Wexford hurled out of their skins and it took Eddie Keher to characteristically win it by a point for Kilkenny with the last puck of the game. What made the defeat so galling was that Kilkenny beat Galway and Limerick very comprehensively in the All-Ireland semi-final and All-Ireland final respectively.

'Unlike today there was no second chance for teams like Wexford because there was no back-door system then. Also back then the only games people saw live on televison were the All-Ireland semi-finals and finals, which meant that the national audience were deprived of the oppprtunity to see the wonderful players Wexford had, like the Quigley brothers and Tony Doran.

'Tony was a great player, a great goalscorer, but I think what made him stand apart was that he was such a wonderful competitor. I think a revealing insight into his personality and psychological make-up was that he once told me that the biggest disappointment of his career was not losing the two All-Ireland finals but losing to Offaly in the 1981 Leinster final. Tony was carried off in the early stages with a severe head injury and only heard the last few minutes on the radio from a hospital bed.'

No matter how high you go, there is something special about playing for your own parish or village, the people you grew up with, the true fans whose life is hurling. The kick you get out of achieving something with your parish – that's the heart of the GAA for giants of the ash like Tony Doran, as one of his old foes Eddie Keher generously acknowledges.

'Tony was one of the greats of the game. He really announced his arrival on the national stage when he scored two great goals in the 1968 All-Ireland final. The fact that they beat Tipperary, who had defeated Wexford in 1965, added to the sense of occasion. Yet it says so much for Tony that the highlight of his career was when he won the 1989 All-Ireland club championship with Buffers Alley at the tender age of forty-two, when they beat a gallant O'Donovan Rossa from Belfast in the final. It shows that the pride of the parish is everything and that is why the GAA is so special.'

48

No Pat on the Back

Pat Hartigan: 1968–1981

Pat Hartigan is one of the greatest full-backs in the history of hurling. He played minor hurling for Limerick for four consecutive years (1965–68) and was on the under-21 side for six seasons (1966–71). He was also a highly accomplished athlete and represented Ireland a number of times as a shot-putter. He won a National League in 1971 and five consecutive All-Star awards in 1971–75 and won Railway Cup medals with Munster in 1976 and 1978. His career was tragically curtailed when he sustained a serious eye injury in 1979. He was at the heart of one of the great moments in Limerick sporting history. The county ended a barren spell by winning their first All-Ireland hurling title since 1940 in 1973. Hartigan's main memories of the game are surprising even to himself.

'Strangely it's the little things I remember about the game. Firstly, I remember the enthusiasm and spirit of Limerick people going on the train and the little games we were playing and the jokes we were making. This was only a front for what was facing us the next day. I remember the effect on people we knew, notably a taxi driver, John Lane, a saint in his own right, who had a tremendous sense of occasion.

'The evening before the match the elder statesman and father figure of the team Éamonn 'Ned' Rea tried to break the ice by talking about glamour boys and the way rooms were being allocated in the team hotel. I suppose we were unusual in that we had two brothers in the squad who were both priests – Father Paudie and Willie Fitzmaurice.'

Hartigan was determined to relax the night before the big name.

'Ned, Jim O'Donnell, Seán Foley and myself headed into O'Connell Street at about 7.30 p.m. It was a sight to behold. Seeing all the Limerick people there gave us a real lift and made us even more determined to win the title, especially the way they were hooting horns at us. Some of them had been there in 1940 and were looking to see us repeat history and others were going to attend Croke Park for the first time.'

Pat credits the importance of the pre-match talk.

'I recall vividly the pep talk before the final. It was given to us by Jackie Power, Ger's father, who had been part of the Limerick All-Ireland victory in 1940. His voice started to falter and he started to cry. Team captain Éamonn Grimes stood up like a flash and took over.'

There are gaps in Hartigan's memory of his biggest day.

'I can't remember leaving the dressing room and I have no memory of going out the tunnel. The next thing I remember was outside on Croke Park and in one din of noise.

'The weather was very bad on the day and we got a little bonus because the wind changed in our favour at half-time. I always feel that the turning point in the game came halfway through the second-half. A high ball broke in behind our half-back line and Mick Crotty looked goal bound. Our goalie Séamus Hogan made a brilliant save and deflected the ball and it went over the bar. A goal for Kilkenny at this point would have finished us but the save spurred us on to victory.

'The real highlight of the All-Ireland for me came after the match and seeing a hundred people crying. It meant so much to them. That was a source of immense satisfaction.'

The following evening was like a curate's egg – a mixed success.

'The post-match celebrations were not all we would have wished for. Such was the throng of people who came to the Crofton Airport Hotel that we were locked inside in the interests of safety. I was doing an RTE interview and was forced to leave by a back window. There was no dance. The tables were cleared and guards were manning the doors so that people couldn't get in. The result was that there was no team celebration as such. There were pockets of us in different rooms.

'However, we made up for it the following day when we got back to Limerick to the reception in the Shannon Arms Hotel. Estimates of the attendance vary – somewhere between 50,000 and 65,000. We didn't get home till 4 a.m. I will never forget the squad-car trying to avoid people as it steered us to our destination and the joy on the crowds' faces.'

49

BERNARD THE BRAVE

Bernard Flynn: 1984–1994

Although he was not the tallest of Meath players, Bernard Flynn had a thrilling cocktail of speed, skill and scoring power that made him one of the great corner-forwards. He won two All-Irelands in 1987 and '88 and was a beaten finalist in 1990 and '91. He won All-Star awards in '91 and '97 and won national League medals in 1988, '90 and '94.

Flynn's inter-county career began when Meath's fortunes were at a low ebb. 'In 1983 I played minor, under-21 and senior. I was a small, scrawny kid at that stage and a lot of people said I wouldn't make it. Big powerful men were in vogue then and I was only five foot nine and ten and a half stone.'

Flynn was to discover in a brutal way that there were severe consequences if you broke the code that drove the squad with the fervour of medieval monks.

'The training in Bettystown and the Hill of Tara was savage. I hated the running up the Hill of Tara sessions. I would always be at the back while fellas like Cassells and McEntee would be up at the front. Even when I was vomiting down my top I kept going because you dared not stop.

'The biggest single lesson I got about Seán Boylan's psyche came one night when he brought us over the sand dunes in Bettystown. It was minus four or five degrees and we were made to go into the water because he loved the healing and therapeutic powers of water, the whole spirituality of that. We were just worried about getting hypothermia. Seán was way ahead of his time because he had a back-up team with him from early on. They had jeeps with their lights on and they were providing the light in the sand dunes.

'It got so bad that night I was scared I was dying. I actually felt death was coming over me. I had never felt so bad before and have never done since. I was at the back and I fell down. I got sick and I hid in a bush, where it was pitch dark. When the lads came running around again, I jumped into the middle and I thought I had got away with it. Seán had been watching me, though, and he saw what I was at and he stopped everybody. He knew I was a young lad and needed a bit of a reality check of what was expected and demanded of me. I was still wiping away the vomit from my top but he gave me such a lecture and a lesson that I never stopped again in my entire life.

'The lads were looking me in the eyes, and some were shaking their heads, and I knew they thought less of me because of that incident. It took me a long while to rebuild some of their trust after that. I felt I had let myself down and I had let them down, but the one thing I learned was that you never give up. It wasn't a case of Seán putting his arm around my shoulder. He devoured me and tore strips off me and had me nearly crying. I got no sympathy from anybody else and that was the kind of thing that was needed. He has the image of being a lovely man but underneath he is a silent assassin. Yet I have the utmost respect for him and without him we would have won nothing.'

50

AN ENGLISH MAN IN TIPPERARY

Nicky English: 1982–1996

Nicky English was Hurler of the Year in 1989, and he won six All-Stars and two All-Irelands as a player before seeing All-Ireland glory in 2001 as coach to Tipperary. However, it was none of those All-Irelands that provided English with his finest moment.

'Winning the 1987 Munster final was my greatest day in hurling,' he recalls with a smile of satisfaction. 'The fact that we beat Cork after extra time in a replay added to it. Tipperary hadn't won a Munster final since 1971, so that's why Richie Stakelum's comment that the "famine days are over" struck such a chord. The emotion our victory unleashed was unreal. Nothing has ever matched that feeling.'

In both 1987 and '88 Galway deprived English and Tipperary of All-Ireland titles. Galway's Noel Lane feels Tipperary did not deploy English most effectively in those years.

'In '87 in the All-Ireland semi-final we were up against Tipperary. When they won the Munster final, their captain

Richie Staklekum said, "The famine is over." That was the motivation we used to beat them. We had lost All-Ireland finals in '85 and '86 and there was no way we were going to lose three in a row. The '88 final is one of the great All-Irelands. There was great rivalry and great duels. One of the decisive factors was that our full-back Conor Hayes had Nicky English in his grip. If they had moved English, we would have been in trouble. I think the captaincy played on Nicky.'

The backdrop to the '89 showdown between Tipperary and Galway in the All-Ireland semi-final was the infamous 'Keady affair', when Galway's Tony Keady was suspended for playing illegally in America before the game. Keady had been the hurler of the year in 1988. The Galway camp were angry about the Keady affair because there were hundreds of footballers and hurlers going to play in America at the time but Tony was the one who was made a scapegoat. After he was suspended for a year there was an appeal, but he lost 20–18.

Before the game and the appeal there was a lot of discussion about whether Keady would play or not, but in an ill-tempered game Tipperary made the breakthrough and went on to beat Antrim in a one-sided final, with English setting a new record of 2–12 in the game. However, the most revealing insight into his character and belief in the importance of team spirit came with Antrim. Dead and buried largely due to his own efforts, English offered to come off the field to give a sub a run. Although they lost their crown to Cork in 1990, Tipperary would win another All-Ireland in 1991.

By then injuries were starting to catch up with English. Babs Keating once said to English: 'Nicky, if I had legs like yours, I'd be wearing nylons.'

Ger Loughnane is a big fan of English:

'I knew he would be a success as a manager. In 1999 in the

Munster semi-final against Tipperary we should have lost, but we scrambled a draw with a last-minute penalty from Fitzie. Nicky English's tactics that day were brilliant: draw Clare out and play the ball in fast behind them, and it almost worked. The replay was set for the following Saturday and we produced our best ever performance to win it. I knew then that it was only a matter of time before Nicky guided Tipperary to an All-Ireland and it only took him two more years to do it. He deserves all the plaudits he has ever got as one of the greatest forwards in the modern game and as a very intelligent manager.'

As one of the greatest forwards in the history of the game, Nicky English keeps a close eye on the great forwards of today:

'I had heard all the hype about Joe Canning and I wasn't sure the first time I saw him playing for Galway minors if it was all justified. Then I saw him scoring line balls for fun in the Fitzgibbon Cup and I began to reassess him. For me the turning point was the 2008 league final. He had excelled for Portumna in the club championship and had just come on to the Galway panel, and I couldn't believe the way he was able to run through the Tipperary defence. It changed the way I viewed him. I thought to myself, this guy can become anything. I was lucky enough to see him play against Cork that summer. It was incredible to watch him almost pushing his own players out of his way because he was so confident he was going to get the scores. In the second half especially he was a one-man show and it was just incredible to see three of the finest players of recent times – John Gardiner, Ronan Curran and Seán Óg Ó hAilpín – in a panic because they had absolutely no idea how to handle him. After that game I felt this is a guy who has the potential to become one of the all-time greats.'

51

A Waterford Wanderer

Jim Fives: 1949–1961

Waterford's sole representative on the team of the century of players who never won an All-Ireland medal is Jim Fives at right full-back – though it was as a forward that he first made his name with Waterford and his club, Tourin. Founded in 1940, his family played a prominent role in the club's development. He was the youngest of five brothers, who all played senior hurling with their native county.

Jim Fives' heroes were the Waterford hurling team that won the All-Ireland title in 1948, particularly centre half-back John Keane, who had hit the headlines for his fine performances against Limerick in the late 1930s. Although Jim played for Waterford minors in 1947, he was over-age to play for them the following year when they went on to win the All-Ireland. With his substantial physical presence, the six-footer played for the county at minor, junior and senior levels.

In 1949 he made his debut for Waterford against Wexford. It was a baptism of fire, as his immediate opponent was no less a player than Billy Rackard. Waterford's defeat that day was to be an omen of things to come.

'The biggest disappointment of my time with Waterford came when we lost to Tipperary by two points in the Munster Championship in 1951,' he told me. 'They were the big power then and we were so close. We never put it together after that.'

Why did Waterford have such little success?

'The Waterford team that won the All-Ireland in 1948 was a relatively old team and it broke up straight after that. We had a poor team while I was there. You have to remember that it is a small county and that the number of clubs playing the game is small. Another problem was that we had not the right management structures. We had far too many selectors and this led to a lot of "political" selection decisions, with selectors sometimes more interested in having players from their club on the team than having the fifteen best players. Of course that was not a problem unique to Waterford but at the time we couldn't afford to be going out with a weaker side.'

After cadet school, Fives was transferred to Renmore in Galway. For four more years he continued to play for Waterford, though he was playing club football and hurling in Galway. He won a Galway County Championship medal with the army, playing at midfield, and played for two years with the Waterford senior football team, though the closest he got to winning a county hurling medal came in 1955, when they lost the county final.

In 1955, Fives made the difficult decision to forsake his beloved Waterford and declare for Galway.

'It wasn't near as easy then to move around from Galway to Waterford as it is now. I was also often caught between the club and county. The club wanted me for a big match but Waterford would want me on the same day for a League match or a tournament game. Really for practical reasons the only option for me was to switch to Galway, although I was very sorry not to be playing for Waterford any more.

'The hardest part was the two times I had to play for Galway against Waterford – in the All-Ireland semi-final in 1957, and in 1959 when we played them in the Munster championship because Galway were "in Munster" then. It's a very, very difficult thing to do to play against your native county.'

As was the case with Waterford, he was on the Galway team in lean times. The highlight was winning the Oireachtas final by a big score over Wexford in 1958. There were a couple of good performances in the Railway Cup: notably a draw with Munster in 1957 and a victory over Leinster in 1959 in the semi-final. The final was delayed until Easter Sunday due to renovations on the Hogan Stand but Munster won the final.

The move to Galway coincided with Fives' switch from the forwards to the backs. 'I was anxious to play in the backs because I always like to be facing the ball. The thing about forward play is that you always have to turn once you get possession.'

A serious back injury caused him to step down from senior inter-county hurling in 1959. Two years later he was transferred to the barracks in Castlerea and came out of retirement to play junior hurling for Roscommon. Having played football for one county and hurling for three counties, Fives came within a whisker of playing for a fourth. He had hardly arrived in Castlebar when he was asked if he would be willing to play for Mayo the following Sunday. The old back injury had returned and Fives was forced to decline the offer, unable to cross the fitness threshold.

―――――

Fives glows affectionately, with the wonder of a baby counting his toes, as he recalls some of the more unusual incidents in his career. 'In 1948 I played a senior club match in Waterford. It was a very niggly game and there was a lot of moaning to the referee, the great Limerick player Garrett Howard. At half-time he brought the two teams together and said, "Let's have no more of this whinging. Hurling is a man's game. It's not tennis. Be men and take your challenges and your punishment. Go back out there and play like men not mice." We took his advice to heart and went out and played like men possessed. Nobody held back and there were some fierce challenges and an awful lot of sore limbs the next day!

'I was playing a junior hurling match for Tourin against Ballyduff in Lismore. Our full-forward "manhandled" their goalie and a melee developed around the goal because they tried to lynch him and he ran. Everyone got involved. What made it unusual was that all of us ended up against the railing of the pitch first and then things got so hot and heavy that we all ended up in the next field. It was the most bizarre sight I ever saw on a hurling pitch – actually not on the pitch! Finally the referee restored order and the match restarted as if nothing had happened.'

Fives' dream team from the players of his era is as follows.

1. Tony Reddin
(*Tipperary*)

2. Bobby Rackard	3. Nick O'Donnell	4. Jimmy Brohan
(*Wexford*)	(*Wexford*)	(*Cork*)
5. Séamus Cleere	6. John Keane	7. Iggy Clarke
(*Kilkenny*)	(*Waterford*)	(*Galway*)

8. Jackie Salmon   **9. Jack Lynch**
(*Galway*)   (*Cork*)

———

10. Josie Gallagher
(*Galway*)

11. Mick Mackey
(*Limerick*)

12. Christy Ring
(*Cork*)

13. Paddy Kenny
(*Tipperary*)

14. Nicky Rackard
(*Wexford*)

15. Jimmy Smyth
(*Clare*)

52

MAGNIFICENT MAURICE

Maurice Fitzgerald: 1998–2002

Maurice Fitzgerald is destined to be forever remembered for the All-Ireland quarter-final in 2001 in Thurles, when his magical long-range sideline drew the match. Mickey 'Ned' Sullivan said of Fitzgerald, 'If he had played in the Kerry team of the 1970s, he would probably have gone down in history as one of the greatest forwards of all time.'

Even as a boy young Maurice's exceptional talents were evident to all shrewd observers. His father, Ned, had played for Kerry and the family were close friends with the legendary Mick O'Connell. Maurice won the first of three All-Star awards in his teenage years, in 1988, having scored ten points in the defeat to Cork in the Munster final. It would be nine years before Fitzgerald won his first All-Ireland medal, when Kerry beat Mayo, their first All-Ireland in eleven years. After such a period of plenty in the 1970s and 1980s, the lack of an All-Ireland title since 1986 seemed unnatural. Some are obliged to work hard for their place in the sun; others have greatness thrust upon them. In the All-Ireland final Maurice wrote his name into the national consciousness, regularly breaking through, with Mayo defenders falling around him like dying wasps, and kicked ten incredible points from all angles. On that performance he was chosen as Footballer of the Year.

Peter Ford was a selector on the Mayo team for that game. 'Maurice Fitzgerald scored three points from play that day. Pat Holmes did what any good defender is told to do in these situations. He forced him out to the sideline and normally there would be no danger, but Maurice could kick points from there. It's very hard to find anybody to mark any player that good in that sort of form. It's almost freakish.'

The then Mayo manager John Maughan has never been let to forget what happened that day. 'I took a lot of flak after the game for the way we didn't replace Dermot Flanagan directly but made a series of switches, and above all for leaving Pat Holmes on Maurice Fitzgerald. The best man to have marked Maurice would have been Kenneth Mortimer, but we needed him up in the forwards. With the benefit of hindsight we maybe should have put someone else on Maurice with ten or fifteen minutes to go, but we felt then it was best to stick to our guns.'

In 2000 Maurice would win his second All-Ireland medal. This time, though, he was cast in the role of supersub. Enda McNulty observed him at close quarters when his Armagh team lost an All-Ireland semi-final replay to eventual champions Kerry. He recalls with a sad shake of his head, 'We knew we were good enough to beat Kerry that time, but I'd say we just weren't smart enough. I think if we'd had a bit more cuteness on the pitch, we would have won either of those games. The master Maurice Fitz created all sorts of havoc when he came on as sub in both games. Looking back, if he had been there in 2002 when we beat Kerry in the All-Ireland final he could have done something special, either a score or a pass, to win the game for Kerry.'

The later years of Fitzgerald's career were overshadowed by the controversy created by his relationship with the team manager, Páidí Ó Sé. Pat Spillane watched the storm that unfolded between two of the two giants of Kerry football.

'The wheels came off the wagon in the 2001 All-Ireland semi-final when Meath beat Kerry by no less than fifteen points. Kerry went through a twenty-nine-minute spell in the first half without scoring and then could only muster a single point from substitute Declan Quill in the second half. Inevitably when a Kerry team loses by fifteen points in Croke Park, serious questions were asked, particularly when Páidí refused to start Maurice Fitzgerald.

'Maurice is very quiet. However, some of the people surrounding him liked publicity. The people advising him had Maurice's best interests in mind, but not necessarily the best interests of Kerry football, although they purported to have the good of Kerry football at heart. He had two very high-profile people backing him in the media, founder of the charity GOAL, John O'Shea, and then-editor of the *Sunday Independent*, Aengus Fanning.'

Spillane continues: 'You can argue that Páidí was right or wrong. At the end of the day Páidí was proved right. There is a very thin line between success and failure, and on the basis of your decisions you have to be judged on whether you were right or wrong. Páidí was proved right in 2000. Maurice was most effective as an impact sub. It was a big gamble, but it delivered an All-Ireland.

'I was looking forward to reading Páidí's autobiography because I thought it would be the perfect opportunity for him to finally tell us what his problem with Maurice was, but on the single issue that most exercised Kerry people he said absolutely nothing. Ronan Keating was wrong. You do not say it best when you say nothing at all. Along with Mike Sheehy, Maurice was the most skilful player I ever played with in the Kerry jersey.'

53

TIPPERARY'S TREASURE

Ciara Gaynor: 1997–2005

When the celebrity economist David McWilliams said if Ireland leaves the EU it will become 'England with camogie', it was an interesting affirmation of the centrality of the sport in Irish life.

It is often said, usually by Tipperary people, that Tipperary is the home of hurling. In the noughties Tipperary became one of the powerhouses of camogie as the county won three consecutive senior camogie All-Irelands. One of the stars of the team was centre half-back Ciara Gaynor. For Ciara, her fascination with camogie began at the same time as she began to talk – too early to remember.

'I can't recall when I actually started playing camogie,' she states. 'Back home my sisters and I would be playing around the yard. My interest developed further when I got to primary school. Our principal, Albert Williams, won an All-Ireland club hurling medal in 1986 and he was a big influence. I went to St Mary's secondary school in Nenagh. We had great success winning junior and senior All-Irelands.'

No camogie player has more right to distorting vanities or ever showed less trace of them than Ciara Gaynor. Being cursed by neither arrogance nor pride, she was selfless in pursuit of the remedy and never above seeking advice. From the outset, though, there was one voice whose whisper was worth more than the shouts of most other critics. No one is more attuned to the nuances of the game than her father, Len Gaynor. He won three All-Ireland senior hurling medals and trained both the Clare and Tipperary senior teams and took Tipp to the All-Ireland senior final in 1997.

'When I was young, Dad was still playing at inter-firms level. When he got into management then with Clare and Tipperary, we'd all head off with him when he was going to training or to matches. As a result hurling was always talked about back home and I suppose that was part of the reason why I became so passionate about camogie.'

There is one jewel of memory from the sport's greatest theatre that outshines all others for Ciara. She lurches into nostalgia about a victory that will leave bubbles of pleasure that will never disappear.

'The highlight of my career was winning my first All-Ireland in Croke Park in 1999,' she recalls with a smile. 'The buzz was great in winning each of the All-Irelands, but the first one was really special.

'I suppose it was a bit of a fairy tale really. We were only playing at senior level for four years and we quickly won three All-Irelands. The team had been building for many years. A lot of us played together at minor and junior level in the 1990s. The junior team won an All-Ireland in '92. The talent was there – it was just a question of getting the blend right. Then Michael Cleary, who had been a great hurler with Tipperary, got involved in training us and he was the biggest influence of all. He put the emphasis on the skills.'

Ciara's immense stature in camogie did not come without sacrifices far away from the clamour of Croke Park.

'You have to be disciplined in a lot of areas: diet, keeping fit, getting plenty of sleep and so on. There was no point in me going down to training for an hour and a half and then going in for a burger and chips or going drinking or heading off to a nightclub. My job as a garda involved shift work all the time, so I had to take a lot of time off work, which ate heavily into my own holiday time. Camogie takes time, money and effort, but it was worth it in the end.'

In autumn 2001 a major controversy developed when it emerged that a huge sum of money had been provided to enable the Tipperary hurlers and their partners to take a two-week holiday in South Africa. Meanwhile the camogie players were not getting any tangible reward, even though they had just won an historic three-in-a-row. Was Ciara annoyed by the obvious inequality?

'It doesn't bother me at all. I was at the hurling All-Ireland like all the Tipperary camogie players that year and we were delighted to see the hurlers win. I think it's great that they went to South Africa and that their wives and girlfriends were going with them because they made a lot of sacrifices too. After our second All-Ireland we got a week's holiday in Lanzarote. It was great, but in all honesty I would have preferred if we got the basic things like a cup of tea and a sandwich after training and proper travelling expenses for training and matches rather than a holiday.'

For Ciara, the rewards for playing camogie were not about medals. 'The biggest achievement we had was not to win All-Irelands but to play as well as we could. That was the ultimate ambition. I think the biggest compliment is that in Tipperary now camogie is very strong with young girls and a lot of them are now swinging hurlies for the first time. We know that whatever happens the future of camogie in the county is secure.'

54

MANAGERIAL MAESTRO

Kevin Heffernan: 1948–1962

Tony Hanahoe imagined Kevin Heffernan picking the 'team of the Heavens' at Heffo's funeral in 2013. 'I'll have Lar Foley, Paddy Bawn Brosnan, Enda Colleran, Páidí Ó Sé, Tim Kennelly ... they're the backs. Des Foley, John Timmons, Purcell, Freaney ... Dermot Earley, Frankie Stockwell ... I'll build around the rest.'

Such was Heffernan's passion for the game it was impossible to imagine that it would not be carried on to the next life. Without him it is doubtful if Gaelic games would enjoy the same profile as they do today.

Heffernan initially came to prominence as one of the finest players in the history of the game. As a consequence he was selected at left full-forward on the Team of the Century in 1984 and the Team of the Millennium in 1999. The tactical acumen he would later showcase as a Dublin manager was already evident in his playing days when he pioneered the role of the roving full-forward. The high point of his playing career came when he captained Dublin to a 2–12 to 1–9 victory over Derry in the 1958 All-Ireland final. He also won three league medals and seven Railway Cups. He scored no less than fifty-two goals and 172 points in his career with the Dubs. Heffo was central to St Vincent's dominance of club football in Dublin, when they won an astonishing thirteen consecutive senior championships from 1949 to 1962.

Those of us who watched Dublin's unconvincing win over Wexford in the opening round of the Leinster championship in 1974 could not have dreamed that they were watching the future All-Ireland champions. Heffo's transformation of Dublin was Gaelic football's equivalent of the Eliza Doolittle story in *My Fair Lady*.

The ingredients of his success were simple: 'What I set out to do was to try to get a team that could win. We had a poor record in the preceding years, and morale was at a very low ebb. What we wanted to do was simply start games again. To begin with, we got a fairly large group of players together, many of whom we knew from earlier days and many of whom were recognised as good footballers but had had no success at county level.

Surprisingly, Heffo's managerial style was to play a significant role in the philosophy of Ger Loughnane. 'In 1974 Clare were playing Dublin in a National League hurling match in O'Toole Park,' he remembers. 'When we arrived, the Dublin footballers were already training and we watched them. It left a lasting impression on me. The Clare players went out on the sideline. There was a match going on between two teams of footballers. On the sideline was a man in an anorak. He came down along the field and you could see he was serious about what was going on. There were no words spoken but, as he came down, everyone instinctively started to move back because this man in the anorak had the teams out on the field in a mental grip. The exchanges were absolutely savage, physically. But you knew that the man in charge was the man in the anorak. Kevin Heffernan taught me that day the greatest lesson of all time for a coach. When you are coaching a team, *you* are in charge. Players don't want a committee. They always want a man in charge. There must be one central voice.'

Having returned to manage Dublin to All-Ireland success in 1983 against Galway, Heffo went on to enjoy one of his proudest moments in the Compromise Rules series against Australia. The series really entered the popular consciousness in 1986 following a major controversy.

One of the Irish players on that tour was Pat Spillane. 'There were storm clouds before we went to Australia, when the Dublin coach Kevin Heffernan was appointed as tour manager ahead of Mick O'Dwyer. Micko is the most successful Gaelic football coach of all time and he has never managed the International Rules team, which is extraordinary.

'The GAA owes Heffo a lot. Gaelic football was not fashionable before his Dubs came on the scene, but they did a massive PR job for the game, as was seen in the number of Dublin jerseys being worn at the time, which later spread to jerseys in the other counties generally, when they had a taste of success. Heffo's Dublin team made Gaelic football sexy because of the hype they generated.'

Heffo agreed to pick his dream team for me.

1. Danno O'Keeffe
(Kerry)

2. Enda Colleran	**3. Paddy O'Brien**	**4. Seán Flanagan**
(Galway)	*(Meath)*	*(Mayo)*

5. Seán Murphy   6. John Joe O'Reilly   7. Stephen White
(Kerry)   *(Cavan)*   *(Louth)*

8. Mick O'Connell   9. Jim McKeever
(Kerry)   *(Derry)*

10. Seán O'Neill   11. Seán Purcell   12. Pat Spillane
(Down)   *(Galway)*   *(Kerry)*

13. Peter Doherty   14. Tom Langan   15. Mike Sheehy
(Down)   *(Mayo)*   *(Kerry)*

55

For Nudie Reason

Eugene 'Nudie' Hughes: 1979–1991

Monaghan's most famous footballer, Nudie Hughes, is part of an elite few who won All-Star awards as a forward and a defender, winning three Ulster senior football championships in 1979, 1985 and 1988, as well as a National League title in '85. Michael O'Hehir immortalised him with the famous line: 'And here comes Nudie Hughes for Nudie reason.'

In any list of the greatest players never to have won an All-Ireland medal Nudie's name features prominently. Who was the greatest player he ever saw?

'I've often been asked that question and I've always answered by saying that there were many great players, but the one I respected most was Offaly's Matt Connor. I'm certainly not saying this because of sympathy because I said the same when he was playing. When the chips were down, he rose to the occasion. Some players, like myself, could do it when you're winning by twenty points, but I saw him in a Railway Cup final in Breffni Park in 1983 when it was gone. Ulster seemed to have won it and they needed a goal. He manufactured a goal from his own 21-yard line and finished it by scoring it at the other end. His free-taking ability and point-taking from play with either foot was extraordinary.

Nudie was well able to hold his own in any company. One player who gave him a lot of problems, though, was the Kerry forward John Egan. Ulster were playing a Railway Cup match against Munster and Nudie was marking John. They were standing talking to each other because Nudie always talked to opponents, even though he would be told not to. At one stage John said, 'What's that man writing down on that piece of paper? He's a right-looking eejit, isn't he?' As Nudie turned to answer, John was sticking the ball into the net.

In 1988 Nudie used that same trick on Cavan's Damien O'Reilly. He was marking him in the Ulster final. At one stage in the game Nudie said, 'Jaysus, there's an awful lot of people up on the hill. How many people would you say are up there?' As Damien looked up to make his guess the ball came in-between them and Nudie caught it without any obstruction and stuck it over the bar. O'Reilly was taken off him immediately.

Since his retirement Nudie has become a distinguished pundit on Northern Sound radio. He brings the same brio to the task as he did as a player. In 2016, when Monaghan got two goals to haul back Donegal's five-point lead, he shouted, 'Forget the Euros. Forget the Leinster Championship. Forget the Iraq War. This is a real war in Cavan tonight.'

As a player Nudie won three Railway Cup medals and chose the Ulster team in 1984 as his dream team.

1. Brian McAlinden
(Armagh)

2. Joey Donnelly   **3. Gerry McGarville**   **4. Tony Scullion**
(Armagh)   *(Monaghan)*   *(Derry)*

5. Ciarán Murray   **6. Paddy Moriarty**   **7. Jim Reilly**
(monaghan)   *(Armagh)*   *(Cavan)*

8. Joe Kernan   **9. Brian McGilligan**
(Armagh)   *(Derry)*

10. Greg Blaney   **11. Eugene McKenna**   **12. Peter McGinnity**
(Down)   *(Tyrone)*   *(Fermanagh)*

13. Martin McHugh   **14. Frank McGuigan**   **15. Nudie Hughes**
(Donegal)   *(Tyrone)*   *(Monaghan)*

56

Sligo's Supreme Stylist

Micheál Kearins: 1961–1978

Micheál Kearins put Sligo football on the map. He first played for Sligo minors in 1960, losing out in the Connacht championship to a Galway side that went all the way to win the All-Ireland powered by Noel Tierney and Johnny Geraghty. The following year he made his competitive debut, being marked by Gabriel Kelly, against Cavan in a league game in Ballymote and he played for the county at all three levels that year. He played in seventeen successive championship seasons with Sligo from 1962 to 1978.

His introduction to championship football in 1962 was the story of his career in shorthand: so near yet so far. Sligo led by a point against the reigning champions, but Roscommon stole victory with a goal in the last kick of the game and went on to contest the All-Ireland final.

Football was in his genes, as his father played a lot of club football and lined out a few times for Sligo, beginning something of the Kearins dynasty. Not only did Micheál and his brother James play for Sligo, a generation later Micheál's son, Karl, lined out for the county.

Micheál's place in the lore of Gaelic football is made additionally secure by his phenomenal scoring feats. He was the country's leading marksman in competitive games in four different years (1966, 1968, 1972 and 1973). In the drawn 1971 Connacht final, he scored a record fourteen points: five from play and nine from placed balls, including two 45s and one sideline kick. He won two Railway Cup medals in a thirteen-year career with Connacht, in 1967 and 1969. Two years later he scored twelve points for Connacht against the Combined Universities in the Railway Cup, all from placed balls. With the Combined Universities leading by 3–9 to 0–17, Connacht got a line ball 45 yards out in the dying seconds and Kearins calmly slotted it over the bar to earn Connacht a replay.

He was a natural rather than a manufactured talent.

'Especially in the early years I did a lot of physical training on my own,' he explained. 'I would run a few miles early in the morning, maybe four times a week. I never bothered practising my free-taking much, not even taking a practice one in the kickabout before a match.'

Despite the longevity of his career Kearins never shed the burden of having the weight of expectation of Sligo fans on his shoulders. 'I was always nervous before a game, knowing Sligo were depending on me. To slot the first free between the posts was always very important to help me to relax.'

He won an All-Star award in the inaugural year of 1971 at left-half forward. In 1972 Kearins was also a replacement All-Star, though a major controversy ensued when he was ommitted from the original selection. He also played in three National League-losing semi-finals with Sligo. He played in three Connacht senior football finals, losing to Galway in 1965 and 1971 before finally winning the title in 1975.

'Winning the Conacht Championship in 1975 was a great honour, but it was not the highlight of my career. Winning the senior County Championship with St Patrick's Dromard in 1968 was my best moment in football.'

A cattle dealer, Kearins has been a familiar sight at many a cattle mart down the years. After his retirement from playing, he became a referee. Kearins did not have to think too deeply when asked about his most difficult game in that role.

'It was an All-Ireland semi-final between Cork and Dublin in 1989. I had to send Keith Barr off that day. He was involved in an incident, then five minutes later he ran 30 or 40 yards to get involved in a second incident. There was an awful lot of off-the-ball stuff that day and it's very hard to manage those games.'

In fact, the tension escalated to such an extent that Kearins publicly pulled the captains, Dinny Allen and Gerry Hargan, aside before the start of the second half and instructed them to warn their players about their behaviour. He didn't exactly get the response he'd hoped for from Allen, who, when quizzed by the Cork lads about what the referee had said, claimed Kearins had simply wished them well for the second half and hoped the awful weather would improve!

Kearins' dream team is as follows.

1. Johnny Geraghty
(*Galway*)

2. Donie O'Sullivan   **3. Noel Tierney**   **4. Tom O'Hare**
(*Kerry*)   (*Galway*)   (*Down*)

5. Paídí Ó Sé
(Kerry)

6. Gerry O'Malley
(Roscommon)

7. Martin Newell
(Galway)

8. Mick O'Connell
(Kerry)

9. Jim McKeever
(Derry)

10. Matt Connor
(Offaly)

11. Seán Purcell
(Galway)

12. Pat Spillane
(Kerry)

13. Mike Sheehy
(Kerry)

14. Seán O'Neill
(Down)

15. Paddy Doherty
(Down)

57

Larger than Life

Michael 'Babs' Keating: 1964–1975

Such were Babs Keating's abilities as a footballer that he played for Tipperary for thirteen years and he won a Railway Cup medal with Munster in 1972. However, it was hurling that made him a household name. He won three All-Ireland medals, was chosen at centre half-forward on the inaugural All-Stars hurling team in 1971 and also won the Hurler of the Year award.

The GAA is part of Babs' DNA.

'Coming from where I was in rural Tipperary, we all had the dream of wearing the jersey, of walking behind the Artane Boys Band and playing in Croke Park. The one thing we had was the confidence that if we got to an All-Ireland we would win it because of the power of the Tipp jersey.

'Football was in my blood. My grand-uncle Tommy Ryan won two All-Irelands with Tipperary. He was playing in Croke Park on Bloody Sunday and helped remove Michael Hogan from the pitch after he had been shot by the Black and Tans. I played football for ten consecutive years with

Munster. The fact that I came from a football family meant the sport came easier to me. I could play football just by togging out because I was brought up with it, whereas with hurling I had to work a bit harder.

'I experienced huge disappointment at under-age, losing four All-Ireland finals at minor and intermediate level. Then, having won an intermediate All-Ireland in 1963, three of us arrived on the Tipp senior team for the first league game against Galway. We played in most games in the league, but of the three new boys, I was the most vulnerable because the Tipp forwards were so strong.

'The highlight for me was playing in my first All-Ireland against Kilkenny in '64. Séamus Cleere was the hurler of the year in '63 and he was an outstanding wing-back. The one thing about that Tipp team was that they had the forwards thinking like backs and the backs like forwards. Séamus Cleere had scored a couple of points from the half-back line in the final the previous year. When you have a half-back scoring like this, he's a seventh forward. My role was to stop Séamus. Luckily enough, the first ball that ran on between us, I got it and scored a tricky point. I made a goal for Donie Nealon as well as doing my own job, so I ended up as Sportstar of the Week and on a high. The hype at home then was as big as it is now. The only difference was the media coverage wasn't anything like as intense as it is now. I was back at work on the Tuesday morning. There was no such thing as banquets here, there and everywhere. Having said that, there was a better atmosphere in Croke Park then because you were closer to the ground.'

While there were many plaudits for his performances, Babs had a few critics also. Famously after the 1968 Munster final when he gave a magnificent performance, scoring 1–3 for Tipperary, Christy Ring congratulated him by saying,

'Great performance, Babs, but imagine what you would have done if you had concentrated for the whole game.'

For Babs, the '71 All-Ireland final has special significance.

'Long before players were handed out gear for free, we were very conscious of the importance of equipment. I had the very best pair of football boots, but the night before the final my bag was stolen with the boots in them. I got a spare pair, but they didn't suit the conditions so I took them off. Michael O'Hehir famously described me in his commentary as 'Barefoot in the Park'. I was marking Fan Larkin and guys like Fan and Ted Carroll were not the sort of fellas to be walking around without some sort of protection. Fan never stood on my feet. He tried it a few times, but I was gone before he could make contact!'

In 1986 Babs was appointed Tipperary manager after a rare lengthy barren period in the county's fortunes. His unique magic worked quickly and in the 1987 Munster final replay his Tipperary team defeated Cork in one of the most memorable matches between the two old rivals. Galway would deprive Tipperary All-Irelands in 1987 and 1988, but Babs marched the team to the Liam McCarthy Cup in 1989 and 1991. After his spell ended in Tipperary he later managed Offaly, Laois and had a second spell with Tipperary but without the same success.

With the obvious exception of Ger Loughnane, few hurling managers have inspired as many quotes as Babs, such as Tom Humphries' observation: 'The miracle of Babs is his tongue. You can be expelled from the NUJ if you are within half a mile of Babs when he speaks and you don't record it. Babs loves microphones. If he could grow them in his garden he'd be out there all the time, talking to them like Prince Charles to his daffodils.'

Heffo's Heroes: Kevin Heffernan (wearing the number 14 shirt) in the thick of the action.

Harry's Game: Roscommon legend Harry Keegan (on the right) tackles Dublin's Kieran Duff. Pat Lindsay is on his knees.

On the ball: Carlow's dual star Paddy Quirke chases another score.

© INPHO/BILLY STICKLAND

JBM: Jimmy Barry-Murphy tangles with Kilkenny's John Henderson.

Supermac: Liam McHale is goalward bound against Cork in the 1989 All-Ireland final.

A Corker: Ross Carr takes on the Cork defence, including a bloodied Tony Davis.

Tougher than the Rest: Larry Thompkins in possession with Gerry McEntee in pursuit. Teddy McCarthy (far left) provides back-up if needed.

SPORTSFILE/BILLY STICKLAND

© INPHO

Camogie's Queen: Angela Downey looks for yet another score

Neither in Fiji nor Fermanagh: Sean Og O'Halpin tackles Tipperary's Eugene O'Neill.

© INPHO/PATRICK BOLGER

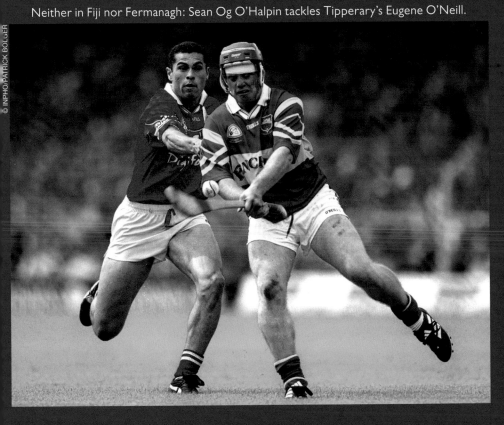

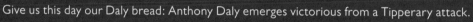
Runaround Sue: Sue Ramsbottom tastes All-Ireland glory with Laois.

Give us this day our Daly bread: Anthony Daly emerges victorious from a Tipperary attack.

© INPHO/TOM HONAN

Peter the Great: Peter Canavan breaks Armagh's hearts . . . again!

The eyes have it: Davy Fitzgerald clears with characteristic conviction.

© INPHO/MORGAN TREACY

Captain fantastic: Kevin Moran has been central to Waterford's efforts in recent years.

Geezer: Kieran McGeeney kicks to safety in Anthony Rainbow's farewell game for Kildare.

King Henry: Henry Shefflin is tackled by Tipperary's John O'Keefe.

© INPHO/CATHAL NOONAN

Earley Days: Dermot Earley tries to shake off Cork's Denis O'Sullivan.

© INPHO/RYAN BYRNE

© INPHO/LORRAINE O'SULLIVAN

A Touch of Class: The Gooch Cooper shoots for goal
with Cork's James Loughrey left stranded.

Jeepers Keepers: Stephen Cluxton saves what looked a certain Meath goal.

© INPHO/RYAN BYRNE

58

HARRY'S GAME

Harry Keegan: 1972–1988

During his seventeen-year inter-county career Harry Keegan was a pillar of the Roscommon defence. Despite his toughness he only got one booking in his playing days. Yet his career almost perished before it had begun.

'I made an inauspicious debut for Roscommon in a league match in 1972 against Kilkenny. A few months later we played Galway in the Connacht semi-final in Roscommon. We were leading by twelve points at half-time and the perception was that the referee gave everything to Galway. John Tobin kicked frees for fun and the match ended in a draw. The crowd were incensed and broke through the fences to attack the referee. It was a real mob scene. John Morley was on duty that day and stood in front of the referee and only for that he might have been killed or certainly very badly injured. The ref was struck, though, and Martin Silke and myself were accused of hitting him. Martin was a sub for us that day. In fact, the ref *was* hit, but by another Roscommon sub. We were brought up before the Connacht Council. It was very serious for Martin, as he was a garda, and if he had been found guilty of assault it would have had major repercussions for his career. Likewise I had just begun my nursing career in St Ita's, Portrane, and if a finding of assault was upheld against me it would have been very damaging professionally.

'The maddening thing was that when the incident happened I was 30 yards away. I had been marking Seamus Leydon that day and he wrote a letter to the Connacht Council. The night of the inquiry Seán Purcell spoke on my behalf as well. The frustrating thing was neither the referee nor the umpires turned up. We were put through all that stress for nothing.

'We beat Galway in the replay in Tuam. Tom Heneghan was put on John Tobin that day and Tobin didn't get a smell of the ball. Heneghan was the perfect man to put manners on a player like Tobin.'

The All-Ireland semi-final that year proved significant for Keegan.

'I got my right ankle injured that day and the injury was to persecute me for the rest of my career,' he says with a shudder. 'I had to go off and we were badly beaten. We trained very hard for that game but left our fitness on the training ground. We were really flying two weeks after. The game is probably most remembered for Mick O'Connell sitting down in the middle of the pitch and taking a long time tying his laces. To some people in Roscommon it was a bit disrespectful.'

Keegan is the only Roscommon player to have won three All-Star awards. He is very appreciative of the role played by the Roscommon County Board, though their methods were unorthodox.

'They always looked after us, even if the money wasn't too generous. One incident stands out for me. After a Connacht final in the '70s I went to one of the top officials in the County Board and told him that I needed money for expenses. He brought me out to his car, opened the boot and pulled out a £100 note from a green wellington and handed it to me. He then told me to send in the docket for it.'

In 1977 Roscommon played Armagh in the All-Ireland semi-final. It is not the loss in the replay that most irks Keegan today. 'Everybody keeps talking about the Kerry–Dublin semi-final that year and it's regularly shown on TV, but people forget that we produced two great entertaining games, which almost 100,000 people came to watch. Yet neither of the games is ever shown on television. The other so-called "classic" was really a game of rugby league, there was so much hand-passing. We played Armagh again in the 1980 semi-final and that was a very entertaining, high-scoring game, but it is never shown on TV, whereas our final in 1980 *is* shown, even though it is a much poorer game.'

Keegan has one particularly strong memory of playing Armagh. 'We played them in a fierce match in the league at the height of the Troubles,' he recalls with bewilderment. 'There was a skirmish and a lot of "scelping" in that match. They beat us by a point. We were delighted they beat us because there were rocks and stones reigning down on us after the game in the dressing room. What would they have done if we'd won? It was not one of my favourite places to go, as they were one of the few crowds I found abusive. I'm sure the Troubles did have an impact on them, but I couldn't understand why they took it out on Roscommon above any team.'

A more crushing disappointment came in 1980, when Roscommon lost the All-Ireland to Kerry by three points, having raced in to a good lead early on – as if to prove Joe

Brolly's assertion: 'Kerry would steal a worm off a blind hen.'

The reaction to that Kerry victory is still a bone of contention in Roscommon today, as Keegan's teammate Tony McManus recalls with feeling: 'Kerry used their power in the media to convince everyone that Roscommon used dirty tactics on the day and that we didn't attempt to play football. Tyrone and Armagh have suffered similar fates in later years at the hands of the media after Kerry objected to the way they play. Tyrone and Armagh beat Kerry in their own ways in recent years and Kerry didn't like it one little bit. What a lot of people don't realise is that Kerry have huge power in the national media, which is not good for the game in general. How a partly rehabilitated Paul Galvin could be chosen as Footballer of the Year in 2009 is beyond me. He was rewarded for behaving himself.

'Then Tadhg Kennelly was given an All-Star he did not deserve at all. We had the spectacle of all the former Kerry players lining up, one by one, to defend his actions in the All-Ireland final. Then Kennelly blamed the Australian ghostwriter of his biography for revealing that he intentionally went out to injure a player in the All-Ireland final – bizarre! Anyone who knows anything about Gaelic football and who looks at the incident in the first minute of the 2009 All-Ireland final knows that it should have resulted in a red card. The incident may even have decided that All-Ireland final. Kerry knew that an inexperienced referee would not send anyone off in the first minute of an All-Ireland final. If Tadhg Kennelly had done the same thing to a Tyrone or Armagh player, the reaction would have been somewhat different, I would say. The northern teams as well as Dublin have shown in the past that they have the mentality to beat Kerry and Kerry don't like it.'

A league match against Dublin provided Keegan with the most amusing moment of his career.

'The week before I had played against Charlie Redmond in a club match and he was sensational. Charlie, though, did not like close attention. He was a big man but was a bit soft and didn't like the physical stuff. If you gave him a yard, he would destroy you. I managed to get a clatter in on him and he went down like a sack of spuds. One of his own players came running up to him and said: "Get up, you f**ker, he didn't hit you half hard enough."'

Keegan's dream team is as follows.

1. Charlie Nelligan
(*Kerry*)

2. Jimmy Deenihan   **3. Mick Lyons**   **4. Robbie Kelleher**
(*Kerry*)   (*Meath*)   (*Dublin*)

5. Kevin McCabe   **6. Kevin Moran**   **7. Liam Currams**
(*Tyrone*)   (*Dublin*)   (*Offaly*)

8. Jack O'Shea   **9. Brian Mullins**
(*Kerry*)   (*Dublin*)

10. Matt Connor 11. Denis 'Ogie' Moran   12. Pat Spillane
(*Offaly*)   (*Kerry*)   (*Kerry*)

13. J. Barry-Murphy 14. Jimmy Keaveney   15. John Egan
(*Cork*)   (*Dublin*)   (*Kerry*)

———

59

THE MARVEL OF THE MARBLE CITY

Eddie Keher: 1959–1977

Kilkenny are the aristocrats of hurling and one of their greatest princes was Eddie Keher. His skill, dedication and attention to detail earned him Hurler of the Year in 1972, six All-Ireland medals, nine Railway Cups and five consecutive All-Stars (1971–75). Keher played senior for Kilkenny for the first time in 1959, having starred in the minor All-Ireland final that year. The senior final ended in a draw and he was drafted on as a sub for the replay. He was still playing for the seniors in 1977, so, apart from his superb skill, the fact that he remained at the top for so long is also an element in evaluating his stature in the game. A prolific scorer, he amassed a grand total of seven goals and seventy-seven points in All-Ireland finals alone.

One victory ranks highest in Keher's memory bank. 'The honour that meant most to me was my first-ever All-Ireland senior medal in 1963,' he recalls with pride. 'Beating Tipperary in the '67 final was also very important because we hadn't beaten them at that level for forty years, I think.

There was an attitude then that you'll never beat Tipperary in a hard game. Although we always play a certain type of game in Kilkenny, I think we toughened up a bit for that game and it made for a very satisfying victory, particularly as we proved our critics wrong.

'From a personal point of view, 1971 was very satisfying. Things went well for me on the day in the All-Ireland final and I made a then record score in an All-Ireland final of 2–11 – a record which was broken by Nicholas English in 1989. I rang him up a few days later to congratulate him. Coincidentally it was Tipp who beat us in the final in '71 and we can have no complaints with that because they had so many great players, like Babs Keating, who was Hurler of the Year that year.'

Keher did have some disappointments along the way. 'In 1966 Kilkenny lost the All-Ireland to Cork, although we were red-hot favourites. Cork won by 3–9 to 1–10. The papers the next day were full of talk about "the year of the sleeping pill". It was the first year players had taken them before an All-Ireland final. There was a lot of smart comments afterwards that we took them too late because we hadn't fully woken up until after the match!'

In 1979, Keher was manager of the Kilkenny team that defeated Galway in the All-Ireland final, when the westerners made a present of two soft goals to the men in amber and black. 'Kilkenny were spurred on by the defeat at the hands of Cork the previous year and didn't want a second successive defeat.'

For a perfectionist like Keher, routine is everything. You have to get the little things right. A famous incident occurred in the 1974 Leinster hurling final with the sides tied. With seconds to go Kilkenny's legendary corner-forward had an opponent tread on his foot and his lace was broken. Almost immediately Kilkenny were awarded a free. As a meticulous player Keher knew he wouldn't be able to score with the lace not attended to, so he bent down and tied it. The Wexford fans thought he was engaged in gamesmanship and running up the clock and let him know with a chorus of booing, but Keher kept his concentration and slotted the sliotar between the posts to win the match.

Kilkenny hurling has sired many characters and Eddie Keher has seen plenty of them. 'Ollie Walsh was a wonderful character,' he says with a smile. 'After we lost the All-Ireland in 1966 we came home from Dublin on the train. At the station Ollie got on board the luggage car and started driving it around the platform. It's a wonder he wasn't arrested!'

When I asked Eddie to pick his dream team he asked for a dispensation to pick two goalkeepers because he could not separate them.

1. Ollie Walsh/Noel Skehan
(Kilkenny)

2. Fan Larkin **3. Nick O'Donnell** **4. John Doyle**
(Kilkenny) *(Wexford)* *(Tipperary)*

5. Mick Roche **6. Pat Henderson** **7. Mick Jacob**
(Tipperary) *(Kilkenny)* *(Wexford)*

8. Frank Cummins **9. Theo English**
(Kilkenny) *(Tipperary)*

10. Jimmy Doyle **11. Pat Delaney** **12. Frankie Walsh**
(Tipperary) *(Kilkenny)* *(Wexford)*

13. Charlie McCarthy **14. Tony Doran** **15. Christy Ring**
(Cork) *(Wexford)* *(Cork)*

60

Mr Darcy

Declan Darcy 1988–2004

Declan Darcy should have been another Ross O'Carroll-Kelly. Growing up in Sandymount in the heart of Dublin 4, an inhospitable – barren, even – hinterland for the GAA, it was difficult to have foreseen in his childhood that he would become the face of Leitrim football's finest hour, as captain of their historic Connact final win in 1994. The fact that both his parents were from Leitrim was the catalyst for his immersion into club football in the county, though initially the move was shrouded in controversy:

'I was playing illegally with Aughawillian. I was not living or working there but I put my father's home place down as my address. Some people in other clubs didn't want me because I was giving Aughawillian an advantage but it was arranged by the club for me to play with Leitrim and that certainly made things easier. The great thing about playing with Aughawillian was that I found myself playing in big club tournaments at the age of sixteen or seventeen, like playing in a final in Cavan against Navan O'Mahonys up against Joe Cassells,

Finian Murtagh and David Beggy, which was surreal for me.'

A senior inter-county debut soon followed.

'I made my debut against Fermanagh wearing some ridiculous thing on my nose, having broken it just beforehand in a hockey match. I then played against Offaly. I started at wing-forward and was doing OK but then moved to centre half-back. Every ball seemed to come to me then and I was the hero of the day and that was where I lined out from then on.'

Darcy soon learned an important footballing lesson.

'I was marking Greg Blaney in a Railway Cup. I was just a nipper and because I respected him so much I was marking him very tightly and hanging onto him for dear life. Eventually he lifted me with an elbow and it was lights out. I couldn't see a thing. Greg is a dentist but he knocked out two or three of my back teeth! He remembers the incident well and we've often laughed about it since. It taught me an invaluable lesson that when you are marking a top player, you can't be hanging out of him. I learned that day that you don't cross the line and the next time I played on Greg I marked him very differently.'

Some of the same fans who were throwing bouquets at Darcy were swinging cleavers when he decided to transfer to Dublin, though many of his friends and Leitrim fans wished him well.

'Once the offer was made I had to give it serious thought. At the time the '94 Leitrim side that I captained to the Connacht final was disintegrating. The changes weren't to my liking. One little incident encapsulated it for me. The day before we played a Connacht championship match we were having lunch and were given steaks. In pretty much his last championship game Mickey Quinn said he wouldn't eat steak, he would only eat chicken because it was the best meal for the match the next day. Here was this Leitrim legend on his last legs worrying about his diet but when I went out of the hotel I saw two of the new players, very talented guys, smoking. That was their way of preparing for the biggest game of their lives. To be honest, if Mickey was going to continue playing, I wouldn't have been able to walk away from Leitrim because I looked up to him so much and so admired his great commitment to the county.'

Darcy is no Édith Piaf. He has some regrets about his time with Dublin.

'I had a good first year or two with Dublin but I made a big mistake when I came into the dressing room first and didn't say to players like Keith Barr: "Get the finger out of your arse and start playing." They were all experienced and gifted players and part of me thought who was I to be telling them what to do. I should have let loose but Dublin is a closed shop and I wanted to make friends. Mickey Whelan was the trainer in my first year and I felt his training was very advanced but it needed the players to take some of the responsibility themselves but they were letting him down. I felt I was a newcomer and held my tongue. Towards the end I did say what I felt ought to be done but I should have done that so much earlier.'

The Dublin experience did provide Darcy with the most amusing incident in his career.

'We were staying in the Horse and Jockey and I went out for a walk with one of the lads. A car pulled in beside us and my colleague said, "There's your man."

"Who?"

"Your man from *Star Trek*."

It was Colm Meaney and he was walking into the car park.

The next thing I knew I heard a booming voice shouting: "Hey, Colm, Beam me up Scotty." It was Vinny Murphy standing at the window. He was as naked as the day he was born!

'Vinny was a character. He loved a fag. Some wag changed the sign in Parnell Park from: "No Smoking" to "No Smoking, Vinny!"

Darcy's dream team is:

1. John O'Leary
(Dublin)

2. Seán Og de Paor   **3. Darren Fay**   **4. Tony Scullion**
(Galway)   *(Meath)*   *(Derry)*

5. Paul Curran   **6. Kieran McGeeney**   **7. Seamus Moynihan**
(Dublin)   *(Armagh)*   *(Kerry)*

8. Darragh Ó Sé   **9. Jack O'Shea**
(Kerry)   *(Kerry)*

10. Peter Canavan   **11. Greg Blaney**   **12. Maurice Fitzgerald**
(Tyrone)   *(Down)*   *(Kerry)*

13. Mickey Linden   **14. Kevin O'Brien**   **15. Tony McManus**
(Down)   *(Wicklow)*   *(Roscommon)*

61

THE LIMERICK LIONHEART

Gary Kirby: 1987–1999

Gary Kirby first came to prominence in 1984, winning an All-Ireland minor medal with Limerick and taking his first senior medal with Patrickswell. Three years later he helped Limerick to an All-Ireland under-21 title and captained the Irish under-21 shinty team. In 1986 he made his senior debut for Limerick. In 1991 he won the first of his four All-Stars. In 2009 he was chosen at centre half-forward on the Munster team of the previous twenty-five years and he ranks among the greatest hurlers never to have won an All-Ireland senior medal. The high point of his hurling career came in the Munster final in 1994.

'My greatest and fondest memory would have to be looking down on the Thurles field, seeing it full with Limerick people waving their green and white, and as captain lifting the Munster Cup after we beat Clare,' he says. 'There was a huge sense of excitement because it just meant so much to the fans because hurling means so much to Limerick. Although we had won the match, the significance of the occasion didn't sink in for a while.'

The All-Ireland hurling final that autumn was one of the most dramatic matches in the history of the game. Limerick outplayed Offaly throughout the match and with just minutes remaining had an apparently unassailable five-point lead. Limerick floundered, and Offaly triumphed. A new joke was born. Why are Limerick magic? Because they can disappear for five minutes.

Kirby had won a National League medal in 1992, when Limerick made a dramatic comeback against Tipperary to snatch a one-point victory in injury time. What was it like to be on the opposite end of the experience?

'It's a feeling I wouldn't wish on anyone. With seven minutes to go, I felt I would be going up to be presented with the Liam McCarthy Cup. Then, all of a sudden, it was gone. Something happened in the last five minutes. You can't analyse it. It was a huge disappointment.'

Two years later, Limerick again won the Munster final after snatching victory from All-Ireland champions Clare in the final minutes of the semi-final. Limerick went all the way to the All-Ireland final again that year, but it was to be Liam Griffin's Wexford that claimed the title.

The match itself was a personal disappointment for Kirby. 'I got a broken finger in the first five minutes,' he recalls with a shudder. 'I remember going over towards the Cusack Stand to take a free from near midfield. I was trying to stop the bleeding before I took it, but as I took the free I felt a searing pain go up my hand.'

For Kirby, 2007 was an unforgettable year. He was on the Limerick backroom team that reached the All-Ireland final against Kilkenny. 'I remember just before we took the pitch our manager Richie Bennis came into the dressing room and he said Kilkenny were just after running out to a silent Croke

Park and that we'd run out to a massive roar. "Prepare for it, lads," he said, but you couldn't be prepared for that. I couldn't believe the roar. Brian Cody and his players were very clever. They don't have so many All-Ireland medals in their pockets for nothing. Every one of them was flying and buzzing the same day. There was no space at all. All their hits were hard. Our lads could hardly catch their breath there sometimes.'

His experiences in management have made Kirby more philosophical about his own playing disappointments. 'Missing out on the All-Ireland hurling finals in 1994 and '96 were probably the low points. Yet at the same time I did not allow myself to get shattered by the whole thing. I had to go on with my life. Looking back they were great years for hurling. Although we lost the Munster final to Clare in 1995, it was obvious that it meant so much to Clare people. Those years brought new life to hurling and really brought a whole new popularity to the game and won a new audience for hurling.'

Selecting his dream team was difficult and he would have loved the space to include players like Brian Whelahan, Brian Corcoran and Leonard Enright.

1. Tommy Quaid
(*Limerick*)

2. Sylvie Linnane **3. Brian Lohan** **4. Martin Hanamy**
(*Galway*) (*Clare*) (*Offaly*)

5. Pete Finnerty **6. Ger Henderson** **7. Tom Cashman**
(*Galway*) (*Kilkenny*) (*Cork*)

8. Frank Cummins **9. John Fenton**
(*Kilkenny*) (*Cork*)

---

10. D. J. Carey   11. Joe Cooney   12. Nicky English
      (*Kilkenny*)   (*Galway*)   (*Tipperary*)

13. J. Barry-Murphy   14. Ray Cummins   15. Eamonn Cregan
       (*Cork*)   (*Cork*)   (*Limerick*)

62

FROM A JACK TO A RING

Jack Lynch: 1936–1950

After his great success in sport the late Jack Lynch went on to achieve even greater success in politics; he used his celebrity as a sportsman to great effect in that role. Celebrity and politics do not always make for happy bedfellows. When the acclaimed film director Ken Loach, who is also known for his left-wing political views, came over to Ireland for a premier of one of his movies and he heard that the then Taoiseach Bertie Ahern would be attending, he said: 'Make sure no one takes a photo of me with that b****x.'

Jack Lynch has a unique distinction of winning All-Ireland senior medals in six consecutive years, from 1941 to 1946, five in hurling and one in football in 1945. A personal highlight came when he captained the hurlers to All-Ireland glory in 1942. He also won three National League medals and ten county championships with the famed Glen Rovers. His status within the game of hurling was reflected in his selection at midfield on both the Team of the Century and the Team of the Millennium.

When I asked him about the highlight of his career, he came up with an unexpected answer. 'It may be paradoxical, but the games of which I have the most vivid memories are the ones we lost,' he told me. 'Of these I remember best the first All-Ireland hurling final in which I played. It was Cork v. Kilkenny on 3 September 1939. I was captain of the team and hopeful of leading Cork out of a comparatively long barren spell. Cork had not won a final since 1931, when they beat Kilkenny in the second replay of the final.

'The match I refer to has since been known as the "Thunder and Lightning" final. We had all kinds of weather, including sunshine and hailstones. It was played on the day that the Second World War commenced. I missed at least two scorable chances – of a goal and a point. I was marking one of the greatest half-backs of all time, Paddy Phelan, and we were beaten by a point scored literally with the last puck of the game. I can remember more facets of that game than almost any other in which I played.

'Although I was lucky enough to play in many All-Ireland finals, all the Munster finals were special. It was always about more than sport. It was a social ocassion where men drank in manly moderation but probably more than any other moment in the calendar it defined our identity. Looking back there was a lot of hardhips in those days, with rationing and so on. To take one example, both Tipperary and Kilkenny were excluded from the 1941 hurling championship because of an outbreak of foot and mouth disease. Yet no matter how bad things were, like Christmas the Munster final was always guaranteed to put a smile on people's faces.

'I specially remember the finals during the Emergency years, when petrol was rationed. People thumbed lifts on lorries bringing turf to the city; others walked and set out days beforehand, and some would cycle through the night to get there.'

When asked of his opinion of himself as a hurler, Jack Lynch was understandably reticent. 'I would prefer to leave this assessment to people I played with or against or who saw me play.'

It was with the greatest reluctance that Jack Lynch picked what he termed his 'hypothetical dream team' for me.

1. Tony Reddan
(*Tipperary*)

2. Bobby Rackard   **3. Nick O'Donnell**   **4. John Doyle**
(*Wexford*)   (*Wexford*)   (*Tipperary*)

5. Jimmy Finn   **6. John Keane**   **7. Iggy Clarke**
(*Tipperary*)   (*Waterford*)   (*Galway*)

8. Frank Cummins   **9. Joe Salmon**
(*Kilkenny*)   (*Galway*)

10. Christy Ring   **11. Jimmy Langton**   **12. Jimmy Doyle**
(*Cork*)   (*Kilkenny*)   (*Tipperary*)

13. J. Barry-Murphy   **14. Nicky Rackard**   **15. Eddie Keher**
(*Cork*)   (*Wexford*)   (*Kilkenny*)

63

THE LAUGHING CAVALIER

Mick Mackey: 1928–1951

Mick Mackey won three All-Ireland Senior titles in 1934, '36 and '40, five National League titles and 8 Railway Cups. Long before Ger Loughnane pulled the same stunt in the 1995 Munster final with Seánie McMahon, Mackey showed himself to be an exponent of lateral thinking in the 1936 Munster final. Earlier that year Mackey had visited the United States and sustained a bad knee injury. Suspecting that the injury might attract some 'attention' in the Munster final, Mackey wore a heavy bandage on the healthy knee. His tactic worked and he went on to score no less than five goals and three points in the match as Limerick won by 8–5 to 4–6.

Nicknames are not part of the culture of the GAA, unlike rugby. There is no question that this is a good thing. There have been a few exceptions, like former Antrim manager Liam Bradley who is known as 'Baker' because back in the 1970s he always wore a white sports jacket. One current inter-county hurler was nicknamed 'Butter' – on the basis that butter is found in bread – and that his father married his first cousin. What makes Mick Mackey unique amongst the giants of Gaelic games is that he had three nicknames. He was often described as 'the Laughing Cavalier', occasionally as 'the King of the Solo Run', but most often as 'the Playboy of the Southern World'. He always seemed to have a smile on his face – both on and off the field. He was one of those exceptional talents who made the crowd come alive because of his swashbuckling style; the higher the stakes, the better he performed, which is a sure sign of greatness.

One of Mackey's finest hours came in the 1944 Munster final, which has gone down in history as the 'bicycle final' because it occurred during the Emergency when private cars were off the road because of rationing during the war effort led by Seán Lemass. People arrived in Thurles in their droves on their bicycles. The fact that it was against old rivals Cork added to the lustre of the occasion. One of Mackey's most valuable contributions was to temporarily challenge the traditional established order in Munster between Cork and Tipperary, and the 'big three' on a national scale with Kilkenny added to the mix.

When he died in 1982, such was his reputation that the funeral cortege was three miles long. Mackey's name lives on in the Mackey Stand in the Gaelic Grounds in Limerick. He won the Hall of Fame award in 1962 and a Bank of Ireland Special All-Star award in 1980. His place in folkore is assured by the many incidents that set him apart on the pitch. A case in point was when Limerick played Kilkenny in the 1940 All-Ireland final. Mackey fired in his first shot, and it was saved by Jimmy O'Connell, but Mick kept running in and as he turned at the edge of the square, he shouted, 'You're in good form, but you won't smell the next one.'

Mackey could also be a great diplomat and when necessary could switch on the charm to his own advantage. In a Limerick county final after a schemozzle, the referee was about to send Mackey off with his brother, John, and their immediate opponents. Before the deed could be completed, Mick interjected: 'Why would you do that? What will the crowd think? They came to see a county final and this a county final, you know, and not a lawn tennis tournament.' As a result of his comments no one was sent off.

64

THE VIKING

Cormac Bonnar: 1983-1992

His is not your typical GAA story. He did not play his first full senior inter-county game until he was thirty, but Tipperary forward Cormac Bonnar still managed to rack up the honours. In four years the full-forward won three Munster championships, two All-Irelands and two All-Stars. Although Bonnar had a brief stint on the Tipperary seniors in 1982–83, injury prevented him from making his mark. Then, in 1988, after impressing for his club, the selectors called him back onto the panel for the Munster final against Cork. He came on as a sub and scored the winning goal.

He was also very distinctive looking because there have been few more fearsome sights in hurling history than the spectacle of him going goalbound with his protective helmet and missing teeth. Hence his nickname 'the Viking'. He finds it difficult to say whether the 1989 or '91 All-Ireland victories meant more to him.

'One All-Ireland meant as much to me as the other. I know people felt we hadn't really won an All-Ireland when we beat Antrim in '89. People spoke of the Woolworth's final because we had only beaten a Cinderella county. That was a bit of an insult to us but it was a much bigger insult to Antrim who had got there on merit. Antrim never got the recognition they deserve for what was, for them, a marvellous achievement. They were a bit unlucky insofar as they came up against Nicky English on one of his best games for Tipp apart from the '87 Munster final.

'For a lot of our supporters the big win that year was really over Galway in the semi-final. All that talk about it being a dirty match was overplayed though there were a few nasty incidents in it. There was a great standard of play in that match and Galway really put it up to us'

He believes Babs Keating was important to the revival of Tipperary's fortunes.

'After losing to Clare in '86 Tipp was in the doldrums. I would have my differences with Babs down through the years but the one thing he did though was to change the attitude to players from those at the top. He got a supporters' club going. Players were treated with dignity and respect. He recognised that if you were to get the best out of players they had to be treated with respect. Players respond to this treatment and it does a lot for morale in the camp and in turn confidence. Having said that I was on the Tipperary panel in 1982 and the difference in the attitude of the players to working hard in training was non-existent.'

Why did Tipp 'blow it' in 1990?

'The League campaign went badly for us. We only stayed in Division One by a whisker and a bizarre combination of results on the final day. Because there had been such a gap between our All-Irelands there was a lot of pressure on players to attend functions and so it was difficult for them to

---

stay in shape. Our attitude was not perhaps exactly what it should have been.

'We were really disappointed to lose to Cork in 1990. You have to win two All-Irelands back-to-back before you are considered a great side and it would have set us up well if we won the Munster final. I think we should have gone all the way that year if we had beaten Cork but it wasn't to be. Things just didn't go right for us on the day. In hindsight I think the fact that Pat Fox was taken off was the deciding factor. It was Mark Foley's final. The finger was pointed at John Kennedy in particular for leaving him too much room. That was most unfair. Four players marked Foley that day and he scored off each of them. The tragedy from our point of view is that we won't go down as a great team, even though we were a very talented side who accomplished a lot.'

1991 ended up as a great year but the omens in the spring were not favourable:

'We played Offaly in the League semi-final and were dismal. We only scored seven points. Things were falling asunder. We had a crisis meeting of the panel and that helped clear the air. After that in the summer things came right and we mushroomed.

'We got a great draw with Cork on their home patch and then we pulled them back in Thurles when they led by nine points midway in the second half to beat them by four points 4–19 to 4–15. It was a wonderful match – a real thriller. It was a real pressure match for us. If we had lost, it would have been the end of the line for the team because some of us were pushing on. That win set us up to beat Galway handy enough in the semi-final. It was a real thrill for me to beat Kilkenny in the final particularly as my brothers Colm and Conal were also on the Tipp team.'

_____

65

Teddy Boy

Teddy McCarthy: 1985–1996

In September 1990 Teddy McCarthy wrote himself into the annals of the GAA. He starred in Cork's historic double: defeating Galway in the All-Ireland hurling final and a few weeks later he would add the second leg to a remarkable double when he helped the Leesiders to beat old rivals Meath in the All-Ireland football final.

With the Keady affair if not exactly behind them, but at least in the background, Galway had a seven-point lead over Cork in the 1990 All-Ireland final and appeared to be cruising to another All-Ireland final, particularly as Joe Cooney was giving a torrid time to Jim Cashman and calling the shots. However, two goals from Cork's John 'Schillaci' Fitzgibbon turned the match decisively in Cork's favour and they ran out comfortable winners. While obviously winning such a unique double meant a lot to him, neither All-Irelands were necessarily his fondest memory of the year as McCarthy explained to me.

'Nobody outside the county expected us to beat Tipperary

in the Munster final in Thurles. They looked as if they were going to be winning All-Irelands back-to-back, particularly having got their Galway bogey out of the way. It was a sweet victory for us particularly in Thurles and bearing in mind that Tipp were going for their first four-in-a-row in Munster.'

He was glad to win the football final as much for Billy Morgan's sake as his own:

'Billy is really serious, I mean totally passionate, about football. Somebody said once that listening to his team talks was more like war than sport. If you watch him he gets red and then purple as he tries to psyche you up before a game. It says a lot about him that he kept going after the disappointments of '87 and '88 and brought us to the titles in '89 and '90.'

He chooses his words carefully when asked about the 1990 victory over Meath. Did it bring particular satisfaction to the Cork side to put one over on Meath after the allegations that there was a history of 'bad blood' between the sides following their ill-tempered clashes in the '80s?

'Winning an All-Ireland final at any time is great no matter who you beat. I'm not sure that there was as much bad blood, to use that term, as people thought. There were tensions certainly – much more so with some players in both camps than others. I would say though most of us had a lot of respect for the Meath guys ... having said all that it would be fair to say that we were glad that after 1990 we had put the Meath thing to rest.'

Like other players featured between the covers of this book Teddy's collection of football medals is much lower than it should be because his career coincided with the golden era of Kerry football. How difficult was it for him to keep going when Cork were losing the Munster final every year?

'God, there were times when it was hard. It did get demoralising. However, I would have to say that we never went into
any of those Munster finals not thinking we were going to
win. We never had an inferiority complex, even though they
beat us well a few times. We always enjoyed those matches.
Mick O'Dwyer always hyped us up by saying Cork was the
most difficult opposition he expected to meet all year. We
always got on well with the Kerry lads. I played with most
of them on the Munster team and I always felt they gave the
Cork lads plenty of respect.

'I suppose what kept us going was the enjoyment we got
from playing. We were all passionately in love with the
game. We had a lot of craic and fun. Although we had a lot
of disappointments in the Munster championship we at least
had the consolation of winning those All-Irelands.'

Jimmy Magee pays a nice tribute to McCarthy which sums
up his place in the pantheon of GAA greats.

'He will always be remembered for his high-fielding in
both codes. He is a man apart with an achievement apart in
the modern games.'

66

Peter the Great

Peter McGinnity 1972–1989

When the GAA opened its museum in Croke Park, Peter McGinnity was one of the main players profiled in the hidden heroes section. It reflected the fact that although he had never won a national honour, he was one of the giants, metaphorically and literally, of Gaelic football in the 1970s and 1980s. At the tender age of sixteen he played under-21 football for Fermanagh in 1970, playing in the All-Ireland final at that grade though they were to lose to Cork. The following year he would lose another under-21 All-Ireland final. In 1978 it was a case of so near yet so far when he played for Belfast team St John's but they lost the decider to a Thomond College, Limerick team dripping with inter-county stars. The closest he came to wining a senior medal with Fermanagh was when the county lost the Ulster final to Armagh in 1982.

In 1988 McGinnity played his last senior game for Fermanagh after a nineteen-year career with the county, which began when he was seventeen. He won four Railway Cup medals. In 1982 he became the first Fermanagh player to win an All-Star, being selected at right half-forward. He jokes: 'I'm not a great man for individual awards, but I dare anybody to try and take it from me!'

After his retirement from the playing fields, McGinnity ventured into management. 'When my playing days with Fermanagh were coming to an end, I became player-manager,' he says with a tone of some regret. 'It was a stop-gap measure. I had been captaining the team and I thought it would be a natural progression for me to become a player-manager – but I was very wrong. I don't think the player-manager system can work. I was too close to the players and I wasn't prepared for the politics that goes on behind the scenes, in terms of clubs wanting their players on the team. I was glad to be finished with it and I made it clear then that I didn't want to go through the experience again.'

So why, then, was he persuaded to take the Leitrim job?

'Persuaded is the key word,' he answers vigorously. 'The Leitrim county secretary, Tommy Moran, had been very helpful to me down through the years, helping me to organise pitches and so on. He more or less made it clear to me that he was going to keep hounding me until I accepted the job.

'It was a real learning experience from the point of view of observing the changes that have taken place in the game, even in the ten years since I started playing. It's become a lot more scientific now and much more time-consuming for both the players and the manager. I also learned that you need great man-management skills to have a successful team. I was always told that if you had organisation and money you were on the road to success, but I was to learn that you need the players as well.'

His reasons for stepping down were complex. 'In the early

months of 1999, I was having serious health problems. I was coaching a ground of young fellas one day and a ball struck me on the side of my head. It left me with a detached retina, which required major surgery. It got detached again in July 1999. So the fact that my general health was not good was one of a combination of factors.'

Who was his most difficult opponent? 'I would have to say that the player I found toughest of all was in club football – Paddy Reilly from Teemore Shamrocks. One of the funniest incidents in my career happened when I was marking Paddy. Paddy's brother, Barney, and I played for Fermanagh under-21s together. We came up the ranks together and I always had great time for him. In one club match the ball went up between Peter and myself and a kind of ruck developed. I snatched the ball as Barney came charging in to give Peter some "assistance". Happily for me, but not for Peter, in the melee and confusion Barney struck his own brother instead of me. It still sticks in my memory, as I was heading up the field with the ball before Barney started chasing me. He said, "Sorry, Peter," as his brother lay stretched out on the ground!'

McGinnity prefaces his dream team selection by referring to the problem of picking players from different eras. He has decided to include one player he never saw playing, but whom he has met and has heard much about his exploits as a player – Seán Purcell.

'One other player in this category who very nearly made my team was Derry's Jim McKeever. When I went to college, he was my coach, but my earliest football memory is listening to commentaries of big games on the radio back in 1958. It always seemed to be that Jim McKeever was on the ball. So when I started playing imaginary games as a very young

boy, I was always "Jim McKeever on the ball".'
McGinnity's dream team is as follows.

1. Brian McAlinden
(*Armagh*)

2. Robbie O'Malley   **3. John O'Keeffe**   **4. Páidí Ó Sé**
(*Meath*)   (*Kerry*)   (*Kerry*)

5. Paddy Moriarty   **6. Kevin Moran**   **7. Henry Downey**
(*Armagh*)   (*Dublin*)   (*Derry*)

8. Jack O'Shea   **9. Brian Mullins**
(*Kerry*)   (*Dublin*)

10. Seán O'Neill   **11. Seán Purcell**   **12. Matt Connor**
(*Down*)   (*Galway*)   (*Offaly*)

13. J. Barry-Murphy   **14. Eoin Liston**   **15. Nudie Hughes**
(*Cork*)   (*Kerry*)   (*Monaghan*)

67

Tyrone's Towering Talent

Frank McGuigan: 1972–1984

Frank McGuigan is celebrated as one of the most skilful players of all time, even though injury and a spell living in the United States curbed his career. Without these disruptions it is almost inevitable that he would have added to the All-Star award he won in 1984. One of the proudest moments in Frank McGuigan's eventful life came in 1972.

'It was a great honour for me to be captain of the Tyrone minor team and to lead my county out in Croke Park, where we narrowly lost to Cork in the All-Ireland final,' he says. They were powered by the great Jimmy Barry-Murphy.

'I believe that sportsmanship is very important. At the end of a match the winners should always console the losers. Cork were very gracious that day. Our full-forward was Mickey Harte. Thankfully for the sake of the county and my own sons, he has had happier experiences in Croke Park on All-Ireland final day since.'

In 1972, shortly after collecting the Ulster minor trophy, McGuigan played for the senior team in the Ulster final, only to lose to Donegal. Frank McGuigan was only the second player in history to play inter-county football at minor, under-21, junior and senior levels in the one year. The first was Roscommon's Dermot Earley.

The following year McGuigan would captain the senior team to their first Ulster title in sixteen years. Assuming the captaincy at such a tender age did not create the fuss that might have been expected. 'Earlier that year our manager, Jody O'Neill, announced out of the blue: "By the way, Frank McGuigan is captain this year." It happened as simple as that.'

In 1977 McGuigan's status in the game was reflected when he went to New York with the All-Stars. As he recalled to me it was a tour that brought some shocking news. 'At the time, instead of us staying in hotels, we often stayed with host families. On one of those trips Tom Prendergast from Laois went to stay in an apartment owned by a Laois man. There was a foreign man staying there and Tom decided to stay with some friends. The next day when we went to play our match there were police everywhere. The guy staying in Tom's apartment had been shot dead there the night before and Tom was a suspect. We often wondered what would have happened if Tom had stayed there that night.

'We were managed by Seán Purcell. Seán called out the team before the first game and announced that he was playing centre half-forward. That got a great laugh, but Seán turned on us and said in all earnestness: "What's so funny, lads?" Because it was Seán Purcell, everybody wanted to play their best.'

So enjoyable did McGuigan find the experience that he stayed on in the States for the next six years. On his return home, the Ulster final in centenary year would see him write his name on the pages of football immortality when he scored a stunning eleven points from play against Armagh. His preparation for the game was less than ideal: 'I did not have any breakfast that morning. All I had was an egg and onion sandwich in a hotel in Clones during the pre-match talk.'

Later that year tragedy would intervene. 'I played a club match for Ardboe and afterwards had a few drinks and on the way home my van went out of control and hit a wall. My leg felt the full force of the impact and was broken, at both knee and hip. I waited a long time before help arrived and when I finally arrived in Altnagelvin Hospital in Derry I was told I would never play football again, but it was the fear in the eyes of my wife and children that bothered me the most. I spent no less than twenty weeks in bed. A year later I was out walking again, but with a limp that would endure. I have no memory of what happened on that night because I think that I had a bit too much whiskey on me! I have learned since that my life is better without drink.'

The only bit of good news that emerged during those dark times was that he had won an All-Star on the back of his stunning performances earlier that year. Though he never won the All-Ireland medal, his rich talents deserved he at least had the pleasure of seeing his sons, Tommy and Brian, win All-Irelands with Tyrone.

Colm O'Rourke sums up his career perfectly: 'He will rank as one of the best two-footed players in history, and his performance in an Ulster final when he scored what seemed like twenty points from play will rank as one of the great all-time displays.'

68

Touched by Greatness

Jim McKeever: 1948–1962

In 1958 the GAA world witnessed a shock of seismic proportions when Derry beat Kerry by 2–6 to 2–5 in the All-Ireland semi-final. The Foylesiders were led to the promised land by a prince of midfielders, Jim McKeever. His ability to jump and catch the ball was the hallmark of his play. He could jump so tidily that he would be almost like a gymnast in the air, toes extended and fingers outstretched as he grabbed the ball, way above the heads of anybody else, then he would hit the ground, turn and play. McKeever's mastery of his position was recognised in 1984 when he was chosen at centre-field on the centenary team of greatest players never to have won an All-Ireland, partnering the legendary Tommy 'the Boy Wonder' Murphy of Laois.

Born in Ballymaguigan in 1930, his love of football was nurtured as a boy when his father brought him to games on the bar of his bike. The bonus of talking to him is the quiet, self-effacing warmth with which McKeever talks matter-of-factly about a glittering career. At the age of seventeen, McKeever made his senior debut for Derry.

'I remember listening to the famous All-Ireland final in the Polo Grounds in 1947. I didn't think then that a year later I'd be playing in a challenge game for the county against Antrim. It wasn't until the following year, though, that I made my championship debut. When I was in my teens, Derry used to play in the junior championship. We didn't have a senior team then. At that stage there was a tremendous gap between Cavan and Antrim and the other seven counties in Ulster. We played in the Lagan Cup at the time, which featured the eight counties in Ulster apart from Cavan.'

The high point of McKeever's career came against Kerry in 1958. 'I have no recollection of great excitement when we won the Ulster final,' he told me. 'However, when we beat Kerry in the All-Ireland semi-final the response was sensational. I remember the great John Joe Sheehy saying to me, "That's a rattling good team you have there."'

Dublin beat Derry by 2–12 to 1–9 in the All-Ireland final, despite an imperious display from McKeever in midfield. 'I have no recollection of great disappointment when we lost the final to Dublin. We were happy just to be there. If someone'd told us a few years before that we would play in an All-Ireland final, we would have been absolutely delighted.'

McKeever was chosen as Footballer of the Year in 1958 much to the chagrin of some Dublin supporters who felt that the honour should have gone to one of their stars, like Kevin Heffernan.

In the following years McKeever led Derry to National League finals, which they lost to Kerry, in 1959 and 1961, before his retirement in 1963.

It is fascinating listening to a player of his stature and hear that it is not his own achievements that really ignite the passion in his voice but his vivid description of the juvenile club match in Derry he watched the evening before that really enthuses him. Derry's first All-Ireland win in 1993 was a source of great pride to McKeever.

'It was very emotional when the full-time whistle went. The fact that all the years of disappointment had been wiped out with the 1993 side gave me a certain amount of pleasure. It was a unique occasion. The first time that something great happens is special because there can never be another first time.'

Who was the greatest player of them all? 'It's so difficult to judge. The greatest fielder and the most stylish footballer was definitely Mick O'Connell.'

Who was his most difficult opponent? 'One of the toughest guys to play against was Galway's Frank Eivers,' he explains. 'He was just massive. You couldn't get near the ball with him standing there beside you.'

After his playing days were over McKeever went on to become a trainer and a manager with both St Joseph's College and Derry. 'I didn't enjoy it near as much as playing. Most times it's two nights training, but you've got to be thinking about games and planning ahead for them. Of course it's a great buzz when you win, but it can be very, very demoralising when you lose and you know your team has passed its peak. I know there are a lot of people interested in administration, but it was never for me. I don't think people appreciate how much stress is on the manager, especially trying to do the job in bits of free time. Anybody who says it's easy is not talking about the job I recognise.'

McKeever has noted some major changes in the game

since his own playing days. 'I think the players of today are better than the players of my time in terms of fitness, but not in terms of the skills. It takes a team five years to develop. Nowadays a bit of a 'win at all costs' mentality has crept in to the game and only experienced players can handle that.'

Many of his happiest memories are of the club scene. 'Ballymaguigan were playing Coleraine in a club game in Coleraine. The pitch wasn't very well marked. The crossbar was only a rope and there weren't any nets. The ball was bobbing around and somebody pulled on it. One umpire gave it a goal, the other a point. Our umpire gave the decision against his own team. Likewise with the other. The referee split the difference and awarded two points. The really comic part of the story was that one of our best players, the late Michael Young, did not want to play as he had hay ready for baling and the weather forecast was not good. However, he was persuaded. When the controversy emerged, Young went up to the referee and told him that he should hurry up and make a decision as he had to go home to bale the hay!'

69

THE DOOLINI FACTOR

Joe Dooley: 1982–2000

Clareen's Joe Dooley played his first senior All-Ireland final for Offaly in 1984 when they lost to Cork. However, a year later Joe won his first All-Ireland medal as a nippy, intelligent left corner-forward on a team which beat Galway. In the 1994 final Joe scored 1–2 as Offaly beat Limerick. In 1998 Offaly became the first team in history to win the All-Ireland hurling title having lost a provincial final. Joe gave a sensational performance against Clare in the third of their epic All-Ireland semi-final clashes, which was instrumental in him winning an All-Star later that year.

The 1994 All-Ireland hurling final was one of the most dramatic matches in the history of the game. One of the many noteworthy aspects of the game was that three Dooley brothers played in the Offaly forward line, with Billy and Johnny joining Joe in the attack. Joe believes though that the most important match in the championship was not the All-Ireland final but the victory over Kilkenny. 'It was all or nothing in that match. They had defeated us in the previous two years. Another defeat would have led to the break-up of that team. It's very hard, especially for older players, to keep going when you are on a losing streak. The win generated huge expectations in the county which accelerated as we got to the final and this was reflected in a big attendance at training sessions.

'After Offaly won that historic Leinster title in 1980 there was a big increase in interest in hurling in the county. Most of the lads on the '94 team would have been in national school at the time and were bitten by the bug.'

It could have been very different for Joe Dooley in 1994.

'We went into the final as a form side though we had lapses in all of our games. Limerick too were a form side. On the day we didn't perform the way we expected. I suppose we had a lot of young, inexperienced players who were a bit intimidated by the occasion. While many of them had played in minor or under-21 finals, it's a big step up to play in a senior final. We kept in touch for most of the match but I have to say I thought it was gone from us before Johnny's free. Hence the reference to the Doolini final because his goal was the start of our Houdini act.

'I expected him to go for a point because we would still have time to get back a four-point lead but he stuck it in the net. Within a minute Pat O'Connor had a second goal. Then Limerick seemed to go into a shellshock whereas we all had a new pep in our step and it seemed that we could score points at will.'

How important was Éamonn Cregan to Offaly's success?

'He played a key role in our triumph. When he came he brought a very different method to training which created a very disciplined structure. He had a very simple approach and believed in fitness, skills and teamwork. He was not into a lot of the psychology business that other managers are.

'It was a very awkward position for him – having hurled for so long with Limerick himself and because he lived down there but it didn't affect his preparations for Offaly. He didn't use his in-depth knowledge of the Limerick players unless we asked him about them.

'I can't remember anything he said to us before the final. But I recall very vividly his team talk at half-time. I can assure you it was unprintable! He was very worked up. None of us dared to speak – except briefly among ourselves.'

Dooley assumes the mantle of a diplomat when queried about Cregan's dramatic walkout from a training session in the run-up to the 1995 championship. Each word is carefully chosen: 'A few players hadn't turned up for training that night. He decided to make a stand and left for home. It had the desired effect. From then on it was business as usual.'

70

STAR QUALITY

Lory Meagher: 1924–1937

A regular feature of Kilkenny's matches throughout the 1920s and '30s was Lory Meagher wearing a bloodstained jersey or head bandage, making scything tackles, immune to the threat to his own safety. As his only protective gear was a peak cap, he collected many stitches, mostly facial, in his inter-county career and lost enough blood to keep Dracula going for months. The message to his opponents was loud and clear: 'The black and amber will not be beaten.'

Kilkenny's Lorenzo Ignatius Meagher was perhaps the first true star of hurling. Meagher could not have chosen a better or more nurturing environment to begin his career. Over the next decade he would both feed off and fuel the fires of passion in one of hurling's greatest shrines. The obsession created in Kilkenny is the envy of nearly every hurling side in the country and Lory was always quick to acknowledge the debt of gratitude owed to the most benevolent of patrons. He was to hurling aficionados in the county what Nureyev was to the ballet enthusiast.

He won three All-Irelands in the 1930s and entered the club of GAA immortals on foot of his towering performance in dreadful weather in midfield when Kilkenny beat the hot favourites and reigning champions Limerick in the 1935 All-Ireland, having previously won All-Irelands in 1932 and '33.

Croke Park on a September afternoon separates the strong, the enduring and above all the brave from the rest. It is a licence to thrill and be thrilled. In full flight in countless training sessions, Meagher was something to behold and those recorded demonstrations of his talents implanted the thought that on a Sunday in September Kilkenny would be just about unbeatable. On that wet September day in 1935 Meagher answered all the questions with an outstanding exhibition from midfield. Nine years earlier he had lost an All-Ireland final to Cork when his brothers Willie and Henry were also playing for Kilkenny.

In his later years Meagher would delight in recalling an amusing postscript from the 1935 final: 'A few days later a stranger approached me and said: "Well, Lory boy, you did all right on Sunday."'

Lory was brought up in a very nationalistic family. As a boy he was inculcated into the beliefs of Michael Davitt, the driving force behind the Land League in the later part of the nineteenth century. One of Meagher's favourite passages was Davitt's comment that 'old men have forgotten the miseries of the Famine and had their youth renewed by the sights and sounds that were invoked by the thrilling music of the camán'. Meagher did make magnificent music with the camán whenever he lined out in the black and amber.

Lory was a great reader of the game and one of the few hurlers of his time who could actually sidestep, whereas many of his peers seemed content when they got the ball just to drive into their opponent.

In Ireland we don't like players or personalities to get too big for the boots. This was best illustrated in the 1970s, when someone said to Gay Byrne, 'There are no real stars in Ireland. You are the nearest thing we have to it, but you are not there yet.' Lory experienced this unique Irish trait when a fan approached him and said, 'You are a great forward. You always get great scores, but you shoot the wides as well.'

He had a funeral fit for a prince when he died in 1973, such was his status within the game. For years, young Kilkenny hurlers chanted 'Over the bar said Lory Meagher' when they scored in training sessions. His legacy is commemorated in the Lory Meagher Heritage Centre, which was opened by former president Mary Robinson in 1994. Apart from his genius on the field, Meagher is renowned for his modesty off it. This character trait was most vividly illustrated when a journalist met him on the roadside one day and asked where he might track down Lory Meagher. The Kilkenny ace's reply was, 'You've just missed him. He passed up this way a few minutes ago. If you hurry, you've a good chance of catching him.'

71

MISSING IN ACTION

Jimmy Deenihan: 1973–83

Jimmy Deenihan was a success on both the football field and the political arena, serving as a Junior Government Minister after a trophy-laden career with Kerry. His importance to Kerry was most starkly emphasised when he was injured for the All-Ireland final in 1982. The consensus is that Dennihan would never have allowed Séamus Darby to score that famous winning goal.

According to Deenihan Kerry's 1978 All-Ireland final victory was inspired by their defeat the previous year.

'Losing the '77 semi-final to Dublin was a terrible blow for us, worse almost than losing the five-in-a-row in '82. We got a worse reception than we got in '82 when we came home. There was sympathy for us that year but there was none in '77. For the League campaign I was rested as well as Pat Spillane, Ger Power and Paud O'Mahony. I had gone through a run of injuries and I think that they may have felt Spillane was too individualistic and not enough of a team player at the time, Ger had not been playing well for a while and I think the selectors blamed Paud for Dublin's first goal. Kerry had a very poor League campaign and only the width of the post prevented them from being relegated in their final match.

'There had been a lot of criticism of management. A challenge had been made openly on Ger MacKenna's position as county chairman. Some of the selectors were replaced. Mick O'Dwyer was booed at a league match in Killarney, I think it was against Galway. That hurt him a lot. We were all irked at the media adulation of the Dubs and the way Kerry were presented as not being in the same league.'

Deenihan believes that there was a definite turning point in the county's fortunes in 1978.

'A big plus for Kerry came in May of that year when we beat Dublin in a game at Gaelic Park, New York. It was a very red-blooded match in every sense! I got my nose broken. Tommy Doyle, Eoin Liston and Pat O'Neill were sent off. We took it very seriously but they took it less so. It was a milestone for us – psychologically we proved to ourselves that we could beat them.

'There was a lot of pressure on us to beat Cork in the Munster final particularly as Cork had a strong side at the time but we did and cruised past Roscommon in the semi-final. The final was a big confrontation for us. We were superbly fit for the game. Most of us lived like hermits. None of the lads went near Tralee races nor to the craic in Ballybunion, and there were no late nights nor alcohol. People who later became heavy drinkers were not drinking at that stage.'

The press were singled out for special treatment.

'We were very careful with the media that year. O'Dwyer pleaded with us to be very cagey with journalists. We had a press night when all the journalists came down but O'Dwyer changed the training routine just for that night! In both '76 and '77 Kerry were affected by the media. There was a lot of hype and we believed it. We were a mature outfit for victory in '78. There were a lot of damaged egos in the side, among both the players and the management. O'Dwyer acknowledged that he had been badly hurt by the booing in Killarney.

'We went into the final with a very changed-about team from the previous year with a lot of positional switches and a much better balance. We were really just hanging on in the first fifteen minutes. I thought it was going to be an avalanche. I remember Robbie Kelleher, their corner-back, had a shot for a point at one stage which summed up how bad things were for us. I think that was Dublin's downfall. Their defence all felt they should be in attack. I think they were deluded by the media attention and all the adulation so much so that they left John Egan unmarked. He stayed in his position and his goal turned the tide. Then came Mike Sheehy's goal, which only he could have scored, and we had the impetus and in the second half we destroyed them. I knew then we would win more All-Irelands and we won the next three. When we went back home to Killarney in '78 we got a tumultuous reception having defeated the unbeatable Heffo machine.'

72

Keeper of the Flame

Billy Morgan: 1966–1981

The high point of Billy Morgan's illustrious playing career came when he captained Cork to an All-Ireland in 1973.

'It was hugely important for Cork to win that year. It had been twenty-eight years since we had last won a senior football All-Ireland and the longer it was going on, the harder it was becoming. We beat Galway easy enough in the end, but what I most recall was the homecoming. When we got into Cork there were crowds in the station and all the way up MacCurtain Street. The biggest thing is when we turned Barry's corner; looking down on Patrick Street it was just a sea of people. I never saw anything like it before. You couldn't see the streets; it was just people all the way down to the Savoy.'

The emergence of the greatest team of all time in Kerry deprived Morgan and Cork of many opportunities for further glory. After their eighth All-Ireland in twelve years in 1986 the great Kerry team went into decline. That same year Billy Morgan was appointed as Cork manager. Kerry's difficulty would be Cork's opportunity and Morgan led the county to four consecutive All-Ireland finals – initially losing to Meath in '87 and '88 before beating Mayo in '89 and old rivals Meath in 1990.

'In 1988 I had thought we might be getting such a home-coming when we played Meath. They had deseveredly beaten us the year before but we had a year's experience behind us in '88. We drew the game, even though we should have won it. In the drawn game Dinny Allen caught Mick Lyons with his elbow and Barry Coffey tackled Colm O'Rourke and caught him with his shoulder behind the ear. People said Niall Cahalane had "caught" Brian Stafford. All the talk between the drawn game and the replay was that Meath were going to sort us out. My own instructions were that if that was the case, if there was any trouble, stand together and be united.

'It didn't come as a huge surprise when Gerry McEntee hit Niall Cahalane,' he says. 'All our lads got involved in the flare-up. When it was over and McEntee was sent off, I said to our fellas: "OK now, that's it, we'll play football from here on in, no retaliation." I repeated the same message at half-time. It was the biggest mistake I ever made as a manager. What I should have said was: "Meet fire with fire, and if necessary we'll finish this game ten-a-side." Fair play to Meath – they beat us with fourteen men.

'I suppose it was sweet then to beat them in the final in 1990. It was a great feeling to manage my county to an All-Ireland in 1989. It was one of the more open All-Irelands. When Mayo took the lead in the second half they looked as if they were in the driving seat but we got the extra couple of points up to have the cushion there at the end of the game. When Mayo put the gun to our head, we rallied and pipped them in the end. It was a very sweet moment, especially after the disappointment of losing the two previous years to

274

Meath. As the '88 final and the replay were such tough and dour games, it was nice that both teams played such pure and positive football. Mind you, of course, I have heard it said that Mayo were "too nice" in that game.'

The late Dermot Earley got to know Morgan when they studied physical education together in Stawberry Hill College in London, winning the first All-Ireland 7s together. 'Billy was as good a goalkeeper as we've ever seen,' he claimed. 'Actually, he is the best I have ever seen. He had this mighty leap off the ground and was the archetypal safe pair of hands. In those days you'd forwards and backs all coming in on top of him and Billy would come out on top of everything and soar through the air, through the melee, and grab the ball or at least punch it to safety. He had great guts. He was scared of nothing and would go in where no sane person would to protect the goal. The best thing, though, was that he had the sharpest eye I've ever seen, which left him with such great anticipation that he could make a really difficult save look very easy.'

Pat Spillane came up against Billy Morgan as a player and as a manager. 'Any time I have ever been asked to choose my greatest Gaelic football team of all time, Billy Morgan has always been my automatic choice for goalkeeper,' he explained to me. 'He was a great reader of the game, superb organiser of defenders, inspirational leader and had excellent reflexes, and he brought all of these qualities to the manager's job. I attribute much of Cork's success in the late 1980s and early 1990s to Billy Morgan. He brought in a very professional approach, which involved drawing on the expertise of other experts.

'After the disappointment of Larry Tompkins' management Billy Morgan's return was expected to be the second coming of the Messiah, but it did not work out that way. It is a great tribute to Billy that when Kerry played Cork in the Munster semi-final in 2004 Kerry fans were worried not because of any of the Cork players but because of the admiration they've had for Morgan's record against Kerry down the years. Their fears were totally unjustified as Cork had little to offer.

'I have heard it said that he would die for Nemo but would only get wounded for Cork. His leadership and motivation is second to none. He will probably rank as one of the greatest club managers of all time with Nemo Rangers.'

73

Brave Brian

Brian Mullins: 1974–1985

Brian Mullins was only nineteen years old when Kevin Heffernan dropped him literally at the centre of his plan to bring back the glory days to Dublin in 1974. The towering, blonde-haired Mullins almost immediately became one of the best known players of his era and beyond. His talent lay in his twin abilities as a superb fielder and passer of the ball. He won four senior All-Ireland medals in 1974, '76, '77 and '78 and '83. The last one was particularly noteworthy because he did so after surviving a serious car accident. All-Star awards came his way in 1976 and '77. To add to his medal collection he also won an All-Ireland club championship with St Vincent's in 1976.

Pat Spillane was a big admirer of Mullins as a player. 'I believe the central components of success are commitment and belief, but they are no good in football if you can't kick a ball. Success as a player is due to a combination of factors: inner drive, belief, hard work and commitment. Brian Mullins made sacrifices, worked hard and was also focused and single-minded. You have to be to make it to the top. He was very keen to improve himself. We take for granted many skills we have without realising they can be developed further. Brian was motivated to become the best he could be. Of course he was only one of fifteen, but when it came to commitment and a willingness to die for the cause, nobody surpassed Brian Mullins.'

Mullins also had success as an inter-county manager, managing Derry to an Ulster championship in 1998. Joe Brolly was to discover that he came from the 'tough love' school of management.

'It became a thing that if I scored a goal in the Ulster championship it had a demoralizing effect on the opposition. I remember watching the TV one night when we had played a championship match against Monaghan. I got a goal after fifteen minutes and ran the length of the pitch blowing kisses and the cameras swept up along so I could see the whole Derry crowd laughing, so it was fun. I must say I enjoyed it but I wouldn't do it now.

'My flamboyant celebrations were not universally popular among opposing players though. I had my nose broken twice after scoring goals. The physical exchanges used to be a lot heavier then.

'I remember lobbying the Meath keeper in Celtic Park. He was a big, tall fella and I just popped it over his head. A Meath player came charging over to me as I began my celebrations and drove his boot into me. I needed about thirteen stitches. Brian Mullins was managing us at the time and said: "You deserve that, you wee b****x!"'

74

CAPTAIN SENSIBLE

Jimmy Murray: 1936–1949

Kevin McStay describes the late Jimmy Murray as 'the father of Roscommon football'. Jimmy had the distinction of leading his team on five occasions on All-Ireland final day, twice in 1943, once in 1944 and twice in 1946. When he got his first football, though, the omens did not suggest that such a glittering career lay ahead of him.

'Santa brought it to me. I spent all of Christmas Day and St Stephen's Day kicking it with my neighbours. To preserve its grandeur I thought I should grease it with Neat's foot oil, which farmers used to soften leather boots. When I had it greased, I left it, in my innocence, in front of a big open fire to dry. After a few minutes there was a loud explosion and the ball was in bits. Happily Santa came back again two nights later with a new and better ball.'

Religion was invoked to help Roscommon win their first All-Ireland: 'Our county chairman, Dan O'Rourke, and our county secretary, John Joe Fahy, just as we were about to go to bed the night before the 1943 All-Ireland, led us in a recitation of the Rosary. I don't think that would happen now.'

For Jimmy Murray the experience was the culmination of a dream. 'I always looked at the newspapers on a Monday morning after a final and stared in wonder at the photograph of the teams marching behind the band,' he told me. 'Now here I was, not only in the parade but also as captain of my beloved Roscommon, about to lead it. In addition, my brother Phelim was in the parade, as he was a member of the team. When the actual parade began, I momentarily became very afraid and wished that I was away from the pitch and sitting up in the stands. I then looked up at Michael O'Hehir in the commentary box. I imagined he was probably saying: " …and here comes Roscommon, led by the fair-haired Jimmy Murray from Knockcroghery …" My spine started to tremble and I immediately thought of my home village and my mother saying the rosary for us, and my father and all our neighbours would be huddled together, listening intently to the radio.'

Although he tasted glory in 1943 and '44, it was a tale of disappointment in 1946. With just minutes to go, Roscommon were leading by six points but, with Murray forced to leave the pitch with a broken nose, Kerry forced a replay with two late goals. 'That was our greatest ever display as a team, yet I do not know how we managed to lose such a commanding lead.

'One of my most vivid memories of my playing career is my brother Phelim telling me that the prince of midfielders, Paddy Kennedy, came over to him in the 1946 All-Ireland final and said: "Phelim, I think it's your All-Ireland." Phelim replied: "You never know, anything can happen, there's still over five minutes to go." Phelim's words were prophetic because Kerry drew the game and they went on to win the replay. It will always rate that as my greatest regret.'

Murray's pub-cum-grocery in Knockcroghery, now run by Jimmy's son John, is arguably the spiritual home of Roscommon football, with all its memorabilia from the county's only All-Ireland successes in 1943 and 1944, including the football from the 1944 final. The football survived a close shave some years ago when Jimmy's premises were burned down – as he recalled to me with mixed feelings. 'The ball was hanging from the ceiling and of course the fire burned the strings and the ball fell down and rolled safely under the counter. The fire happened on a Saturday night and when the fire brigade came one of the firemen jumped off and asked me, "Is the ball safe?" As I was watching my business go up in smoke, the ball wasn't my main priority! But the fireman came out later with the ball intact. The next day I got calls from all over the country asking if the ball was safe. I was bit annoyed at the time that all people seemed to be concerned with was the safety of the ball and nobody seemed to be too bothered about what happened to the shop!'

Jimmy's son John describes his father as 'a GAA Catholic': 'He went to one Mass on a Sunday and two matches!'

Jimmy selected his dream team for me.

1. Danno O'Keeffe
(Kerry)

2. Enda Colleran   **3. Paddy Prendergast**   **4. Seán Flanagan**
(Galway)   *(Mayo)*   *(Mayo)*

5. Brendan Lynch   **6. Bill Carlos**   **7. John Joe O'Reilly**
(Roscommon)   *(Roscommon)*   *(Cavan)*

---

8. Mick O'Connell **9. Paddy Kennedy**
(*Kerry*) (*Kerry*)

10. Mick Higgins **11. Seán Purcell** **12. Pádraig Carney**
(*Cavan*) (*Galway*) (*Mayo*)

13. Seán O'Neill **14. Tom Langan** **15. Kevin Heffernan**
(*Down*) (*Mayo*) (*Dublin*)

75

WATERFORD'S WIZARD

Paul Flynn: 1993–2008

Waterford's ace forward and sharpshooter Paul Flynn is one of the greatest hurlers never to have won an All-Ireland medal. Flynn was one of the most prolific scorers in modern times.

Waterford almost made the breakthrough in 1998 under Gerald McCarthy. Even though Clare were leading all through the Munster final, Paul Flynn got a late goal and then he had a chance to win the game from a long way out, but he put the ball wide.

There's a story told about the two grasshoppers who came onto the field before the 1998 Munster final replay as the pulling and dragging started between the players on both teams. One said to the other, 'We're going to be killed here today. Do you feel the tension?'

The other replied, 'I do. Hop up here on the ball. It's the only place we'll be safe!'

In one of the most infamous games in living memory, where the intense aggression began even before the match started, Clare came out on top after an explosive start which saw a lot of 'incidents' on and off the ball. The match spawned the infamous 'Colin Lynch Affair', which saw the Clare midfielder suspended for three months; the Peter Pan of hurling Tony Browne would provide a crumb of comfort for Déise fans when he was chosen as Hurler of the Year in 1998.

Babs Keating has a firm view on the reasons for their failure to go all the way: 'I would say the Waterford team of recent years was very unlucky. Waterford had three massive players: Tony Browne, Ken McGrath and Paul Flynn. On the crucial days they never got the three of them to play well at the same time. If you take 2004, Paul Flynn got thirteen points in the All-Ireland semi-final against Kilkenny. If he had got any help at all, they would have won, but neither Browne nor McGrath backed him up properly. That was their undoing. They were so dependent on those three. They were like the Waterford team of the late 1950s and '60s. They were just short of two or three players.'

Disappointingly Flynn found himself on the subs bench in 2008 when Waterford reached their first All-Ireland final since 1963, only for the Déise to be humiliated by Kilkenny in a twenty-three-point defeat. Before the match Kilkenny's Christy Heffernan was asked if he thought the Waterford players would be fit enough. He replied: 'They should be fit enough, they've been training for forty-five years!'

GAA pundits are the people we love to hate – except on those rare occasions when their prejudices resonate with ours. Yet they have become an integral part of the sporting landscape and folklore. After his retirement in 2008, Flynn became a pundit on *The Sunday Game*. For media bosses, the temptation to plunder the thoughts of former star players and successful managers and benefit from their judgements is overwhelming. For those personalities who have retired, media involvement affords them the platform to continue their happy addiction to the small and large dramas created by hurlers when they suspend accepted reality in favour of a private, if heightened, version of it on the pitch. As a television pundit Flynn drew on the depth and authenticity of his own playing experience. He knows the mood of the players, the way they speak and what's important to them. He can read faces. He can appreciate the subtle difference between when a player blinks in acknowledgment and the moments when the lashes touch for a fraction longer, suggesting a softening, a form of encouragement. Above all he is constantly alert for glances which are veiled and hostile when the story is told in the silences.

As a pundit Flynn has raised eyebrows himself in particular in criticism of Davy Fitzgerald's management of the Waterford team, specifically the type of drills done in training. While acknowledging that Flynn was one of the greatest hurlers of modern times, Davy's risposte was succinct: their training was 'up to speed' he said, but 'I am not sure Paul Flynn was'.

Flynn's place in hurling history is secure with a string of top performances. In 2002 he was one of the chief architects of Waterford's first Munster title in thirty-nine years, beating Tipperary in the final. Over the next five years the Cork–Waterford rivalry would light up hurling and produce some of the finest games in recent history, notably Waterford's triumph in the classic 2004 Munster final. Flynn's scoring prowess was central to Waterford's success in the noughties.

76

Keys to the Kingdom

Mick O'Dwyer: 1957–1973

Mick O'Dwyer is universally acknowledged as the greatest Gaelic football manager of all time because of his achievements of winning eight All-Irelands with Kerry, two Leinster finals with Kildare and a Leinster final with Laois. In 2007 he marked the occasion of his seventieth birthday by becoming manager of Wicklow, where yet again he sprinkled his magic dust. Despite a rare health setback, O'Dwyer continued to coach the squad during the summer of 2007 and transformed them from being ranked the second-worst team in the country to the dizzy heights of a place in the top twelve in 2009.

Many managers' career statistics have been grossly distorted by an addiction to the game that caused them to go on managing far past their prime. O'Dwyer has mantained his unashamedly romantic vision of what his team could accomplish on the pitch, his insistence that they could not settle for simply winning matches but must try to fill every performance with flair, verve and originality.

Even without his achievements as a manager, O'Dwyer would be guaranteed his place among the GAA immortals because of a glittering playing career: winning four senior All-Ireland medals, eight league medals and being voted Footballer of the Year in 1969.

His early days in the green and gold jersey were not without disappointment, though. He played minor football for Kerry against Waterford in the Munster championship and was replaced, to his great surprise, in the next match by Ireland's favourite poet Brendan Kennelly, who recalls the incident with amusement: 'Dwyer told me that I would never amount to anything because my togs were too long! I heard, though, he told someone else that I would never make it because my arse was too close to the ground.'

Shortly after he retired O'Dwyer took over a young squad and quickly turned them into the greatest football team we have ever seen. Surprisingly he had a major impact on the philosophy of Ger Loughnane. 'Tony O'Reilly tells a great story about Brendan Behan,' he says. 'Behan turned up on a chat show on Canadian television totally drunk. The presenter was very unimpressed and asked him why he was so drunk. Behan replied, "Well, a few weeks ago I was sitting in a pub in Dublin and I saw a sign on a beer mat which said: 'Drink Canada Dry.' So when I came over here I said I'd give it a go!" O'Dwyer deftly uses that incident to speak of the need to have the kind of positive attitude that says, "I'll give it a go." That's the kind of upbeat mentality he brought to his teams coming into Croke Park.'

Micko tells a story of how in 2002 he attended a social function when he was still Kildare manager, and met the then Dublin manager Tommy Lyons. Tommy said to O'Dwyer at one stage, 'Micko, you and I will fill Croke Park this year.'

O'Dwyer replied, 'Tommy, you and I wouldn't fill a toilet!'

O'Dwyer is amused at the kind of highbrow analysis his former protégés Páidí Ó Sé and Pat Spillane sometimes produce in their high-profile role as pundits. Hence his love of the story of the two former Kerry players attending a Mensa convention for people with high IQs, which naturally had its annual convention in Tralee. Spillane and Ó Sé were the star guests at the official dinner. While dining, they discovered that their salt shaker contained pepper and their pepper shaker was full of salt. How could they swap the contents of the bottles without spilling, using only the implements at hand?

The two Kerry immortals debated and finally came up with an ingenious solution involving a napkin, a straw and an empty saucer. They called the waitress over to dazzle her with their brilliant plan. 'Miss,' they said, 'we couldn't help but notice that the pepper shaker contains salt and the salt shaker...'

'Oh,' the waitress interrupted. 'Sorry about that.' She unscrewed the caps of the bottles and switched them.

77

THE LIFE OF O'REILLY

Gerry O'Reilly: 1949–1962

Wicklow's Gerry O'Reilly occupies that special place in the GAA reserved for hidden heroes. It is a testimony to his ability that although he lined out for a county which failed to win any silverware over his long career, he nonetheless is universally acknowledged as one of the greatest wing-backs in GAA history. In fact during his entire Wicklow career he never even lined out in a Leinster final. The one silver lining for O'Reilly was that he played at a time when the Railway Cup was a massive competition. With Leinster he was able to take his place alongside the giants of the game and show himself to have no peers in his position. He won three Railway Cup medals in 1952, '53 and '54. It was largely because of his impact in this competition that O'Reilly was chosen on the Team of the Century of greatest players never to have won a senior All-Ireland medal in 1984.

O'Reilly was a romantic about the game and was in thrall to those who inspire a love of Gaelic games. He pays particular tribute to one man.

———

'Michael O'Hehir was the man who brought hurling games in vivid form to the people of rural Ireland at a time when television was unknown and transistors unheard of. He showed that hurling is a game that is an art apart, its extent and depth perhaps not fully realized, rather merely accepted. He was a national institution. As we march, not always successfully, to the relentless demands of a faster, more superficial age, just to hear his voice was to know that all was well with the world. He painted pictures with words like a master craftsman. Young boys listening to him decided immediately they wanted to join the ranks of the football and hurling immortals. Irish sport is not the same without him. He was irreplaceable.'

O'Reilly did not play in an era of significant managerial influence and was a little nonplussed by the emergence of the modern cult of the manager. When I asked him about the secret of motivation in Gaelic football, he responded by telling me a parable:

'The Notre Dame American football team found that their fortunes had declined enormously and their playing standards had reached rock bottom. The school decided that the team was not worthy of wearing the traditional Notre Dame colours. For years they played in the second strip. Then a team came together and qualified for a minor final. In accordance with the custom in American football, the team went out and were introduced to the crowd. Then they went back into the dressing room for their final instruction. There, hanging on every player's peg was the traditional jersey of Notre Dame. The coach told them to throw away their old jerseys and put on the traditional colours. When the team left the dressing room, they felt like kings. It's all about knowing what buttons to push and when to push them.'

78

CAVAN'S COLOSSUS

John Joe O'Reilly: 1940–1950

Through the commentaries of Michael O'Hehir, Cornafean's John Joe O'Reilly became one of the most famous names in Ireland in the 1940s. He won back-to-back All-Irelands in 1947 and 1948, National Leagues in 1948 and 1950, and four Railway Cup medals in 1942, '43, '47 and 1950. Born on a farm near Killeshandra in 1918, after receiving a scholarship to St Patrick's College in Cavan he went on to the army cadet school at the Curragh, where he showed promise as a sprinter and as a basketball player.

His career coincided with the most glorious era in Cavan football. In 1933 Cavan became the first Ulster team to win the All-Ireland. Further titles followed in 1935, '47, '48 and 1952. Initially, though, John Joe would taste the bitter pill of defeat in three All-Ireland finals before getting his hands on the ultimate prize. They lost to Kerry in 1937, Roscommon in 1943 (after a replay) and Cork in 1945.

The replay against Roscommon was mired in controversy, as Roscommon's wing-back Brendan Lynch recalled: 'We beat Cavan in the All-Ireland final after a replay. I marked Mick Higgins, who was very quiet and a very clean and good footballer. What I remember most was the mayhem at the end. First Cavan's Joe Stafford was sent off after having a go at Owensie Hoare. We got a point but Barney Culley didn't agree and put the umpire into the net with a box. Big Tom O'Reilly, the captain of Cavan, came in to remonstrate and threw the referee in the air.'

At first John Joe played at wing-back, but then he switched to the pivotal role of centre half-back and made the position his own. The most famous of his matches was the Polo Grounds final against Kerry in 1947, when he captained the side, having taken over the captaincy from his brother, 'Big Tom'. Right half-back on that team was the late John Wilson, who went on to become Tánaiste in the Irish government who recalled the occasion for me.

'The final was held in New York as a gesture of goodwill by the GAA to the Irish people in America. Once it was announced it aroused great interest in every county. To get there was a great prize in itself. The teams left Cobh together for a six-day trip on the SS *Mauritania* to New York after getting our vaccinations against smallpox, which were compulsory at the time. The fact that we were playing the aristocrats of football, Kerry, added to the occasion for us, but the fact that it was the first final played abroad gave it a much more exotic quality, so it really grabbed the public imagination.

'The pitch, which was used for baseball, was much smaller than the usual Gaelic pitch. The grass was scorched and even bald in a few places, and there was a mound in the playing area. The ground was rock hard and the weather was hot. Kerry got off to a great start, but Peter Donohoe was on fire for us that day. The American press described him as

292

"the Babe Ruth" of Gaelic football after the greatest star in baseball of the era. We had an amazing leader and one of the all-time greats in Gaelic football in John Joe O'Reilly – the young army officer who died so tragically after a short illness in 1952 at the tender age of thirty-four. We won by 2–11 to 2–7. By coincidence, one of the biggest stars of our team, Mick Higgins, who scored a goal and two points in that match, was born in New York.

'In 1950 P. J. Duke died suddenly from pleurisy in St Vincent's Hospital. Two years later on 21 November 1952, the thirty-four-year-old Commandant John Joe O'Reilly, after being diagnosed with a kidney complaint, died unexpectedly in the Curragh Military Hospital.

'It was very difficult for all of us to believe that those two great servants of Cavan football, who had played in the county's glory days, had gone to their eternal reward so prematurely. Whenever I talk to GAA fans, there are always great arguments about who had the best half-back line of all time: the Roscommon half-back line of 1943–44 with Brendan Lynch, Bill Carlos and Phelim Murray, or the Cavan back line of 1947–48. I can still hear Michael O'Hehir calling them out, "On the right is P. J. Duke, in the centre Commandant John Joe O'Reilly and on the left Lieutenant Simon Deignan."'

John Joe's son, Brian, recalls the trauma for the family: 'My mother was left with four young kids. I was just five when Dad died and I had two younger sisters. It was very tough times. My mother was told she was not entitled to a widow's pension. Years later I investigated on her behalf and discovered that she had been.

'I played minor football for Cavan but it was hard to escape from my father's shadow. I retired from the game at a very young age.'

———

John Joe's status in the game is reflected as centre half-back on both the Team of the Century and the Team of the Millennium. His hold on the public consciousness is nurtured in a popular song, 'The Gallant John Joe'.

79

ROYAL O'ROURKE

Colm O'Rourke: 1975–1995

It was a time when Meath and Dublin were drawing more often than Michelangelo, and Colm O'Rourke was voted Footballer of the Year. O'Rourke won two All-Ireland medals, three league titles and three All-Stars. However, the games he will probably be best remembered for are the four-game saga against Dublin in 1991.

Colm O'Rourke was at the heart of Meath's triumph. 'What I remember most is the intensity of the games,' he says. 'Kevin Foley's goal would have been the most dramatic in anybody's sporting life. There were stages in all the games, particularly in the last one, when I thought it was gone, but we were mentally strong, having been together so long. We didn't play well in some of the games but did just enough to hang on. Morale was very good in the camp. We did very little training between the matches. It was mainly rest and recuperation. There was a very simple explanation why we emerged victorious in 1991 – we were the best team.'

Despite their intensity, the four-game saga did produce

one moment of light relief. Paul Curran was dropped for the third game but came on in the second half and scored the equalising point. A few nights later Dublin manager Paddy Cullen had a team meeting with the players and did some video analysis with them. Cullen was severely critical of the forwards' first-half performance and turned to Curran and asked him: "Where were you in the first half?" To the hilarity of his teammates, Curran replied: "Sitting beside you, as a sub on the bench, Paddy!"'

The 1991 victory did not mean as much to Colm O'Rourke as the victories over Dublin in the mid 1980s. 'For a long time in the '70s and '80s Dublin had a hold over us,' he explains. 'There was a feeling of the inevitable in our camp about Dublin's victory. But 1986 changed all that. We reversed that pattern and that paved the way for our All-Ireland titles in 1987 and '88. We had a settled team at the time and they hadn't, which gave us a significant advantage.

'Winning the first All-Ireland was obviously a very sweet one for me, but '88 was even better when we won the league and championship. I felt that what made my greatest triumphs all the sweeter was that they came towards the end of my career, particularly as I had so many disappointments and injuries early on.'

The importance of O'Rourke to the Meath side was never more clearly demonstrated than when he came on as a sub in the second half of the 1991 All-Ireland final, having gone down with viral pneumonia in the week leading up to the game. 'For me, the year ended on a real downer – no pun intended! – when we lost the final to Down, particularly as I missed most of the match.'

Paradoxically O'Rourke feels Meath's place in the affections of the Irish people was greatly heightened by the defeat.

The ill-tempered clashes with Cork in the '87 and '88 finals had left Meath with a reputation, at least in certain quarters, of being a dirty side.

'It would be fair to say I noticed a big change in the attitude of people outside the county to Meath after the game. I think we won a lot of friends because we didn't crow about it or rub it in when we beat the Dubs and accepted our victory graciously and our defeat to Down equally graciously.'

Sligo's greatest footballer, Mickey Kearins, became a referee after he retired from football. He reminded me that his career with the whistle is probably best remembered for the time he sent off Colm O'Rourke.

'It was an incident after half-time and he got a heavy enough shoulder while in possession. It knocked the ball out of his hands, but he didn't try to retrieve it – he came after me. The play moved down the field and he followed me the whole way down, sharing "pleasantaries" with me! I had no option but to send him off.'

The two giants of the game had another heated exchange subsequently, in the 1988 All-Ireland semi-final, when Kearins was a linesman.

'There was a line-ball incident and he felt I gave it the wrong decision,' he recalls. 'I know myself now that I was wrong and he was right, having seen the replay on telly. I would have to say, though, he was a great player and actually made the Meath forward line while he was in his prime. He was their playmaker.'

Colm O'Rourke has been a media analyst since 1991 when he was still the best player in the country. In his autobiography, Liam Hayes deals with the ripples of discord that were created on the Meath panel back in 1991, but O'Rourke has been an inspired choice and to this day is one of the best pundits you will find anywhere. His mind is as agile as an Olympic gymnast. When he talks about football, he nearly always seems, quite simply, to hit the right note. You cannot ask any more of an analyst than that. He does not mince his words. 'Aidan O'Shea has become a personality of the game but without the big-day performances to warrant it.'

He is equally honest about his own days: 'A forward might return the favour [a rough tackle] with a good wallop in the snot. I have to admit to being guilty on a few occasions. It is amazing how an elbow to the ear can put manners on a defender.'

80

THE CHOSEN FEW

Páidí Ó Sé: 1974–1988

The late Páidí Ó Sé was part of an illustrious quintet – the 'magnificent five' – with Ger Power, Mike Sheehy, Pat Spillane and Ogie Moran, who won eight All-Ireland medals with Kerry, captaining the team to All-Ireland glory in 1985. In his fourteen years on the Kerry team, Ó Sé won five consecutive All-Stars from 1981 to '85. However, his most impressive statistic is that in the ten All-Irelands he played in, he conceded just one point to his immediate opponent, David Hickey of Dublin in 1976.

Páidí was a first-class storyteller and was well able to tell stories against himself. Many go back to his time as a garda. In 1979 after a league match against Cork he went for a few drinks. The next morning when he went in to report for duty in Limerick he was feeling a bit off colour. He decided that the best way of concealing his discomfort was to take out the squad car and pretend to go on patrol, but instead he pulled into a quiet field for a nap. A few hours later he was awoken by a great commotion and suddenly there were squad cars all over the field. Páidí stumbled out of the car to find himself face to face with the Assistant Commissioner, who said, 'Páidí, did you nod off for a little while?'

'I'm sorry. I'd an auld game yesterday and I just pulled in for a few minutes. What are all of ye doing here?'

'We're checking out the venue for the Pope's visit to Limerick next September. The Holy Father'll be saying a Mass out here. We're sussin' out the place for the security plan. Sorry to have disturbed you.'

After a shift ended it was customary for a garda to go out for a drink. Sometimes, though, this posed problems when the session carried on after closing hours. Early in his career Páidí was dispatched one night to inspect a pub that was reportedly selling after hours. When he arrived at the premises, he was told to check it out before entering.

'I'm here now, over,' he radioed back to the station.

'Is there any activity there?' questioned the officer.

'Yes,' he replied. 'I can hear people shouting, I can hear laughter and I can hear glasses clinking.'

'And can you hear a cash register going?' asked the officer.

'No,' Páidí replied.

'Ah, you better leave it off, Garda Ó Sé, it could be our own crowd.'

In 1985 everyone on the Kerry team had their hearts set on winning the All-Ireland. None more so than Páidí, as he was captain. As he was trying to gee up the troops before the game, he said, 'We really need to win this one.'

Mick O'Dwyer asked: 'For who?'

'For me.'

'Not for Kerry?'

'Well, for Kerry as well.'

In an effort to add impact to his words, Páidí smashed the

ball as hard as he could on the ground. It bounced so high that it shattered the lights overhead. Glass flew all over the dressing room. Yet so absorbed were the team in the team-talk that not a single player noticed the incident.

Páidi went on to manage Kerry to All-Ireland success in both 1997 and 2000. His style of management was very direct. Once his half-time talk to his team finished with the immortal words: 'Get the lead out of your arses now and shake your heads up and get out there now.'

Páidí was never afraid to talk about his famous friends, like Martin Sheen, Gregory Peck, Tom Cruise and Dolly Parton. He was close to the late Charlie Haughey. He had a fund of stories about the former Taoiseach. One of his favourites went back to Italia '90. After the Italy game, Haughey came into the Irish dressing room and for the players brought up in Ireland gave a rousing speech about the sporting sons of Ireland.

Loudly, Tony Cascarino asked Niall Quinn, 'Who is that bloke?'

'He is the Taoiseach.'

Then Andy Townsend asked Cascarino who their visitor was.

Cas replied, 'I don't know, but Quinny said he owns a teashop.'

One of Páidí's stories was about a Kerry footballer of yesteryear who was in serious need of some love and affec-tion but he had no wife or money. So one evening he met a lady of the night in Tralee and asked her the cost of her services. When he explained he had no money she enquired if he had anything in his pockets. He replied that he had two All-Ireland medals. As it was a slow night, she agreed to exchange her services for the two medals.

A few weeks later some Mayo footballers came to Tralee on a stag night. One of their number met the same lady of the night. The conversation unfolded as follows:

'How much do you charge?'

'Two hundred euro.'

'That's an awful lot.'

'But I'm worth it.'

'How do I know you're any good?'

'Here. Let me show you my two All-Ireland medals.'

81

KERRY'S GOLDEN BOY

Jack O'Shea: 1976–1992

Jack O'Shea is one of the giants of Gaelic football, with seven All-Ireland medals, six All-Star awards and an incredible four Footballer of the Year awards. In 2009 he was chosen by the *Irish Independent* as the greatest footballer of all time.

Why was the Kerry team he played on the greatest of all time? 'I always think of the great Kerry team as the proto-type of the successful team,' he explains. 'We had the four obvious things: we were fit, we trained hard, were talented and gave 100 per cent. We had six other ingredients, though, that made us so successful. First, we never depended on one or two individuals to produce the goods. If Sheehy and the Bomber were having an off day, the likes of John Egan and Ger Power produced big performances. Second, we were very much a team. Third, we were able to handle success and we used this capacity to motivate us to achieve even more success. We enjoyed it when it came. Fourth, we had a positive attitude. Each of us always believed that we would beat our man, even when we were marking a more skilful player, and collectively as soon as we put on the Kerry jersey we believed no team would beat us. That is not arrogance but positive thinking. Fifth, all the Kerry players were very intelligent. It is vital to a team to have fellas who think about the game, especially about improving their own game, but in particular lads who can read a game and when things are going badly never lose their composure and can turn things around. Sixth, we had inspired leadership from Mick O'Dwyer. His man-management skills were excellent – he instilled belief and got us right physically and mentally for the big day. He also knew how to motivate us. When it comes to motivation, it is different strokes for different folks. Dwyer knew what buttons to push to motivate us individually and collectively. He always provided us with good feedback. It was always positive feedback, which is more effective than negative. Above all he was a winner. Winners have critical skills, don't leave winning to chance, leave no stone unturned and make things happen.'

After his retirement from playing, Jacko managed Mayo to a Connacht title in 1993 but now does some work in the media as a pundit, while his son Aidan went on to play for Kerry.

How does he feel the great Kerry team he played on would fare today in this era of packed defences? 'When it comes to comparing standards from one generation to another, the pundit who is an ex-player is always on difficult ground,' he says. 'It is easy to lose track of the boundary between proud self-belief and triumphalism. Training methods, tactics, diet and general preparation for the game have altered dramatically from when Mick O'Connell stopped playing in 1974. It makes it almost impossible to make judgements on how players from the distant past would have performed had they played in a different time. But there are players who would have survived in any era. They had that X-factor that set them apart in their own dreams. They had the vision, determination, imagination and above all the sheer skill to rise above the players around them, and great players like Mike Sheehy would do just the same if they were playing today.'

During our conversation Jacko described more in sadness than in anger an incident which nearly ended his career before it began. 'We played Roscommon in the under-21 All-Ireland final in Roscommon in 1978. The Roscommon fans gave us a hard time that day. We were motivated, but Roscommon were really hyped up and a Roscommon player did me. I ended up in a bad way, but I was lucky that there was no permanent damage. Others haven't been so lucky. It will spoil the game if the thugs are ever allowed to take control.'

Despite his glittering career Jacko had a few disappointments on the way. One of the Cork stars when they regained the All-Ireland in 1989 was John Cleary – a very accurate forward, though not the biggest man in the world. Before Cork's clash with Kerry that year Jack O'Shea came up to him and in an effort to psyche him out said, 'You're too small and too young for a game like this.' Cleary said nothing until after the game, when Cork emerged triumphant, and as he walked off the pitch past Jacko he softly said, 'You're too old for a game like this.'

Micheál O'Muircheartaigh has a special memory of Jack O'Shea: 'When you think of the Kerry team, they had great characters like Eoin Liston, Páidí Ó Sé and Jack O'Shea. I remember the Munster final of 1983 for a particular reason. Jack O'Shea was the captain and I was training Jacko and the

Kerry lads in Dublin. Kerry had won the Munster final from 1975 and in '83 most people expected them to win again. I travelled to the match with Jacko and we had worked on his victory speech and we were very happy with it. The only problem was Kerry lost the match because of a late Tadhg Murphy goal. Jacko's great speech was never made!

'But there was another twist to the story. Kerry forgot to bring the Munster Cup with them and it was only quick thinking by Frank Murphy, the Cork secretary, that saved the day. He went into some press in the back and found some cup. I think it was the Cork junior championship trophy. That's the cup that was presented to the Cork captain, Christy Ryan, but I don't think anyone noticed!'

82

THE OFFALY ROVER

Willie Nolan: 1954–1963

Willie Nolan captained Offaly to a place in the 1961 All-Ireland final. In front of a record crowd that exceeded 90,000 his team lost by a solitary point to the reigning champions, Down.

Nolan is keen to give much of the credit to Offaly's emergence to an outsider. 'There was no such thing as a manager then, but Peter O'Reilly had trained the Dublin team to win the All-Ireland in 1958, then he fell out with Dublin,' he said. 'Some of our boys knew him from playing club football in Dublin and knew he was at a loose end and asked him to take us on. He loved the idea of the chance to get back at Dublin.

'In 1960 Carlow were leading us by six points at half-time in our first match in the championship but we beat them by three points at the finish. That meant we would be playing in the Leinster semi-final against Dublin. I had seen them play in the previous round against Longford and they beat them by seven goals. I thought to myself, "We're rightly bunched."

We beat them by 3–9 to 0–9. It was one of the biggest thrills of my life. Peter was the figurehead and was a lovely man, so we were really fired up to win the match for him.'

In the Leinster final Offaly were unable to raise their game to quite the same standard but scraped a one-point victory over Laois. It was an historic occasion, as it was the county's first Leinster senior title in either football or hurling. Their opponents in the All-Ireland semi-final were Down, who had the advantage in terms of experience, having contested the All-Ireland semi-final the previous year, and the northerners eventually narrowly came out on top after a replay.

In 1961 Carlow were accounted for again in the Leinster championship, paving the way for a Leinster semi-final clash with Kildare, which they won. Having accounted for Dublin in the Leinster final, Offaly brushed aside the challenge of Roscommon in the All-Ireland semi-final. It was a victory which left Nolan with a tinge of regret.

'I was sorry that Gerry O'Malley had to lose that semi-final,' he recalled. 'He was a great player and had fierce dedication. He was based in Ferbane at the time and the lads there were always trying to get him to play for Ferbane, but he was always loyal to his home club in Roscommon, St Brigid's. He was one of the greatest players. Although he wasn't a stylish player, he had a great heart and gave great service to Roscommon.'

Was he nervous captaining the team in an All-Ireland final?

'If you weren't nervous before an All-Ireland, there was something wrong with you. It was the thrill of my life. But I was as nervous as a kitten. Basically all I had to do was keep the backs from roaming up the field.'

Nolan has many memories of playing with the 'Iron Man

of Rhode', Paddy McCormack, who has gone into folklore because of his interaction with Sligo's Michael Kearins' first Railway Cup game against Leinster in Ballinasloe. At the start, as he was moving into position before the ball was thrown in, Kearins noticed his immediate opponent, Paddy McCormack, digging a hole along the ground with his boot. Paddy said, 'You're young Kearins from Sligo. I presume you expect to go back to Sligo this evening.'

'Hopefully,' Kearins replied.

'If you don't pass the mark, you have a fair chance of getting back!'

At twenty-one, Willie did not foresee then that his one chance of winning an All-Ireland had passed him by in 1961. Although in 1962 he had the consolation of winning his second consecutive Railway Cup medal, Offaly surrendered their Leinster title to Dublin in the final. It was to be Nolan's last game with the county.

'Losing that match was effectively the end for that Offaly team. My great hero, Mick Casey, had been playing for years and Seán Foran likewise and we didn't have replacements for them. Offaly won the minor All-Ireland in 1964 and it wasn't until some of those lads came through that Offaly achieved success again.

'We were invited to America a while after losing the 1962 Leinster final. We played New York twice. My brother, Peter, was playing for them. I stayed on for a few weeks after the tour was over because I had two brothers over there. I came back in November. Offaly had played two matches in the league by that stage. Tommy Furlong, an older brother of Martin, was in goal. The Reverend Chairman of Offaly at the time was very annoyed with me for staying on in America. Although Peter O'Reilly was supposed to be in charge, the

Reverend Chairman had the final say and there was no way he was going to let me play again. My heart was broken because I wasn't playing football, so I went back to America to stay. I started playing with New York.

'At the time every county who won the league came out to play New York. In 1963 Dublin came over and we beat them. That was one of the biggest thrills of my life. Four years later we beat the great Galway three-in-a-row side, which was another great thrill.'

Although he has many happy memories from his playing days, strangely Nolan has none of the medals he won as a player. 'I gave them all away to various people over the years,' he says. 'When you're playing, it's the winning that matters, not the medals, but as you get older the medals start to become important.'

83

A Great Leaper

Willie Joe Padden: 1977–1993

'Will Galway bate Mayo
Not if they have Willie Joe?'

(THE SAW DOCTORS)

Willie Joe Padden is one of the elite group of footballers who have been immortalised in a song, but Mayo's most iconic footballer takes it all in his stride.

'I know some of the lads in the band and I sadly I think they chose me just because my name rhymed with Mayo not because of my brilliance on the pitch! There have been a few strange moments. Five or six years ago this American came over to visit Ireland just because he was a massive fan of the Saw Doctors and as soon as he came in the door of the bar I had in Castlebar at the time he asked me: "Hey man, are you the guy in the song?"'

Having made his debut with Mayo in 1977 and still in his teens Padden found himself playing in a team dogged by defeat.

'We didn't win the Connacht championship in the 1970s but we were affected by what was going on all round us. Kerry and Dublin had raised the bar. If you were really serious about playing football and if you wanted to be in the All-Ireland series, you went from basically two nights' training a week to four. We hadn't been doing the training that was required to make a breakthrough at national level.'

The joy of a Connacht title in 1981 quickly turned into bitter disappointment when Mayo faced Kerry in the All-Ireland semi-final.

'They were at their pinnacle. We were probably well in the game around half-time but in the second half it was a no-show as far as we were concerned. We got beaten by sixteen points in the end. Although it was very disappointing to lose it might have been a blessing in disguise because it really showed us that we had an awful lot to do to be able to compete with the Kerrys and Dublins of the time.'

Mayo's philosophy of the game is a source of pride for Padden.

'Down through the years we have provided some very good entertainment. Unfortunately that's no good to you when you want results. But there would be a great flair in Mayo football. I sometimes think you might be able to compare us to the French rugby team. When we play football to our maximum we are very attractive. We've always had very talented footballers.'

Some players have their careers defined in moments. Willie Joe Padden is such a player. In the All-Ireland semi-final in 1989 against Tyrone he was forced to the sideline with a dangerous cut to his head. In one of the most iconic images in the history of the GAA he later returned to the

---

fray, covered in blood, his head wrapped in a bandage, his shirt splattered with blood.

'Everybody had written us off before the match. I got an injury. I'm not too sure which Tyrone player it was. He was going for a ball and he hit his knee off my head and I got a few stiches in it. You don't mind getting a few things like that as long as you win the game. It was our first experience of getting to a final after all our endeavours from the previous years. From our point of view and from a spectator's point of view, it was a great period because we were basking in the build-up to the final, especially being in our first All-Ireland for so long.'

The disappointment for Padden was heightened because he knew there were not many chances left for him to win a coveted All-Ireland medal.

'It's all right playing in an All-Ireland final but if you don't win no one is going to remember who the runners-up were in ten years' time, if they're asked the question. I remember thinking at the time: "Am I going to get the chance to stand in Croke Park again and have another go at winning an All-Ireland?" Sadly it was not to be.'

There is an undercurrent of sadness in Padden's voice as he recalls the way his Mayo career ended in 1992.

'Jack O'Shea had taken over as manager and I suppose his reading of it was that some of the older lads had enough mileage on the clock. He decided to bring in some new blood. I fet that I still had a contribution to make to the team for another year or two, maybe as a fringe player. When the panel was picked I wasn't included. Maybe it did hurt me a bit. I certainly found it a shock to the system having been involved with the county for so long because your life is built around training and playing. You do miss it. But the time comes from everyone to move on.'

———

With five Connacht medals and two All-Star awards to his name Padden can look back at the disappointments of the past with a wry smile. Padden's quick wit was shown when he was approached by a stranger in an airport who said: 'You're a dead ringer for Ian Botham.' Quick as a flash Willie Joe replied: 'Funny I never get any of his cheques.'

Willie Joe excluded Mayo players from his dream team but claims he could easily pick fifteen Mayo fellas who would beat any dream team.

1. John O'Leary
(*Dublin*)

2. Páidí O'Se   **3. Darren Fay**   **4. Martin O'Connell**
(*Kerry*)   (*Meath*)   (*Meath*)

5. Seamus Moynihan 6. Kieran McGeeney   **7. Seán Óg de Paor**
(*Kerry*)   (*Armagh*)   (*Galway*)

8. Jack O'Shea   **9. Darragh Ó Sé**
(*Kerry*)   (*Dublin*)

10. Maurice Fitzgerald 11. Larry Thompkins   **12. Pat Spillane**
(*Kerry*)   (*Cork*)   (*Kerry*)

13. Mickey Linden   **14. Peter Canavan**   **15. Colm Cooper**
(*Down*)   (*Tyrone*)   (*Kerry*)

84

PADDY'S PLAY

Paddy Prendergast: 1947–1958

Although he is one of the greatest full-backs in the history of football, Paddy Prendergast had an inauspicious start to his career.

'In 1947 I made my debut for Mayo,' he explained. 'I was stationed in Dungloe with the guards at the time and had played Donegal for a year or so at that stage when the invitation came to play for Mayo. I had a severe dilemma because I was very happy where I was and I knew very few fellas on the Mayo team. On the day of the match I travelled down to Ballina for a challenge match against Galway, via bus and taxi, but typical of the County Board they didn't think of getting me a few shillings to cover my travel expenses. I was brought around and introduced to the players before the game.

'I was selected at full-back, but at that stage I was a midfielder. On my right was John Forde, on my left was Seán Flanagan. I was marking Ned Keogh. The first ball that came in, Ned sold me a dummy and scored a goal with his right. The next ball he sidestepped me and scored a goal with his left. Seán Flanagan shouted at me: "What in the name of Christ are you doing there?" With the small bit of dignity I could muster I replied: "To be frank, I have no idea."

'Nobody expected us to go anywhere. Quite frankly, neither did I. We got together for collective training in Mrs Gaughan's guesthouse in Ballina before the 1948 championship. We were under the watchful eyes of Gerald Courell and Jackie Carney, who welded us into a team. They were very disciplined and there was no drinking or womanising tolerated. It was the making of us as a team. Living together and sharing breakfast every morning bonded us together. At night a blackboard was produced and every aspect of the game, offensively as well as defensively, was gone into, as well as the strengths and weaknesses of the opposition. We were not the typical team for the time. We only had one farmer, but he was a big farmer – Henry Dixon. We had four or five lawyers, about as many doctors, an engineer and a priest. Peter Quinn was newly ordained at the time and the lads exaggerated their atheistic elements just to wind him up. They were intelligent fellas who believed in themselves.

'While we won two All-Irelands, I believe we should have won a four-in-a-row from 1948 to '51. We tailed Cavan by a point but were playing with a gale in the 1948 All-Ireland final with three and a half minutes to go when the referee blew for full-time. I am certain we would have beaten them if we had played the full match. There was no objection, but it was savage really that this should have happened.

'In 1949 the belief was that we would win the All-Ireland semi-final by ten points. After twenty-four minutes Seán Flanagan and I had a chat about how much we were going to win by. Then inexplicably the county selectors took off two of our half-backs and replaced them with two forwards. The Meath half-forwards started to waltz through them. The incompetence of the County Board knew no bounds. Their madness cost us an All-Ireland that year. If it was today, we wouldn't have accepted it.'

The ineptitude of the selectors almost cost Mayo the All-Ireland in 1950.

'We had probably the best goalkeeper in the country at the time in Sean Wynne and he was in excellent form for us all year. Then for some crazy reason he was dropped for the All-Ireland final against Louth and Billy Durkin was brought in for him. Understandably Billy was very nervous and the first ball he handled he dropped it. Seán Flanagan knew we were in trouble and pulled Frank aside. He signalled to the sideline that Frank was injured and Wynne came in for him. Only for Seán doing that we would have probably lost that All-Ireland.

'I remember the joy was unconfined after the game. People don't realise how different Ireland was back then. We were on our knees in economic terms. The GAA made an awful difference to people at such a black time. The bonfires that blazed after we won were a sign that people could still have hope.'

Another All-Ireland came in '51 but legend has it that it was then that the seeds of Mayo's woes were sown for decades to come.

'People tell it slightly differently, but the core story is that when we returned with the Sam Maguire Cup in 1951 we interrupted either a Mass or a funeral and the priest was so enraged that he put a curse on the team that we would never win the All-Ireland again while any of that team were on earth.'

Prendergast was to have one more opportunity for glory in 1955.

'We had a great chance of beating Dublin and qualifying for another All-Ireland final. We were lodged in their half throughout the second half but still we couldn't put them away. It was to become an all-too-familiar story for Mayo for decades to come.

'We had great characters in the team. John Forde was very serious. When we stayed in Mrs Gaughan's guesthouse, our routine was to go for a ten-mile walk after breakfast. Before a big game against Kerry, Tom Langan said he was going to skip the walk that day because his stomach wasn't too good. Then Mick Flanagan said he would not go either because his leg wasn't too good. John jumped up and said: "For Jaysus' sake, wire Kerry and award them the game!"

'Since I retired I look at the failures of Mayo as my personal via dolorosa. At the moment I hardly want to see them play. It pains me to see them lose games they should have won, like the All-Ireland against Meath in '96. I am tired looking at their failures and their lack of determination. You won't win All-Irelands unless you have courage and determination.'

One aspect of modern football really bugs him.

'I hate the cult of the manager. A good manager will bring organisation, but it is fifteen good players that win All-Irelands. The financial end troubles me also. Two questions I want to ask about these managers: How much are they getting paid? Are they worth it?'

85

KING SIZE

Stephen King: 1980–1997

As a youngster Stephen King was a precocious talent. 'When I was fourteen, I played under-16 for the county,' he remembers. 'When I was sixteen, I played for the county minors. When I was a minor, I played under-21 for the county, and when I was eighteen I played my first match for Cavan seniors against Meath in a challenge match in Kells. I never really looked back after that.'

For seventeen years King's career progressed without any success at inter-county level. He had the consolation, though, of winning four Railway Cup medals. 'Those cups were hugely important to me, particularly in the 1980s. At the time Ulster football was in the doldrums. The Railway Cup allowed us to rub shoulders with players from the great Kerry team and match ourselves with many of the greatest players of all time. Ulster, probably more so than the other provinces, always took the competition very seriously and it paid off with the success we had.'

One of the highlights of King's career was playing for Ireland in the Compromise Rules against Australia. Despite

319

the disappointments with Cavan, his zest for the dramas of the game was undiminished.

'It probably wasn't as difficult as people might think to keep going,' he states. 'I got great enjoyment from playing and it was a great way of meeting people. Having said that, it was hard to lose Ulster championships year after year. You would ask yourself: Why am I doing this to myself? Then a few months later the league started and after you won a couple of matches the hunger came back as strong as ever.'

The longevity of his career saw him playing under a number of different managers. He admired them all, but one stood out for him.

'I would have to say they were all very good – people like Gabriel Kelly and P. J. Carroll were very committed. Eugene McGee came with a big reputation, having won an All-Ireland with Offaly, and he certainly was a very deep thinker about the game. Martin McHugh was definitely the best of them all. He was the first to really adapt our style of football to the modern era and really move us up with the times in terms of taking us away from a catch-and-kick style of play to a faster style.'

Apart from the change of style and Martin McHugh's influence, I ask, why did Cavan make the breakthrough and win the Ulster title in 1997?

'Ulster is such a minefield that it is very hard to win the title. In Martin's first year in charge of us, we got to the Ulster final. We could have won it, but we were too naive on the day. In 1997 we were a mature outfit and for a few players like me it was the end of the line, so it was do or die. We got out of jail to snatch a draw with Fermanagh, and I think we knew then that it was going to be our year.'

Cavan's victory in the Ulster final prompted celebrations the likes of which had not been seen in the county since the glory days of John Joe O'Reilly. The local media and local radio station, Shannonside/Northern Sound, celebrated the win as the major news story of the year. 'Everyone in Cavan went haywire. I'll never forget the scene in Clones after we won. You couldn't see a blade of grass on the pitch because of the sea of blue and white.'

If 1997 provided King with the highlight of his career, it also provided him with his greatest disappointment. 'Definitely the low point of my career was losing the All-Ireland semi-final to Kerry. As a team we didn't perform to the best of our abilities on the day. We missed the boat. It was all the more galling because I still believe we would have won the All-Ireland that year had we beaten Kerry.'

Having climbed the mountain in 1997, Cavan football went into something of a decline afterwards. King sees it more as a transition than a crisis.

'The change of management probably had something to do with it. Then there were players like myself who stepped down, so a new panel had to be developed and it takes time for things to settle.'

Major controversy erupted when Martin McHugh's successor Liam Austin was forced to resign as Cavan manager because of so-called 'player power'. King was the punters' favourite to take the job, but he declined to run for the post.

'I had just started up my own pub in Killeshandra at the time, so there was no way I could even consider taking the position.'

How does King feel about 'player power'?

'In general I think it's a bad thing,' he explains. 'The one thing I would say, though, is that players should be properly looked after by the GAA because it is the players that generate the big crowds and the revenue for the Association. Once that happens I think players should concentrate on playing and not get involved in politics, if that's what you want to call it.'

When asked about his favourite character in the game, his answer is immediate.

'Anthony Molloy from Donegal. He's got such a great way with people and is so friendly. It's no wonder he's such a popular guy.'

He is equally emphatic when asked about the greatest players he ever saw.

'Jack O'Shea and Brian Mullins. They would have made a fantastic and unbeatable combination, if they had played for the same team.'

Stephen King is a strong believer that Gaelic football must rid itself of its thuggish element. 'The GAA has had a lot of controversies in recent years with violent incidents on the pitch and they must do something about it. Probably the most worrying thing is that some of these incidents have taken place in underage and college matches. I have no time for the off-the-ball stuff that's spoiling the game. We have to face up to some hard choices if we are to stamp this out.

'I also feel that we have to have a long hard look at the rules of the game. I think football is being killed by the stop-start way in which the games are being played. It's ruining the game because the pace is so slow now. When you contrast it with hurling and the speed of that game, football is playing catch up.'

King's dream team is as follows.

———————

King Size

1. Billy Morgan
(Cork)

2. Robbie O'Malley
(Meath)

3. Mick Lyons
(Meath)

4. Tony Scullion
(Derry)

5. Páidí Ó Sé
(Kerry)

6. Paddy Moriarty
(Armagh)

7. Jim Reilly
(Cavan)

8. Jack O'Shea
(Kerry)

9. Brian Mullins
(Dublin)

10. Martin McHugh
(Donegal)

11. Greg Blaney
(Down)

12. Matt Connor
(Offaly)

13. Peter Canavan
(Tyrone)

14. Colm O'Rourke
(Meath)

15. John Egan
(Kerry)

86

Like Father, Like Son

Billy Quinn: 1954–1963

The May sky was bursting with dark, sultry clouds and the green sod was slippery after a morning of heavy rain as raging hot favourites Kilkenny took on Tipperary in the final. A star was born, as the late Billy Quinn's performance was the key factor in Tipp's 3–10 to 1–4 victory.

A member of the Rahealty club but a native of Rossestown, a couple of miles east of Thurles, Quinn was a prodigious talent as a youngster. He attributes much of his success to his coach at Thurles CBS, Limerick man Brother Doody. Genetics also played its part – 'An uncle of mine, Jack, captained the first Harty Cup-winning team and there was a lot of hurling in the family.'

Billy Quinn had the rare distinction of making his inter-county debut in an All-Ireland final. 'I played for four years on the Tipperary minors,' he told me in his family home. 'When I was fourteen, I was brought on as a sub in the All-Ireland final against Kilkenny in 1950. Tipperary had won all their matches up to then by a cricket score. So I had never got a chance to come on and get used to the thing. It was crazy to bring me on for my first match in an All-Ireland final because I had no idea where I was or what I was doing.'

He won his second minor All-Ireland medal (one of his teammates was his brother, Dick) in 1953, when he captained the team. He was a bit blasé about it all.

'There was no real pressure on me as captain. All I had to do was to call the toss and collect the cup! The only work I had to do was before the All-Ireland final when our goalie had a panic attack on the way out. The lads called me back and I got him back up against the wall of Hill Sixteen. He was more afraid of me than of the opposition and he went out and played a blinder.

'We were so used to winning that I got the cup and threw it somewhere else and we went home. There was no celebration as such. The big thing was to win the Munster final. There was a massive crowd at the Munster final then. When you came out of the ground your feet would hardly touch the road because there'd be so many people.

'The big thrill was to be hanging around with the senior team. The Munster final in Killarney was a classic match, though I'd an awful experience when a Cork man dropped dead beside me with the excitement of the match. The crowd invaded the pitch a few times and Christy Ring had to escort the referee off the pitch.'

A decade previously, such was the intensity of one Tipperary–Cork match that a man had to be anointed on the ground. The entire crowd knelt down as a mark of respect.

Within months of captaining Tipperary to the All-Ireland minor title, Billy was making his senior debut. 'My first senior match was for Laois,' he told me. 'It was in the middle of winter and not a suitable day for hurling. All I remember from the match is that we got a 21-yard free. It was blocked down, but I ran in and put the sliotar in the net. The referee disallowed it. To this day I don't know why. I was disgusted.'

Unfortunately Billy's inter-county career coincided with a barren spell in Tipperary's fortunes in the championship. 'We played Cork in 1956 and Séamus Bannon got the best goal I ever saw. He ran down the wing and lashed the ball in the net, but one of our lads threw his hurley 20 yards in celebration and the referee disallowed the goal. Cork beat us. It was the greatest injustice I ever saw in hurling. We got dog's abuse listening in to the All-Ireland in Thurles that year because everyone was saying, "Ye should be there, if you were any good."'

Billy's last year in the Tipperary colours would be 1956. A taxing job in Boland's Bakery in Dublin, working six days a week from 7 a.m. to 10 p.m., restricted the commitment he could give to hurling. Although he played club hurling for Faughs, it was not conducive to keeping the attention of the Tipperary selectors. While he played a few games for Dublin, his commitment to their cause was not total because there was always talk that he was on the verge of a recall to the Tipp side. This indecision cost him the opportunity to play in an All-Ireland senior final.

'Dublin had a great team then, with exceptional players like Lar Foley, Des Foley and Des Ferguson. I thought I was going to go back playing for Tipperary, but I'm half sorry I didn't pursue the opportunity to play for Dublin more. They only lost the All-Ireland to Tipperary by a point in 1961.'

Ireland's World Cup clash with Holland in 1990 marked a restoration in the fortunes of Billy's son Niall – as he scored the crucial equaliser in response to Ruud Gullit's goal and secured Ireland's passage into the knockout phases of the competition. The gloss was taken off the occasion somewhat when a burglar raided their house as the family went out to celebrate – in the process robbing Niall's mother's bracelet, but the most prominent features missing were Billy's two All-Ireland minor medals.

Like his father before him, Niall played in an All-Ireland minor hurling final – for Dublin against Galway in 1983. Despite his pride at Niall's great success in soccer Billy felt the game was no match for hurling.

'I put my foot in it in 1990 when a journalist came to interview me about Niall after he scored the goal against Holland. When he asked me if I was proud of him, I said without thinking, "To tell you the truth I'd rather he had won a Munster medal!"'

The family did pay a price for Niall's devotion to hurling, though. 'Niall always had a hurley in his hand when he was young. One famous day in Killarney, Babs scored a last-minute goal from a free. That was the day when Donie Nealon came on with a towel and was supposed to have switched the ball and swapped a wet one for a dry one to make it easier for Babs to score. Niall was about five at the time, so he was practising frees in the back garden after the match and my wife, Mary, was doing the ironing when the window was shattered to smithereens by Niall's sliotar. Mary nearly dropped dead with the shock of the shattering glass. All Niall said afterwards was, "I was only doing Babs Keating!"'

87

PADDY'S DAYS

Paddy Quirke: 1974–1990

Paddy Quirke hurled for Carlow at senior level from 1974 to 1990 and played senior football with the county from 1974 to 1987. He played in thirty-one senior county finals – hurling, football and replays – and 106 times for the Carlow hurling team.

Quirke played for the Leinster football team in both 1979 and 1981, and in four consecutive years between 1978 and 1981 for the Leinster hurling side. Which experience did he enjoy the most? 'I preferred playing most for the hurlers because I felt more like I was on a par with them than with the footballers,' he says. 'I think I was just one of the lads with them, but it was a bit more difficult with the footballers. In 1979 I played in the Railway Cup final in Thurles against Connacht. I was playing in my favourite position, midfield, along with Ger Henderson. Fan Larkin was the captain. I was marking John Connolly. At that stage I feared no one and I could mix it with the best. I was playing with the best in Leinster – Tony Doran, Frank Cummins, Noel Skehan,

Martin Quigley, Pat Carroll, Mark Corrigan, Peadar Carton
– and enjoying it.'

Hurling was his passport to San Fransisco. 'I played a few
games out there and it was really tough and physical,' he
recalls. 'At one stage I put in my hurley, angled with the bos
to the ground, to block an opponent, and got a severe belt
across the face. I was taken off course and rushed to hospital.
I had no social-security cover, but my friends who were with
me decided I was Patrick Foley (a genuine holder of social
security). So all of a sudden I was somebody else. The only
problem was when I heard the name Patrick Foley being
called out in the hospital I forgot that was supposed to me
and had to be reminded who I was!

'At that stage I was not in very good shape and was
expecting some sympathy from the doctor. Instead all he
said was, "Were you playing that crazy Irish game?"'

The highlight of Quirke's career came in 1990, when he
was chosen as the dual All-Star replacement. He played
for most of the football game against Kerry after injury to
Roscommon's Dermot Earley and marked Eoin Liston. At
the banquet after the game he was shocked to discover that
he was chosen as man of the match.

As Paddy takes a nostalgic trip down sport's memory
lane, one football game lives vividly in his memory. 'In 1985
we qualified for the National League quarter final and lost
to Armagh in Croke Park, but the game that stands out for
me for Carlow was playing against Kerry in the Centenary
Tournament in 1984. The county grounds were packed. I
remember Lar Molloy holding Pat Spillane scoreless and
taking a fine point himself. We ran them very close and I
was marking Jack O'Shea. Mike Sheehy got the vital scores
for Kerry in the end. It was obvious that Carlow had lots of

329

potential. Vincent Harvey was training us at the time and one of his favourite chants was "Get the ball in around the blue grass area!" Kevin Madden was on the team then. I received Christmas cards from him for a couple of years and the PS was: "Quirke, I'm still looking for the blue grass area."'

Paddy experienced some major frustrations on the way. 'Winning our only football title in 1986 and achieving a rare double was a career highlight for me. In '87 we were going for the double again. Éire Óg were the opposition. We were playing great football halfway through the second half when a bizzare thing happened. Seán Kelly, the referee, gave Éire Óg a free. Just after he blew the whistle I could see an Éire Óg supporter running towards him. She had a flagpole in her hand. I tried to bring it to the ref's attention. He thought I was complaining about the free, so he ushered me away. The next second he was floored by a blow from the flagpole. The game was held up for five minutes. We lost the game by the minimum 2–9 to 2–8.'

Who was the greatest character he ever played with or against?

'There were a lot of them. I played a shinty match for Ireland against Scotland in the Isle of Man in 1979 and one of my teammates was Limerick's Pat Hartigan. He was really a great character and mighty craic.

'The late James Doyle – "the Jigger" – from my own club was a great character. In 1985 we played the Westmeath champions Brownstown away in the first round of the Leinster club hurling championship. This was a hard-fought game and a great victory for Naomh Eoin. The Jigger was asked a few days later how bad the pitch was. He replied, "Well, the grass was so long a hare rose at half time!"'

Quirke's dream football team is as follows.

––––––––––

1. Martin Furlong
(*Offaly*)

2. Robbie O'Malley   **3. John O'Keeffe**   **4. Niall Cahalane**
(*Meath*)   (*Kerry*)   (*Cork*)

5. Páidí Ó Sé   **6. Kevin Moran**   **7. Martin O'Connell**
(*Kerry*)   (*Dublin*)   (*Meath*)

8. Brian Mullins   **9. Jack O'Shea**
(*Dublin*)   (*Kerry*)

10. Matt Connor   **11. Larry Tompkins**   **12. Pat Spillane**
(*Offaly*)   (*Cork*)   (*Kerry*)

13. Colm O'Rourke   **14. Peter Canavan**   **15. Mike Sheehy**
(*Meath*)   (*Tyrone*)   (*Kerry*)

He also picked the hurling team he would have liked to have played on:

1. Noel Skehan
(*Kilkenny*)

2. Aidan Fogarty   **3. Pat Hartigan**   **4. John Horgan**
(*Offaly*)   (*Limerick*)   (*Cork*)

5. Mick Jacob   **6. Ger Henderson**   **7. Iggy Clarke**
(*Wexford*)   (*Kilkenny*)   (*Galway*)

8. Frank Cummins   **9. Paddy Quirke**
(*Kilkenny*)   (*Carlow*)

10. Johnny Callinan **11. Martin Quigley**   **12. John Fenton**
(*Clare*)   (*Wexford*)   (*Cork*)

13. Éamonn Cregan   **14. Tony Doran**   **15. Eddie Keher**
(*Limerick*)   (*Wexford*)   (*Kilkenny*)

88

RATHNURE'S ROYALTY

Nicky Rackard: 1942–1957

Few families have had such impact on the game as the Rackards. Nicky's status as the greatest full-forward in the history of the game is reflected in his selection in that position on both the Team of the Century and Team of the Millennium, while his brother Bobby was picked at right-corner back on both teams. Meanwhile their younger brother, Billy, won three All-Ireland medals. Traditionally only Christy Ring and Mick Mackey have been placed ahead of Nicky Rackard in hurling's hierarchy of greats, although his tally of honours is less impressive than Ring's in particular. Rackard won two All-Ireland senior titles, one Railway Cup medal in 1956 and one National League medal in the same year.

He was one of the most colourful characters hurling has ever known. He changed the whole sporting and social structure of Wexford. He went to St Kieran's College in Kilkenny and developed a love for hurling which he brought home to his brothers and to his club, Rathnure. Wexford

332

had traditionally been a football power going back to their famous four-in-a-row side (1915–18). But Nicky Rackard turned Wexford almost overnight into a recognised hurling bastion. He was crucial to Wexford's two All-Irelands in 1955 and 1956. In the 1954 All-Ireland semi-final against Antrim he scored an incredible seven goals and seven points.

The 1956 final between Cork and Wexford was one of Rackard's happiest memories and is acknowledged as one of the greatest hurling finals of them all. It had been history in the making, as Christy Ring was seeking a record ninth All-Ireland medal, but above all the game will be remembered for Art Foley's save from Ring.

It was a match which captured the imagination like few others. Tradition favoured Cork. Going into the game they had won twenty-two titles against Wexford's two. Such was the interest in Wexford that two funerals scheduled for the day of the final had to be postponed until the following day because the hearses were needed to transport people to the match! Over 83,000 people attended. The final had to be delayed until 23 September because of a polio scare in Cork. The authorities did not want a huge crowd assembling in any one place.

The crucial contest was that between Christy Ring, playing at left-corner forward and Bobby Rackard. It was the Wexford man who would win out in every sense.

Wexford had the advantage of a whirlwind start, with a goal from Padge Keogh after only three minutes. Two minutes later Ring registered Cork's first score, with a point from a 21-yard free. Wexford went on to win by 2–14 to 2–8.

Significantly, that Wexford team had a special place in Christy Ring's affections. 'I always loved our clashes with

Wexford in Croke Park. It was a different climate in Croke Park because you didn't have the pressure of the Munster championship on your back. It was the same for Wexford; they didn't have the pressure of beating Kilkenny on them. Both of us could relax a bit.'

89

HOLDING BACK THE TEARS

Lulu Carroll: 1992–2006

There are some moments that are seared in the memory. Although I never had the good fortune to meet her I was shocked to hear of Lulu Carroll's premature death in August 2007 at the age of thirty-five. It seemed that a light quenched when she passed on. Few gave so much so often. If we want to see the true spirit of the GAA her career captured its power, magic and heroism. Nothing epitomised her courage though like her brave fight against her illness.

Lulu won an All-Ireland title with Laois in 2001 and eight Leinster titles. She also won six senior county championships and one Leinster senior club title with Timahoe. She also won two All-Ireland senior 7s titles, an All-Ireland under-16 medal in 1988, one NFL Division 1 and NFL Division 2. Lulu was honoured with an All-Star and one replacement All-Star during her glittering football career. In 2007, she won a well-deserved GAA president's award on St Patrick's Day in Croke Park just a few months before her death.

To get an insight into Lulu I sought the help of the person

who knew her best as a player, her teammate and great friend Sue Ramsbottom.

'It was her persistence and nagging of our teacher, Mr Sayers, that led the way for girls to play on a boys national schools team. Lulu got a great kick out of saving penalties on the boys and would taunt them with: "Ah you couldn't score a goal on a girl." Lulu dreamed of playing in Croke Park on All-Ireland final day – which she did in 1988 against Kerry.

'Lulu played in the forwards, midfields, backs and goals. Many people have done this before and many will do this in the future but the difference is, Lulu was brilliant in all these positions with All-Stars and replacement All-Stars to prove it. We had a wonderful time together on that journey to get an All-Ireland medal. Girls came and went but Lulu's steely determination, focus and energy made sure her dream was realised.'

Lulu had many great moments as Sue recalls.

'The year 1996 was a great year for Lulu as the sports commentators called her "the Liam McHale of ladies' football with her long tanned legs". It was also on the day of the final that Lulu got that marvellous equalising goal for Laois in the last seconds so we could have another bite at the cherry.

'It was in 2001 that the Laois Ladies won that famous All-Ireland. Not many people remember that Lulu got player of the match in the 2001 Leinster Final. This was the hardest game Laois faced and played on route to the All-Ireland in 2001. While all her teammates lay down Lulu rose everybody else that day and ensured the dream was kept alive. Lulu was a real hero and only for her there would be no All-Ireland medal in Laois.'

Sue is the best person to appraise Lulu's legacy.

'Lulu was a proud Timahoe and Laois woman and wore her jerseys with pride. When she finished playing for Timahoe she enjoyed coaching and passing on her skills and knowledge to the new kids on the block. She had eight county medals to her credit. I know the last county medal she won the year she died meant so much to her. The Timahoe club owes a great deal of gratitude to Lulu as a player and a manager, helping it to the dizzy heights of reaching a club All-Ireland in 2000.

'Lulu was the epicentre and the heart and soul of every team she played on. We will all play again some day with Lulu in the great pitch called heaven. The best of things come in ones – one great friend, one Croke Park, one All-Ireland medal and one Lulu.'

90

TOUGHER THAN THE REST

Sylvie Linnane: 1976–1989

The most famous quote in the hurling vernacular is Micheál O'Muircheartaigh's observation: 'A mighty poc from the hurl of Seán Óg Ó hAilpín . . . his father was from Fermanagh, his mother from Fiji, neither a hurling stronghold.'

However, a good contender for runner–up must be 'Sylvie Linnane: the man who drives a JCB on a Monday and turns into one on a Sunday.' Having said that my interview with Sylvie was delayed because he was gone to Mass!

His fire and brimstone approach to the game often concealed his innate talent, though winning three All-Star awards does indicate his craftsmanship. He won five Railway Cup medals, three All-Ireland medals and two National Leagues. However, it was the contests rather than the medals that meant the most to Sylvie.

'For me the colour of a jersey, especially the Kilkenny one, was all I needed to get up for a game. I always had a passion for beating them. Everyone likes to take their scalp. I was never one to say anything to an opponent but I did believe they should know I was there. One time we were playing Kilkenny I received an uppercut from Harry Ryan before the National Anthem. I couldn't see after it but I still let fly at him.

'The other thing I remember was the incredible reception we got when we won the All-Ireland in 1980. It was clear how much it meant to people. The great thing was they were all there again when we lost the next year.'

Linnane lined out at right half-back on the Galway team that won the breakthrough All-Ireland in 1980 and at right-full back when Galway won All-Irelands in 1987 and '88. Of the four All-Irelands he lost, the one that wounded most was the defeat to Offaly in 1981. 'We shot fourteen wides in the second half. You can't afford that.'

Linnane has spent half a lifetime denying some of the dramas attributed to him on the pitch. However, it is a little-known fact that he once created a drama off the pitch.

'We were in Dublin the night before an All-Ireland final and as always we were sent to bed early. The problem is that it's very hard to sleep the night before an All-Ireland. I was rooming with Steve Mahon and we heard a massive row going on in the street underneath. So I went to investigate and saw this fella beating up his wife or his girlfriend. I ran into the bathroom, got the waste-paper basket, filled it with water and ran over to the window and threw the water over the man. It did the trick and he stopped and the woman ran away. A happy ending – or so I thought until the man recovered from the shock and got really, really angry and started to climb up the drainpipe to pay back the person who threw the water on him. I didn't think the night before the All-Ireland was the best time to get involved in a brawl – especially as this guy looked like a pure psycho so I decided discretion was the better part of valour. I turned off the light so he wouldn't know where to find me. I went quietly back to bed and listened attentively to see what would happen. What I hadn't known at the time was that the light immediately below my room was on! The room belonged to the former Galway great Inky Flaherty. Inky was not a man to mess with and a few minutes later I heard him forcefully eject the intruder out the window – which was not the typical way to prepare for an All-Ireland.'

Sylvie's single-minded determination was most tellingly revealed before the 1987 All-Ireland final against Kilkenny when he was marking Harry Ryan. At the special Mass for the team before the game, when the priest offered him the sign of peace, instead of responding with the normal greeting, 'And also with you', Sylvie's response was, 'And peace be with Harry Ryan.'

Sylvie's dream team is:

1. Ger Cunningham
(*Cork*)

2. Brian Murphy	**3. Conor Hayes**	**4. Joe Hennessy**
(*Cork*)	(*Galway*)	(*Kilkenny*)
5. Pete Finnerty	**6. Ger Henderson**	**7. Anthony Daly**
(*Galway*)	(*Kilkenny*)	(*Clare*)

8. Frank Cummins   **9. John Connolly**
(*Kilkenny*)   (*Galway*)

10. Nicky English	**11. John Power**	**12. Joe Connolly**
(*Tipperary*)	(*Kilkenny*)	(*Galway*)
13. Pat Fox	**14. Noel Lane**	**15. D. J. Carey**
(*Tipperary*)	(*Galway*)	(*Kilkenny*)

91

THE KING

Henry Shefflin: 1999–2015

The late Bill O'Herlihy was interviewing John Giles and remarked, 'This is something of a local derby between Holland and Germany.'

Glies replied: 'Yeah, they've been close to each other for years.'

In his new incarnation as *Sunday Game* pundit, Henry Shefflin brings the same no-nonsense approach to anlaysis as Gilesy did for years as a soccer pundit.

'Big, lanky and not much pace' was one description of Shefflin as a teenager. As a seventeen-year-old he played as a forward in the Leinster minor final and was relegated to sub goalie for the rest of the campaign. Shefflin would take over from D. J. Carey as the undisputed king of hurling. Even in his most sublime moments he played with a competitiveness that is as essential to him as breathing.

Shefflin gave an intriguing insight into the intensity of Kilkenny's preparations in his description of the pre-match routine before the All-Ireland final of 2002. 'John Hoyne was warming up in the dressing room and he got a slap of a hurl in the head from someone. He got four staples before he went out. That was just the warm-up.'

Henry bought fully into the Kilkenny culture of team.

'We never depended on one or two individuals to produce the goods,' he recalls. 'If I was having an off day, the likes of Eddie Brennan would produce a big performance. We were very much a team. Brian Cody does not want to see anyone come off the field happy after a defeat. There was no point in saying I played well but the others let me down. We won as a team and we lost as a team. We used defeats to motivate us to achieve even more success.'

Shefflin was central to Kilkenny's historic four All-Irelands in a row. His fourth in 2009, after their thrilling victory over Tipperary, spawned a new joke: What does NAMA stand for in Tipperary? No All-Ireland medal again.

He became the first player to win ten All-Star awards and in 2009 he was chosen by the *Irish Independent* as the greatest hurler of all time.

A revealing insight into Shefflin's mentality came after they lost to Tipperary in the 'drive for five' final in 2010, when he came off early in the game with an injury.

'Six days later I was sitting at home feeling a little sorry for myself, my knee swollen like a balloon, the cruciate ligament and cartilage in shreds and a pair of crutches for constant company. At thirty years of age I was facing a second major knee operation in three years. Already at a low ebb after losing to Tipperary, that prospect of more surgery and long rehabilitation compounded the misery. Watching the All-Ireland under-21 final when Tipp squashed Galway quickly changed my mood.

'My pride was hurting from defeat, my knee was hurting

from the damage sustained, but nothing pained me more that night than the perception that there was a new act in town. The five-in-a-row was dashed and it was as if we were being told with a sympathetic pat: *Move on now, lads, your time is up.*

'If there was any greater motivation for picking it up and going again, I certainly don't recall it. Not even the memory of the final cut as deep. I can recall saying to myself in the aftermath and in the weeks and months that followed how I wasn't letting go here, that we weren't gone.

'It fuelled my recovery and we retained the upper hand on them until 2016. A night that might have represented a changing of the guard, more so than the final itself six days earlier, was worked to our benefit.'

92

GALWAY GREAT

Seán Duggan: 1942–1953

An indication of the late Seán Duggan's status in the game is that his understudy in Galway was Tony Reddin and when Reddin moved to Tipperary he established himself as one of the great goalkeepers and was chosen as goalkeeper on the official Team of the Millennium. In 1984, Duggan would be selected on the official team of those who had never won an All-Ireland senior medal. He captained Connacht to victory over Munster in the 1947 Railway Cup final. Four years later he would win a National League medal.

The start of Duggan's career coincided with the Emergency.

'My abiding memory from the time is of travelling to Loughrea, which was twenty miles away from us. Petrol was restricted, and transport was not readily available. How would we get there? After several meetings it was decided that we could get the use of a turf lorry and with great secrecy we all met there from the city centre at the famous Ballybrit Racecourse. It was eleven o'clock in the morning. We had several detours, trying to avoid all the official checkpoints before we arrived two miles from Loughrea town at the spot which was to be the pick-up point after the game. We walked to the field, played our game and won. As money was tight our refreshments were scarce: sweets, biscuits, and red lemonade. When we got back to the designated spot it emerged that our illicit transport was spotted, and our turf lorry was "on the run". So we started to walk back to Galway, getting to Craughwell village tired and hungry. We replenished ourselves there courtesy of the local orchard. Then we heard the good news that our turf lorry was the Galway side of Craughwell, up a side road. Five miles from Galway city our turf lorry broke down. By that stage it was 2.30 a.m. Two of the lads had a friend in the area and knocked him up, and we borrowed his pony and trap. Some of us leapt in and headed for home. I jumped out at the crossroads and walked into my house. At the time there was no lock on the door and despite the hard times I treated myself to the luxury of a cup of tea.'

Duggan particularly enjoyed the Oireachtas final victories in 1950 and 1952. However, the 1951 National League final against New York at the Polo Grounds was his happiest memory.

'We were one point up with a few minutes to go and New York were awarded a 21-yard free. Up stepped Terry Leahy – great hurler, master scorer. My mind was very uneasy: would it be defeat all over again? Leahy bent, lifted and struck, but his shot was saved and cleared. Then the late great Josie Gallagher sealed our victory with two more points.

'To have won at home against an up-and-coming Wexford team and to win a major national trophy before 30,000 exiles at the Polo Grounds is still clear and vivid and pleasing; and of course a trip to New York in 1951 – when many people never went outside their own county – was the treat of a lifetime.'

After ten years of inter-county hurling an eye injury brought a premature end to Seán Duggan's career in 1953. By that stage 'the agility of youth was fading'. He was keen to see Galway playing Championship hurling in either Leinster or Munster.

'Down the decades when Galway had some great men and very fine teams, games were lost through lack of competition. That vital edge was missing in close finishes – it cost us several games and possibly titles over the years.'

Duggan was confident about the future of Gaelic games.

'The GAA will succeed and progress as long as it has the support of people; the club is the cell of growth and renewal. Hurling is woven into Irish history. The roar of the crowds, the whirr of the flying sliotar and the unmistakable and unique sound of the ash against ash has enthralled sport fans for decades.'

Seán had a nice line in self-deprecation.

'I played minor for Galway at sixteen and spent two seasons in those ranks. In a minor semi-final against Kilkenny Galway lost by about nine goals. After the match I overheard a Galway fan express the hope that he had "seen the last of that fellow in goal".'

93

FROM KILDARE TO HERE

Larry Tompkins: 1979–1996

Larry Tompkins first came to prominence in 1979 when he was selected to play for the Kildare senior team, having also lined out for the minor and under-21 football team that same year. He emigrated to New York and returned to Ireland in the mid 1980s, when he opted to declare for Cork following a dispute with the Lilywhites over the purchase of an airline ticket. On that Cork team he linked up with another former Kildare player, Shea Fahy, who would be chosen as footballer of the year in 1990. Having lost All-Ireland finals in 1987 and '88 to Meath, Tompkins starred in Cork's All-Ireland wins in both 1989 and 1990, captaining the team in 1990. Nine years later he coached Cork when they lost the All-Ireland final to Meath.

The '89 All-Ireland is yet another case of what might have been for Mayo. Their former All-Star midfielder, T. J. Kilgallon, recalls the game vividly. 'After Anthony Finnerty got the goal, we were in the driving seat because, having lost the previous two years, they were starting to doubt themselves, but in the last ten minutes we went into disarray and let them off the hook. They finished strongly and got the final three points.

'When you think back to that team, you have to say that the heartbeat of the team was Larry Tompkins. He was their engine, driving through defences and getting points from play, and always reliable from frees. To win All-Irelands you need a top-class free-taker and Tompkins was certainly that. He was exceptionally committed and would put his body on the line to do anything that was necessary for Cork to win.

'I especially think of their All-Ireland triumph in 1990. Larry picked up a cruciate ligament in that game, but he played through the pain barrier and scored four points to lead Cork to back-to-back All-Irelands. I am sure the fact that Tompkins and the Cork lads were up against their bitter rivals Meath drove him on to push Cork over the line.'

Pat Spillane offers a nuanced assessment of Tompkins.

'Talking to Cork fans after they lost badly to Kerry in the 2007 All-Ireland final, the only consolation, as they saw it, was that at least Larry Tompkins was no longer in charge of the team,' he contends. 'Larry was a great player, but getting a Cork fan to say something nice about his time as Cork manager is as difficult as pushing custard up a hill.

'Larry devoted his entire life to it. But the problem was that even though he had captained the county to an All-Ireland in 1990, people in Cork to this day think of him as a "blow-in", which means he was grudgingly accepted. The failing that Larry had as a manager was that he tried to train the team to be like him, to be as dedicated, determined and fanatical about fitness as he was. He had them running up hills. He brought them on beaches for early-morning runs. Eugene McGee was the first to do this with UCD. Ger Loughnane did it with the Clare hurlers. Since that ploy did not work for Larry, no other team have used it since.

'Larry is a lovely fella and a gentleman. He was probably the first professional Gaelic footballer – not in the sense that he was getting paid but because he trained morning, noon and night, seven days a week.'

94

Back to the Forwards

Brian Whelahan: 1989–2006

For many, an abiding memory of Croke Park will always be Brian Whelahan, after conjuring a performance of exceptional class against Kilkenny, in the 1998 All-Ireland final, with his arm raised aloft in triumph, drinking in the moment, turning defeat into victory.

Whelahan's quality was first readily apparent to a national audience in Offaly's victory over Clare in the 1989 All-Ireland minor final. With his brothers, Simon and Barry, as his teammates, he turned Birr into one of the powers of club hurling, winning four All-Ireland titles. To cement the family connection, the team was coached by their father, Pat Joe.

Brian won his first senior medal against Limerick in 1994. Offaly went into the game full of confidence. In fact, so self-assured were they that the side's greatest character, the effervescent Johnny Pilkington, was making victory speeches before the game – all the more remarkable because he was not even the captain! The end of the game was one of the most dramatic finals ever witnessed when Offaly scored 2–6 in the final five minutes to snatch victory.

Ger Loughnane dominated 1998, along with the many controversies that dogged his Clare team: the clashes with officialdom, the rows with referees, the unprecedented media attention. After Offaly lost the 1998 Leinster final to Kilkenny, Babs Keating controversially described the Offaly players as 'sheep in a heap'. Babs met with the County Board and decided to stay, but the next morning he resigned beause he was 'shocked' by an interview in a newspaper with Offaly's star midfielder, Johnny Pilkington, who had questioned his record with the county, stated that Babs had abandoned Offaly's tradition of ground hurling and questioned the tactics against Kilkenny. In Offaly's hour of crisis they went in search of a secret weapon. His name was Bond, Michael Bond, or as the players christened him 'Double-Oh-O'. A few months later he would make the most sensational positional switch in Brian Whelahan's career and effectively win the All-Ireland against Kilkenny in 1998. Before that there was the small matter of three battles with Clare.

In the All-Ireland semi-final Clare led Offaly by four points with ten minutes to go, but it required a late free from Jamesie O'Connor to tie the match at 1–13 each after Offaly scored 1–2 without reply. Much of Clare's performance in the replay was a monument to patience, nerve, courage and technical brilliance, the mature masterwork of a great team. As normal, Clare concentrated on setting a dominating, draining pace. This was essential for a team in which goals had to be mined like nuggets. Houdini could not have escaped from the pit the Offaly team were in and Mr Micawber would have been hard-pressed to find any reason for optimism. Clare's calculated challenge was intensifying towards its thrilling crescendo but suddenly ...

Nobody knows. That's the mystery, the fun, the drama of hurling. Then came a bizarre incident. Jimmy Cooney intervened and blew full-time two minutes prematurely. A large section of the Offaly supporters staged a sit-in on the field while Johnny Pilkington had a fag, 'Wouldn't you think they'd go off for an auld drink?' he said.

A new hurling soap opera was about to unfold. To nobody's surprise, in the Clare camp they were told that there would be a replay in Thurles on the following Saturday. Hence Johnny Pilkington's comment: 'The statement was that you hadn't had Offaly beaten until the *Sunday Game* was over.' Ger Loughnane's verdict on the game was very economical: 'On the day Offaly were the better team and deserved to win.'

The climax of Whelahan's career came in the 1998 final. Suffering from flu, he was clearly struggling in the half-back line, so Michael Bond boldly moved him to full-forward, where Whelahan's class came to the fore and he scored six points, and then, with just minutes left, a goal that sealed the title, in a 2–16 to 1–13 victory over Kilkenny.

Hubert Ringey, the Offaly captain, in his victory speech after Offaly beat Kilkenny in the All-Ireland final, said, 'We might have come in the back door, but we're going out the front door.' In one of the great GAA ironies, Offaly came through the back door, having voted against it, and Offaly, true to form, voted against the back door the following year.

Although he was voted Hurler of the Year in both 1994 and 1998, Whelahan was sensationally omitted from the '94 All-Star team. Such was the ensuing level of controversy about this decision that the system of All-Star selection was changed for the following year.

———

Whelahan's place in the pantheon of hurling greats was forever secured in 2000 when he was the only player from the modern era to be selected on Hurling's Team of the Millennium, replacing Tipperary's Jimmy Finn from the Team of the Century.

95

THE DONEGAL DYNAMO

Brian McEniff: 1969–2005

The highlight of Brian McEniff's playing career with Donegal came in 1972, though few could have predicted the end of the county's provincial subjugation earlier in the year.

'We played Leitrim in the league in Carrick-on-Shannon,' he says. 'I think the score was 4–13 to 1–3 to Leitrim. I was player-manager at the time. I got the lads into a room in Bush's Hotel and said, "Right, boys. The only way we can go is up. Today was the lowest we could possibly go. The championship is coming up soon and are we going to make an effort for it or are we not?" We all made a vow there and then that we would all train hard for the championship and we did.

'We beat Down after a replay and Tyrone in the Ulster final. It was kind of a fairy tale after so bad a start to the year. As it was Donegal's first-ever Ulster title, the whole county went wild. It was like winning the All-Ireland. We had a great week afterwards! The celebrations probably affected us in the All-Ireland semi-final against Offaly, the reigning All-Ireland champions. We were playing very well up to half-time but we gave away a very bad goal to Kevin Kilmurray. Even though we lost we were probably happy enough with our performance because Ulster teams weren't doing well in Croke Park at the time. I'd say Offaly got a bit of a shock that day.'

In 1989 McEniff took charge of training Donegal again and he had his finest hour in 1992 when he masterminded Donegal's All-Ireland 0–18 to 0–14 triumph over red-hot favourites Dublin to win the county's only All-Ireland.

'We had been so unimpressive in the All-Ireland semi-final against Mayo that nobody gave us a chance against Dublin. I think that gave the Dublin players a false sense of security. The media really built them up and I think the Dubs started to believe their own publicity. In contrast there was no hype about us because we hadn't done anything to deserve it. None of our fellas were going on radio shows blowing our own trumpet.

'You can't win an All-Ireland without leaders on the pitch and we had four of them in 1992: Anthony Molloy at midfield, Martin McHugh at centre-forward, Tony Boyle at full-forward and Martin Gavigan at centre-back. Molloy was a superb leader. He could catch a ball in the clouds and that would lift the team. If you could get past Martin Gavigan, you were doing well. Tony and Martin could get you a score from nowhere. Winning the final was like a dream come true. As it was our first-ever All-Ireland it meant so much to the people at home.'

Jim McGuinness spoke of McEnniff's ability to tap into Michael Carruth's gold medal win that year. 'He pushed back our training session so the boys could listen to the fight on the radio. It felt like a really significant sporting moment for Ireland and it meant that everyone was wired going onto the field for training. In the A versus B game there was an edge that I had never seen between these boys before. I am not suggesting that Donegal won that All-Ireland there and then. But I do believe that a different mentality came into that squad that morning.'

In his time McEniff has seen some unusual sights: 'In 1979 we qualified for the Ulster final against Monaghan, but they beat us well. The match is best remembered for an infamous incident. The referee threw in the ball. Seamus Bonner won possession, sent in the ball to the forwards, and one of our lads popped it over the bar. The only problem was that the band were still on the far side of the pitch and they were playing the national anthem! The referee had to restart the game and our point was disallowed.'

Pat Spillane offers an appraisal of McEniff. 'He would rank up there as being as cute as Dwyer and that would be as high a compliment as you could give,' he states. 'He's the same sort of guy as Dwyer in the sense that when you're talking to him, you think you're asking him questions, but he's really picking your brain. He was a very intelligent and stylish footballer himself and one of the best defenders in the game in the early 1970s.

'In 2003 he was the county chairman and the central council delegate, as well as team manager. He did everything but drive the bus and wash the jerseys. As a manager he really shone after their defeat to Fermanagh in 2003. In that match they gave an abysmal performance, but McEniff picked them off the floor to bring them within a whisker of qualifying for an All-Ireland final – which was an absolutely incredible achievement.'

96

MATT-ER OF FACT

Matt Ruth: 1973–1983

Some managers have a strained relationship with their players. When Tony Book became Manchester City manager, he fell foul of star player Rodney Marsh. It got back to Book that Marsh frequently called him useless. He called in Rodney and invited him to take back the comment. Marsh answered, 'In fact, thinking about it more, you're not that good.'

Kilkenny ace corner-forward Matt Ruth was cut from a more respectful cloth.

Ruth's Kilkenny team of the '70s is considered one of the greatest of all time, with players like Pat Delaney at centre-forward, Frank Cummins in mid-field, Pat Henderson at centre half-back, Eddie Keher prowling with menace near the opposition posts and Noel Skehan in goal. However, Ruth carved a unique place in hurling folklore when he scored perhaps the most infamous goal in hurling history.

In the 1982 Leinster final there was nothing to choose between Kilkenny and the reigning All-Ireland champions,

Offaly. Then comes the most controversial umpiring decision in the history of the GAA.

A long ball is sent in from the Kilkenny defence. The Offaly
goalkeeper Damien Martin advances to shield the sliotar as it
goes harmlessly wide. Martin is absolutely certain the sliotar
is out over the line. Kilkeeny's Liam Fennelly is advancing
rapidly and swings his hurley – making a sweet contact and
sending the sliotar across the goal where the ever-vigilant
Matt Ruth has an empty net to aim at. He does not miss.

Martin cannot believe his eyes when he sees the umpire
raising the green flag. His incredulity is genuine. It is in no
sense an attempt to put the blame on somebody else for an
error of judgement but the indignation of a man who feels
he has been the victim of a travesty of justice. He will go to
his grave with 100 per cent certainty that the umpire made a
terrible blunder.

It is the turning point of the game. Kilkenny win the match
and go on to win the first of two back-to-back All-Ireland
titles. But was their '82 Leinster title based on an error of
judgement by an umpire? Inevitably this was the main area
of discussion when I spoke to Matt Ruth about the incident.
As we talked during Wimbledon fortnight, it was under-
standable that he should use a tennis analogy to explain the
circumstances of the umpire's difficult decision.

'If you watch Wimbledon and see the speed at which the
ball travels, you will notice that both the umpire and the line-
judge have all these fancy electronic gadgets to help them
make the right decision but still there are many times when
the players think they have bad decisions made against
them. The ball is hitting the line at such speed that it can be
virtually impossible at times to say with absolute certainty if
a ball is in or out. The same thing can happen in hurling.

'I know Damien Martin is totally sincere when he says the ball was out. I can't say for sure myself, it all happened so fast. All I can say is that Liam Fennelly doesn't think it was out. Nobody else but Liam could have pulled it off. He is left-handed and he hit the ball at an angle that virtually no other hurler would have done to get the ball across to me. I know that is very difficult to explain to someone who doesn't know Liam's style of hurling and his wrist action in particular. It probably sounds very technical but I think that is probably the reason why he was able to get the ball across the line, even though it seemed he had no chance of saving it. The use of video evidence in GAA matches came too late to resolve this controversy.'

Ruth, though, is more of a glass-half-full type of person: 'I look back at my career and I only think about that game when somebody reminds me of it. I remember the people rather than the matches. I remember the characters above all.

'Fan Larkin was a wonderful player and a great character. On an All-Star trip to America someone challenged Fan Larkin to a race, the whole length of the pitch. "Be the Lord save us, you won't. But I'll tell you what – I will race you to the 21-yard line. That is as far as I have to go!"'

97

CAPTAIN FANTASTIC

Seán Óg Ó hAilpín: 1996–2002

Given the demands on the modern player, the dual star is increasingly rendered an endangered species. There have been eighteen players who have won All-Ireland senior players on the field of play in both hurling and football. Eleven of these are from Cork, including such luminaries as Jack Lynch, Jimmy Barry-Murphy, Brian Murphy, Ray Cummins, Denis Coughlan and, famously in 1990, Teddy McCarthy.

In 2003 in the Munster Championship, after getting over the grievances with the County Board, with a new management team Cork were all out to prove that they were right to strike and the only way to do that was to win something. They won the Munster title. In 2003 in the course of Cork's triumphant march to the All-Ireland final, a new sporting icon was launched on Leeside. Seán Óg's younger brother, Setanta, thrilled the Cork public in the way Jimmy Barry-Murphy inspired Cork to All-Ireland final glory at nineteen years of age in 1973. Cork fans were bitterly disappointed losing the final to Kilkenny. Their sense of misery was compounded when they heard that Setanta had gone down under to carve out a new career for himself as an Aussie Rules player. Yet the following year Cork were able to reverse the previous year's form when they beat Killkenny by 0–17 to 0–9 to win another All-Ireland.

The hand of fate is especially fickle when it comes to sport. Accordingly, after a single victory or defeat, the hurlers on the ditch can change their colours faster than Manchester United. For all the benefits of leading a confident and unchanged side, Cork really struggled in the 2005 All-Ireland semi-final against Clare. With the minutes slipping away, it seemed that Cork were on their way out of the championship. Resignation was actually what the Cork fans in the stands had in common, even if none of them had a language that could express it.

It was a real test on and off the field, Seán Óg recalled. 'Even the Cork fans felt sorry for Clare. They were arguably the better team – they just didn't take their chances. With twenty minutes to go, we were six points behind and hadn't raised a single flag in the second half. Clare had scored points and were rampant. Brian Lohan was giving one of his greatest-ever displays at full-back and was "cleaning" the great Brian Corcoran. Clare's Tony Carmody was on fire and causing us untold damage in the centre half-forward position. Something had to be done. John Allen courageously took off Corcoran and Ronan Curran, two All-Stars the previous year, and sent on Wayne Sherlock and Neil Ronan. Wayne went to wing-back and John Gardiner moved to the centre. Neither Carmody nor Lohan exercised the same dominance again. Neil scored a crucial point.

'John Allen rightly said afterwards, "We had to make the call. We would have been lacerated if we didn't. We were five points down and the game was slipping from us. We have twenty-nine people on our panel. I mean, it was a case of what do we do here – do we throw in the towel or do we try and stem the tide?'

Cork scored seven of the game's closing nine points to sneak a one-point win and then won the All-Ireland against Galway with more comfort by 1–21 to 1–16. To add to the occasion for Seán Óg he captained the team, in the process giving one of the great acceptance speeches in the Irish language.

Seán Óg is universally recognised as one of the greatest wing-backs in the modern age. However, like his teammates on the Cork team, he has also become one of the most famous mutineers since Fletcher Christian, with a series of disputes and strikes with the County Board. The serpentine maneuverings of both parties down the years has been the stuff of a mystery novel where every incident and comment seems to blow into an entity of near biblical importance. The Cork hurling public in the main have been solid in their support for their hurlers. However, their player power, which culminated in the end of Gerald McCarthy's managerial reign, after he received death threats, has not endeared them to everybody.

Babs Keating was one of the most vocal critics of the Cork squad. 'In 2008 we saw that Justin McCarthy wasn't the problem in Waterford, and John Meyler wasn't the problem in Wexford,' he contends. 'Likewise Gerald McCarthy was not the problem in Cork. The problems are more with the present generation, who have an exaggerated opinion of their own importance. I think it would have been better if the likes of Donal Óg Cusack, Seán Óg Ó hAilpín, Ronan Curran or Eoin Kelly, if they had the approach of J. J. Delaney, Tommy Walsh and Henry Shefflin, or Mick Harte's Tyrone, because they are focused. I think it is time many of our players stopped looking for what others can do for them and started asking what they could do for the game.'

———

98

MAYO'S MAN MOUNTAIN

Liam McHale: 1985–1999

It was only when Mayo got to the All-Ireland final in 1989 that Liam McHale decided he was really going to give football a serious go. Before that his focus was on basketball but 1989 would cause his priorities to shift:

'That year holds very strong memories for me. My father died from cancer the day of the Connacht final. I rushed home after the game and he died ten minutes after I arrived. The next Sunday was the Connacht final replay against Roscommon. I scored four points and had one of my best games – though the All-Ireland semi-final against Tyrone was my best game for Mayo.

'In the championship that year we got into the habit of winning tight matches in the last ten minutes. Johnno (John O'Mahony) was always harping on about the last ten minutes and we felt we could really plough it. We felt we were invincible. In the All-Ireland semi-final we gave a very un-Mayo-like peformance when we wore Tyrone down. We thought we had a great chance going into the final.

'We were millimeters from winning the All-Ireland in '89,' he recalls. 'We hit the post twice and the ball bounced back into play. They hit the post twice but each time the ball went over the bar. One of their players double hopped the ball and scored a point but the ref, Paddy Collins, who was normally an excellent referee, missed it. After scoring the goal Anthony Finnerty got another chance but the late John Kerins got a touch to it. The umpire backed away because he was afraid the ball was going to hit him. He missed John's touch and instead of giving us a 45 he flagged it wide. Our freetaker Michael Fitzmaurice was on fire that day and hadn't missed a placed ball, including a 45. If we had got a point at that stage it would have been a big help to us. Cork were a more experienced team than us, having contested the All-Ireland final the previous two years but they were very brittle at that stage of the game. As a forward I could see their nerves in the way the backs were shouting at each other but we allowed them to settle rather than keep them on the ropes.'

McHale's capacity to tell it as it was did not always endear himself to the football constituency in Mayo.

'In 2006 I was on RTE's *Up for the Match* programme the night before the All-Ireland final. Mary Kennedy asked me if I was confident. I replied: "I would be confident if we weren't playing Kerry." I got some abuse because of that.' McHale has played with and coached the great enigma of Mayo football Kieran McDonald. His assessment of McDonald is unreservedly positive.

'He's a very nice and generous guy. He loves Gaelic football and has the number eleven tattooed on his back in Roman numerals. He would be a bit like Roy Keane in that he is very private and is not comfortable with strangers coming up to him looking for autographs. He enjoys a few beers but in a quiet pub where he knows everyone. It's not that he's arrogant but he doesn't like fanfare or the media spotlight.

'Like myself he has taken more than his share of abuse from Mayo supporters. It really disappoints me when I hear that and other players get it as well. If these guys were getting five grand a week it would be different but they are amateurs and the amazing sacrifices they make and we made, training Christmas Day, St Stephen's Day and running through woods on New Year's Day when everyone else is relaxing, it's not fair. Going back to my time as a basketballer, some people continued to question my commitment to the Mayo team.'

In common with a whole generation of Mayo footballers, McHale has special fondness for Anthony Finnerty.

'Three days after we lost the All-Ireland final to Cork everyone was very down. We were in Anthony's local pub, Mitchells, at about 2pm and the place was packed. Someone asked him to say a few words to cheer them up. Anthony got up on a three-legged-stool and said, "I know ye all feel sorry for me and are cringing that I have to stand up like this in public but I've got to be positive and look on the bright side. If I had got that goal I missed ye'd have been talking about me all winter but now that I missed it ye'll never stop talking about me." Needless to say he brought the house down.'

McHale's dream team is as follows.

1. Eugene Lavin
(*Mayo*)

2. Kenneth Mortimer	3. Kevin Cahill	4. Dermot Flanagan
(*Mayo*)	(*Mayo*)	(*Mayo*)
5. Declan Meehan	6. James Nallen	7. Seán Óg de Paor
(*Galway*)	(*Mayo*)	(*Galway*)

8. Kevin Walsh
(*Galway*)

9. T. J. Kilgallon
(*Mayo*)

10. Ja Fallon
(*Galway*)

11. Kieran McDonald
(*Mayo*)

12. Michael Donnellan
(*Galway*)

13. Kevin McStay
(*Mayo*)

14. Pádraic Joyce
(*Galway*)

15. Val Daly
(*Galway*)

99

HEFFO'S HELPER

Gay O'Driscoll: 1965–1979

Dublin's victory over Galway in the 1974 All-Ireland final still evokes fond memories for a Cork-born player (he lived there until he was ten) – Dublin corner-back Gay O'Driscoll. Such was the hype around the game that O'Driscoll and his fourteen teammates became immediate household names. It was not simply that the Dubs were on top of the pile but that they had done so against all expectations and with such speed. Gaelic football had now entered show business and O'Driscoll and his band of merry men were entertainers as well as players.

Surprisingly it is not that final that O'Driscoll remembers most fondly.

'I think the most significant game for that great Dublin team was the Leinster quarter-final of 1974 in which we beat Offaly by a point. Offaly had a great team at the point – having won the three previous Leinster titles and two All-Ireland finals. When the final whistle blew, and I can still remember it as clear as anything, I was about halfway up the field on the Cusack stand side. That was when our great run really began. I will never, ever forget that tingling sensation that went down my back. It was like a premonition that great things were in store for us. Nothing in sport, not even the All-Ireland finals, compared with that moment.

'At the time Dublin football was in the doldrums. I remember in the early '70s we lost to Kildare in the first round of the championship. I was sitting with Jimmy Keaveney on the bus back and he said to me that he would get an awful slagging from one of his mates at work the following day. I thought to myself at least nobody knows that I was playing for Dublin because I never told anyone about it, nor would I ever admit I played for Dublin.'

Asked the reason for Dublin's startling transformation into a team of thoroughbreds from a bunch of no-hopers O'Driscoll pauses for deliberation.

'It's very hard to put your finger on it. There were several reasons and the transformation was like a snowball. Although eight or ten players who played in 1974 were there in '70 and '71 but we got a few new players in '74, notably Brian Mullins who had a big impact. Of course Kevin Heffernan's role is well documented at this stage – though it should be remembered he had great players to work with,' he said. 'One thing I observed, which I'm convinced did make a big difference, was that there were no cliques in the team any more. I had played for Dublin since 1965 and up to '74 there were always cliques in the team, e.g. players from the one club sticking together and togging out together. That changed for some reason in '74 and Heffo capitalised on that by making us the fittest team in Ireland.'

The zenith of Heffo's army came in 1977 in the All-Ireland semi-final against Kerry. O'Driscoll believes it was a victory for Dublin's increasingly professional approach to the game:

'Tactics didn't come into it in '74. After losing to Kerry in '75, tactics came in the following year and a more professional approach like watching videos of our opponents. I remember we watched a video of Kerry beating Cork in the Munster semi-final and picked up one of Kerry's key tactics. They tried to pull out the opposing full-back line and pump the ball over their heads and get their forward line to turn around and run in. We countered that by keeping either Robbie (Kelleher) or myself back to act as a kind of sweeper.

'In hindsight the '77 semi-final was the classic football match. We were trailing all the way until the last few minutes. Never did I think it was gone and never did I think we would win. In that cauldron you never thought about victory or defeat. Such was the intensity of the games against Kerry that you knew you had to give 110 per cent for every ball and your concentration was totally on what was happening in the here and now.'

100

THE LIFE OF BRIAN

Brian Lohan 1993–2006

Brian Lohan's three consecutive All-Stars (1995–97) serves as just a small indicator that he is the greatest hurling full-back in the modern era. His father, Gus, had won a National League medal with Clare in 1977. Brian's brother, Frank, played beside him as left full-back when Clare won All-Irelands in 1995 and '97.

Ger Loughnane was all too aware of his general's contribution.

'In the All-Ireland semi-final against Galway in 1995 Brian Lohan damaged his hamstring,' he recalls with a shudder. 'He was on Joe Cooney, and Cooney had got a couple of points off him. I went down to the sideline and looked at him. I did more than look at him, I needn't tell you! He started to hurl out of his skin. Lohan said afterwards, "I saw Loughnane coming down the sideline and decided it was time to start hurling!"

'In the All-Ireland final that year with about twenty minutes to go he pulled his hamstring again and he gave a signal. We had built up such an understanding that at any time, whether it was in a dressing room or out on the field, a look was all it took. There was no need for words most of the time. It showed the terrific understanding there was between everybody and that applied with the selectors as well. Our physio Colm Flynn said to me, "Jesus his hamstring is gone." I replied, "Tell him he's not f**king coming off." I turned my back and walked in the other direction after Lohan called me. Colm went in and broke the news to Brian. No reaction whatsoever. He just got on with it and pretended nothing was wrong with him. When you talk about mental toughness, what Lohan did in the All-Ireland . . . it was out of this world. It would never happen in soccer. If a player pulls his hamstring in soccer, the stretcher is brought in and there's a big exit.

'In the last twenty minutes he used his head, stayed goalside of John Troy and whoever else came on, and played away with a torn hamstring. He wasn't able to train for three months afterwards. For those last twenty minutes he held out by sheer guts. For a Clare player to do that in an All-Ireland final was incredible and said everything about the difference between the team I played on and the team I managed. There's no way I'd have done that when I was playing.

'He got through it by cutting down the angles. It was a measure of his courage and his intelligence. He used his head to survive with a torn hamstring. He was willing to go through the pain barrier because the team needed him to do so.'

Loughnane was tough on his star:

'I drove Brian Lohan to distraction in training,' he claims with a big smile. 'When I wanted to improve a forward like Barry-Murphy, I always put them on Lohan in training.

Indirectly I was given him the line that he "cleaned" Lohan. Then I'd say, "Barry, move around. He's slow. He won't be able to keep up with you." Lohan would be growling. Then I'd say something like, "Don't let him forward. Drive him back. He's not able to hit the ball when he's going backwards." Brian would be fuming inside but he'd never say anything. He is one of the most loyal people you could meet.'

Asked to provide a snapshot to illustrate Lohan's character Loughnane went for an off-the-field example. 'Lohan and Mike O'Halloran are as close friends as people can be. They always roomed together, but in '98 Hallo didn't make the team. Brian Lohan came to me and said, "Hallo isn't playing. I want to be in the room with somebody who is playing." Lohan was the best man at Hallo's wedding, but this was business. It showed how professional Lohan was.'

Loughnane has the last word on Lohan: 'I just can't find the words to praise him enough. We'll never see his like again. Lohan will become a legendary character, even more so than he already is. The characteristics he showed, the nerve for the big occasion, the intelligent play meant that I've never seen a full-back like him. In all aspects of his life he's ambitious. He's driven to succeed but he is a totally calm, calculating person. His good points are too numerous to mention, but anyone who's seen him play knows what they are. He is simply the best.'

A Fond Farewell

A heavy cloud of sadness enveloped me with the news of the passing of Donie Shine in April 2017 after a courageous battle with illness. He became a household name in the GAA world in the 1980s with his stewardship of the Clann na nGael team that would see them win six consecutive Connacht Club Championships.

In 1994 he succeeded Roscommon's most iconic name, Dermot Earley, as manager of the county senior team. Dermot was one of the first to ring Donie to congratulate him. When I asked Dermot for his summation of Donie his answer was immediate: 'A gentleman to his fingertips.' Five simple words that say so much.

It was after his term with Roscommon had ended that Donie used his great knowledge of the game to forge a new career as an analyst with Shannonside radio. With Willie Hegarty he became the greatest double act since Laurel and Hardy though with the *elan* of Simon and Garfunkel.

Of course his proudest moment came in the 2006 All-Ireland Minor Final when Roscommon took down the Kingdom. The icing on the cake for him was that his son Donie was the undisputed star of the game. His commentary at the end pulsates with the passion of a proud father. In 2010 that sense of pride was again emulated when Roscommon won the Connacht Final against all the predictions of the pundits and Donie Jnr gave a masterclass of forward play. Magic moments that will never be forgotten in Roscommon.

My personal memories of Donie though are away from football – as a devoted husband to Lil and loving father to his children. My hope is that soon they will reach the stage that they are able to smile at the treasure trove of happy memories they have of a remarkable man.

THE LAST WORD

For more than 130 years great women and men have adorned the GAA with their skills, style and substance. This book has sought to celebrate a cross-section of them. I hope their stories have in some small way captured the richness of the bigger GAA story: a narrative of pride, passion and parish. It is so much more than trophies and medals.

In the GAA everyone knows your name in this unique community where we all face the call to unity. Ireland's greatest living writer, Donal Ryan, was not the most talented young hurler in history. Hence he claims that the most common question he was asked is, 'Are you useless?' After he found fame as a writer he was watching his beloved Tipperary in the crucible of dreams that is Semple Stadium when the referee gave a controversial decision against them. He leapt up from his seat and launched into a savage diatribe against the ref, casting doubt on his parentage in the process. After his rant he was mortified that he had gone too far and was hoping that nobody would recognise him. He was about to meekly sit down when he heard a booming voice say: 'Ah, Donal Ryan, would you ever sit down and write a short story about it?'

The unique power of the GAA to be the national soap opera was vividly illustrated in the summer of 2017. Apart from thrillers like Waterford and Kilkenny on the field there were juicy controversies off it. After the minor match of 'Bernard Flynn versus James Horan' came the real deal with the 'Diarmuid Connolly saga'. Connolly was suspended after an incident in the Dublin-Carlow game. Then in the words of Michael Foley the Dublin manager, Jim Gavin, 'stopped the clocks' by 'saying something interesting' and had a cut at Pat Spillane and Colm O'Rourke for their comments about Connolly on *The Sunday Game*. Then two *Sunday Game* pundits, Joe Brolly and Dessie Dolan, rounded on Spillane for his comments. Spillane in turn accused Brolly, Dolan and presenter Des Cahill of 'throwing him under the bus'. Trying to make sense of it all, Paul Galvin claimed that his wife had forced him to watch an episode of *Love Island* but there were much more hormones on *The Sunday Game* than on *Love Island*.

Mayo footballers were yet again the story. Their obituary was written after they were on the ropes in All-Ireland quarter-final against Roscommon. After every shipwreck there is enough wood to build a raft. Eight days later, they came out and gave their near neighbours a twenty-two-point trouncing in the replay. Their manager, Stephen Rochford, was derided after the first game but a hero after the second one. Teams win matches. Managers win replays.

The magic of the GAA is its unique ethos. A parable serves to illustrate.

Offaly are famous for their dramatic endings. Who will ever forget Seamus Darby's sensational goal which deprived Kerry of their five-in-a-row in 1892? The previous year, though, their hurlers had a last-gasp winning goal to claim an historic All-Ireland title. To this day in Galway they are still asking if Johnny Flaherty threw the ball into the net.

After the final whistle the Offaly goalkeeper, Damien

Martin, and the full-forward, Padraig Horan, met at the halfway line and embraced.

Horan said, 'Damien, this makes all the sacrifices worthwhile.'

Martin replied, 'They would have been worth it if we never won anything.'
